LORDSHIP AND FEUDALISM IN THE MIDDLE AGES

LORDSHIP AND FEUDALISM IN THE MIDDLE AGES

by

GUY FOURQUIN

Professor of Medieval History
University of Lille

Translated by Iris and A. L. Lytton Sells

London

George Allen & Unwin Ltd

Ruskin House Museum Street

First published in 1976

ISBN 0 04 9400487

Translated from the French:
Seigneurie et Féodalité
Presses Universitaires de France, Paris 1970

Printed in Great Britain
in 11 point Baskerville type
by The Devonshire Press, Torquay

Translators' Note

Seigneurie et Féodalité has proved an exceptionally difficult work to put into English. Owing to the limitation of length imposed by the series of French publications to which it belongs, the author has been obliged to use an abbreviated language involving many abstract nouns which, if translated direct, are unintelligible in English. Our own language having always preferred concrete expressions, we have often been obliged to expand that of the original. Another difficulty has arisen from the use of legal terms current in medieval France, but which, with some exceptions, have no equivalent in English. Professor Fourquin often assumes, on the part of his readers, a knowledge of these words; but as they, or the context in which they are used, are not all to be found in standard dictionaries of Old French or medieval Latin, we have sometimes been obliged to reproduce the original or explain its meaning in a footnote. This applies to such expressions as *intuitus personae* and a *tenure ingénuile*.

The word *rente* lends itself to ambiguity. It may mean 'rent', a payment by the person in question; or it may mean 'pension' or 'annuity', a payment received. In this work it appears in both meanings. The word *cens* is clear. A *tenure à cens* is a tenure for rent payable to a rural, but not a feudal, lord. It is called a *censive* and the holder a *censitaire*. This kind of tenure appears to have existed in France from as early as the eleventh century, while written contracts became very numerous in the thirteenth; but nothing of the kind as yet existed in England. On the other hand, the scarcity of labour consequent on the Black Death led to a certain amelioration in the condition of tenants and labourers. This improvement could not be successfully restrained by the Statute of Labourers (1349) or other statutes, and the fifteenth century, in fact, saw a steady improvement in the peasant's real wages. When enclosures came to be widespread in the later fifteenth century, with the increasing commercialization of the age, servile conditions of tenure gradually disappeared. Enclosure, particularly for pasture as in the Midlands, raised a new question of security for the rural tenant, and the test of that security came to depend on whether or not he could produce a copy of the appropriate entries in the Rolls of the Manor, showing the conditions of his tenure. Such as could do so were known as copyholders, and were usually able legally to resist eviction or alteration of the conditions of their holding. As the French *censive* may be regarded as roughly equivalent to this kind of tenure, we have ventured to translate it by 'copyhold', whether or not purists may regard it as an anachronism.

It is a pleasure to acknowledge the advice and help of our friends at Durham University, and particularly that of Professor D. S. Reid in respect of the above complex and difficult question.

Contents

Introduction

The word 'feudalism'[1] is ambiguous. This is because the adjective *feodalis* was used in the Middle Ages, while the noun was invented only in the age when feudalism was approaching extinction, that is, towards the end of modern times. Today historians use this term, which is an anachronism in the eyes of medievalists, in two different senses.

One may first take it as designating a type of society based on a very special arrangement of human relationships: bonds of dependence linking one man to another and thus establishing a hierarchy among individuals. One man, the vassal, commends himself to another man, whom he chooses as his master and who accepts this deliberate 'commendation'.[2] The vassal owes his master fealty,[3] counsel, military and material assistance. The master – the lord – owes his vassal fealty, protection and the means of subsistence. This last can be provided in various ways, usually by conceding to the vassal a piece of land known as a 'benefice' or 'fief'. Thus the hierarchy among individuals was very soon accompanied by a hierarchy of rights over land, due to 'an extreme parcelling out of property rights'. Finally, since central authority had also been subdivided, there now existed in every country a hierarchy of autonomous authorities which exercised in their own interest the powers normally belonging to the State. This kind of society is sometimes described as a 'feudal régime', but J. Calmette and Marc Bloch have preferred to replace the word feudalism in this sense by 'feudal society'.

It is thus permissible to reserve the word feudalism for a

[1] *Féodalité.* Until about a hundred years ago 'feudality' was used by such writers as Hallam and Buckle. Subsequent usage has replaced it by 'feudalism' (Translators).

[2] In 1875 Sir Henry Maine, the author of *Ancient Law,* wrote that 'Feudalism had grown up from two great sources, the Benefice and the practice of Commendation' (Translators).

[3] *Fidélité,* almost synonymous with '*foi*', that is, loyalty to a mutual undertaking – a contract (Translators).

second connotation, namely a group of institutions. While the first meaning had mainly a social, and also political, bearing, the second is above all juridical, and it is in this sense that F. L. Ganshof uses it in his excellent book entitled *Qu'est-ce quo la féodalité?* But the two meanings are closely connected. The words *féodal, féodalité* derive from *fief*. Georges Duby observes that the fief is 'only one of the essential components' of the feudal system. But, as F. L. Ganshof writes, it is 'if not the main component, at least the most remarkable, in the hierarchy of rights over land which is included in' feudal society.

The word 'feudalism' survives as a term of invective. People still stigmatize political, administrative, economic and other 'feudalisms'. Everything that characterized the 'Old Régime' in France was stigmatized under this label, and thus on the night of 4 August 1789 the *feudal* rights were supposedly abolished, while the decree of 11 August 'entirely' suppressed 'the *feudal* régime'. For a long time, the invective covered both senses of the word. On one side, absolute monarchy was regarded as equivalent to feudalism, as we see in Proudhon's works; but is not absolutism the antithesis of a system mainly characterized by the disintegration of the State?

On the other hand, men confused feudalism and lordship (*seigneurie*), while feudalism and nobility were also regarded as equivalents. But the latter drew its strength in principle from the possession of lands known as lordships. If one thinks of its ancestral origins, the great domain and the *villa*, lordship may appear as 'an organization more than a thousand years old which permitted the great landowners to exact dues and services from their tenants'. Whether or not the great landowners possessed the right of administering justice had nothing to do with the disintegration of the State. If in 1789 feudalism was moribund, rural lordship remained very much alive; but the Revolution killed it by abolishing the 'feudal' rights which were nearly all 'seigneurial', that is, rights of lordship.

The old confusion between feudalism and lordship does not derive solely from the fact that the nobility shared in the vestiges of feudalism, and in the eighteenth century still possessed a large number of rural lordships. It is also explained by the fact that in certain regions, like England and western and south-western France, the two words served both purposes. For example *fief* described both tenures of vassalage and peasant tenures. It is no surprise then to find Montesquieu, a man of Bordeaux, deliberately confusing feudalism and the system of lordship. Even so, this great thinker saw that feudalism was indeed a phase of history marked by the splitting up of the powers which should normally be exercised by the State.

On the other hand, the Marxists have confused feudalism with lordship from other motives. According to them, 'feudalism' was less a kind of political régime than a type of economic and social organization which came between ancient slavery and capitalism. The essential feature of the system was obviously the substructure, characterized mainly by the subordination of the rural masses to the 'lords', who laid hold of part of their dependants' work as well as of the lands. But that is precisely lordship and not feudalism, because the latter is not at all a mode of production. For the Marxists, 'feudalism' lasted a thousand years, whereas real feudalism subsisted for only three hundred.

The persistent confusion of the two words, so frequently met with, has, however, one advantage. It puts one on guard against the temptation of considering feudalism and lordship separately; which is undesirable, since the fief consisted at the same time of one or several lordships. It would be preferable to see how lordship and feudalism have reacted on each other, without forgetting that lordship, if we extend this term to the great landed estate of the early Middle Ages, subsisted for more than a millenium. Lordship, in most of its features, existed long before feudalism and it was to survive it for long years. One might consider the question of lordship without saying much about feudal institutions, but the opposite would be far more difficult.

To examine feudalism, not limiting oneself to its juridical aspects, two attitudes are possible; and the rôle to assign to lordship will depend on this choice of attitude.

If one emphasizes rather the bonds between man and man,

the study of lordship will be seen in perspective. Marc Bloch has done this in his excellent *Sociéte féodale* (1940), and his conclusion is plain: 'Lordship in itself has no title to a place in the succession of institutions which we call feudal.' Why is this? Because the great domain which preceded it 'had previously coexisted with a stronger State, which had fewer and more tenuous relations with its subjects, but a much greater circulation of money'. And also, no doubt, because these conditions were again to prevail long before the end of the Middle Ages. On the other hand – and this is the second possible attitude – if, without minimizing the power of the bonds between man and man on all levels of the social hierarchy, if one wishes rather to emphasize the economic aspects of society, the fief – and therefore the rural lordship – is not just a simple, or even important element, but the very mainstay of the whole system. The whole of feudal society, from the serf to the feudal lord, lived on the revenues of the lordship. What the feudal lord drew in services and in money from his vassal – himself a rural lord – can only be estimated in terms of the produce of the estate, which was very often both rural lordship and a fief. The adoption of this second interpretation will be found more convenient in relating the study of lordship to the study of feudalism.

The limits imposed on the length of the present work have compelled the author to effect drastic cuts. Not only has it been generally impossible to describe the political, religious and economic environment, but the author has had to limit his study both in time and space. He has been led to suppose in the reader a knowledge of the *villa* and of vassalage in the Merovingian and Carolingian eras, that is, up to the mid-ninth century. Geographically, the study is centred on the old Frankish area, the regions between the middle waters of the Loire and the Rhine; where, like the *villa* and vassalage, lordship and feudalism came into being and acquired their most characteristic features. The part of the work devoted to other countries, like central and southern France, England and Germany, has been smaller; for Italy, very much reduced; while Christian Spain and the Latin States of the East have been altogether omitted.

Bibliography

The bibliography of the subject is immense, but will here be limited to the most important recent works, which often contain their own bibliographies.

I. *On vassalage and feudalism in general:*

BLOCH, Marc, *La société féodale*, 2 vols, Paris 1940. Eng. trs. by L. A. Manyon, *Feudal Society*, Routledge, London, and University of Chicago Press, 1961.

GANSHOF, F.-L., *Qu'est-ce que la féodalité?* 4th ed. Brussels, 1968. Eng. trs. *Feudalism*, Harper & Row, New York, 1961; Longman, London, 1964.

MOUSNIER, Roland, *Problèmes de stratification sociale*. Actes du Colloque Internationale, 1966. Published by the Faculté des Lettres et Sciences humaines de Paris-Sorbonne; Presses Universitaires de Paris, 1968.

II. *On the villa and lordship in general*

BLOCH, Marc, *L'histoire rurale française*, 2 vols, Paris, 2nd ed. 1961–4. Eng. trs. by J. Sondheimer, *French Rural History: An Essay on its Basic Characteristics*, University of California Press, Berkeley, Calif., and Routledge, London, 1966.

DUBY, Georges, *L'économie rurale et la vie des campagnes dans l'Occident médiéval (France, Angleterre, Empire, IXe–XVe siècles)*, 2 vols, Paris 1962. Eng. trs. *Rural Economy and Country Life in the Medieval West*, Arnold, London, and The University of South Carolina Press, 1968.

FOURQUIN, Guy, *Histoire économique de l'Occident médiéval*, Paris 1969.

IMBERT, Jean, *Histoire économique des origines à 1789*, Paris 1965. Recueils de la Société Jean-Bodin, Brussels: Vol. I, *Les liens de vassalité et les immunités*, 2nd ed. 1958; Vol. III, *La tenure*, 1938; Le domaine, 1949.

III. *Works on lordship and feudalism which, however, treat of only part of the period or the régions in question.*

BOUTRUCHE, R., *Seigneurie et féodalité; le premier age des liens d'homme à homme*, Paris, 1968.

DUBY, Georges, *La société aux XIe et XIIe siècles dan la région maconnaise*, Paris, 1953.

ELLUL, J., *Histoire des institutions, de l'époque franque à la révolution*, Paris, 1964.

GENICOT, L., *L'économie namuroise au bas Moyen Age*, Vol. I, *La seigneurie foncière*, Namur 1943; Vol. II, *Les hommes, la noblesse*, Louvain, 1960; Vol. III, *Le XIIIe siècle européen*, Paris, 1968.

HEERS, J., *L'Occident aux XIVe et XVe siècles; aspects économiques et sociaux*, Paris, 1970.

LOT, F., and FAWTIER, R., *Histoires des institutions françaises au Moyen Age*, Vol. I, *Institutions seigneuriales*, Paris, 1957; Vol. II, *Institutions royales*, 1958; Vol. III, *Institutions ecclésiastiques*, 1962.

TABACCO, G., *Fief et seigneurie dans l'Italie communale* (*Le Moyen Age*), Paris, 1969.

Certain important research studies to which the author is greatly indebted, and which contain no bibliographies, have not been printed. These consist in multicopied works, including C.-E. Perrins's *La seigneurie rurale en France et en Allemagne du début du IXe siècles à la fin du XIIe siècle; La sociètè allemande et ses institutions due X^e au XIIIe siècle;* and *La sociètè allemande a la fin du Moyen Age* (*XIVe and XVe siècles*). Several other works treat of the history of Germany and Italy from the ninth century to the end of the Middle Ages. Note finally E. Perroy's *Les Carolingiens*, *La féodalité en France du Xe au XIIe siècle*, and *La société féodale en France et en Angleterre au XIe et XIIe siècles.*

IV. *On the influence of lordship and feudalism after the fifteenth century.*

MOUSNIER, R., *Les hierarchies sociales de 1450 à nos jours*, Paris, 1969.

MOUSNIER, R., LABATUT, J. P. Z., DURAND, Yves, *Problèmes de stratification sociale. Deux cahiers de la noblesse pour les états généraux de 1649–15.* Faculté des Lettres et Sciences humaines de Paris-Sorbonne. Textes et Documents IX. Paris, 1965.

Additional bibliographies will be found at the ends of Parts One and Two, and suggestions for further reading are at the end of the book.

PART ONE

THE GROWTH OF LORDSHIP AND FEUDALISM

From the Mid-Ninth Century to the Year One Thousand

Chapter I

TRANSFORMATION OR EVOLUTION?

I. THE DISINTEGRATION OF THE STATE

The formation in the Carolingian period of a society based on vassalage was a spontaneous movement which took no account of political divisions but which officialdom could not ignore. For the consequences of this phenomenon, soon to make themselves felt, leave no doubt that vassalage led to the disintegration of the Carolingian Empire and 'State'. With hindsight one might suppose that the first Carolingians deeply distrusted this social change; but in fact, from the time of Pepin the Short, and certainly from the time of Charlemagne, vassalage was deliberately favoured by the sovereigns.

A. The Carolingians and Vassalage

Far from trying to thwart this social evolution – which would have been a practically hopeless task – Pepin and his successors favoured it. Bonds of vassalage were only private arrangements which the royal officials could have ignored in the exercise of their functions. And from the reign of Charlemagne onwards, at least the kings wished to use vassalage as an instrument of government. This systematic use of vassal relationship can only have been due to the very inadequacy and inefficiency of the 'State' government.

As a consequence of the wars of Pepin and Charlemagne, the Frankish kingdom had attained vast proportions. Communications being very slow, this Carolingian western Europe would by our standards resemble a continent. It was therefore impossible to recruit a civil service sufficiently numerous and competent, since the literary renaissance was to be slow and limited; or sufficiently reliable, if only because of the great distances to be covered and the presence of the aristocracy, the more so as the resources of the kingdom remained irregular and limited. Charlemagne and his heirs could control only a small number of their subjects.

They had therefore no choice but to seek as much co-operation as possible from this minority, an aristocracy. Their policy was in line with the ideas of the age. The king had the same mental attitude as the magnates, who felt no interest in the rural population as a whole, whether they were 'un-free' or 'free' (*francs*). Moreover, with very rare exceptions, the 'non-free' depended solely on their masters, and the free husbandmen were in much the same situation, especially if their *dominus* enjoyed immunity from royal dues. It was only the peasants on his personal domains who interested the king; and he thus found it convenient to have the rural population governed by intermediaries – in other words, by the great landowners.

For the king, therefore, only one social class had any importance – the landed aristocracy. He thought that by attaching it solidly to himself he would, with these magnates on his side and through their mediation, control the whole of the West. But he would also have to impose the royal authority on the whole of this class by using the bonds of vassalage in two ways: first, by multiplying as far as possible the number of his direct vassals, to whom he would grant important benefices and privileges; and, secondly, by inducing the other aristocrats, those whose estates were of average or modest extent, to become royal vassals or *vassi dominici*. The aristocracy would thus be involved in a hierarchy on three levels (the king, the *vassi dominici* and the vassals of the latter), these three ranks being bound together 'by a sort of chain of oaths of fealty, of which the king held one end, and which he relied on using in order to increase his control over his subjects' (E. Perroy), in default of being able to gain any practical advantage from the oaths of fealty which were constantly exacted from all free men.

The progress of royal vassalage is explained also by military considerations. Charlemagne and his early successors widened their 'recourse to vassalage in military matters'. Their armies did not consist only of their vassals, but the latter, with their own vassals, greatly increased the numbers and the fighting-value of the 'ost', especially when they were established in 'colonies', that is, in garrisons established in frontier zones and in turbulent regions, never fully subjected, like Aquitaine, Bavaria and Italy.

In political and administrative matters the use of vassalage proved very dangerous. By extending a custom that dated from his father's reign, Charlemagne brought into the system of vassalage those counts and prelates who were not already there. But this vassalage of *honores* was completed only under Louis the Pious. Thus, over the whole of Charlemagne's Empire administrative functionaries and high religious dignitaries were diverted from their proper pursuits.

One must distinguish here between the laymen and the clerics. As a *vassus dominicus*, a count received extensive benefits. As a count, he received the *res de comitatu*,[1] lands which were part of the domain and which constituted the endowment of this function, for its duration. In 817 a diploma of Louis the Pious, which relates to the endowment of the Count of Tournai, describes it as a *ministerium* and distinguishes it from the *beneficia* which were granted to the royal vassals. But in the course of the ninth century a kind of fusion took place, within a count's patrimony, between the *honor* and the *beneficium*; hence it became increasingly difficult to displace a count or revoke his functions, the more so as the *honor*, like the benefit, was very soon acquired for life and then became *de facto* hereditary. In 877, at Quierzy, the same provisional measures were taken in respect of a count's *honores*, when they fell vacant, as for the vassal's benefits. In both cases heredity prevailed, the son succeeding his father.

Ecclesiastical functions evolved in the same way – except of course in the matter of heredity – because, at least since the reign of Louis the Pious, all bishops and certain abbots had

[1] Or *comitatus*, or *ministerium* or *honor*. Here *honor* designates not merely the public function, but also its endowment.

been constrained to become royal vassals. Those prelates whose lands were given immunity were regarded as functionaries. This state of things is reflected in the writings of Hincmar, Archbishop of Reims, who uses the same word, *honores*, to cover both the functions and the endowments of the bishops, and even the beneficiaries of the royal vassals: the function (*episcopatus, abbatia*) is assimilated to the benefice. As to the homage and the oath of fealty taken by the prelate, these were the same as for laymen. In 860 Hincmar did indeed protest against the rite of placing his hands between the king's and taking the oath, probably without success; but he accepted the rule of *commendatio*. The prelate was given *seizin* of his bishopric or his abbey according to the rite of *vestitio*, the symbolical object then being the crozier. The mode of tenure of its properties was thus bringing the upper clergy almost into line with the lay aristocracy, from which its members (the younger sons of powerful families) were drawn in increasing numbers.

Willingly or perforce the Carolingians instituted a policy which almost at once proved prejudicial to the power of the Crown. Bishops and abbots, particularly those who enjoyed immunity, acquired greater and greater freedom of action. This was not very dangerous. What was more dangerous was that the counts, far from being more submissive, freed themselves from the king's control and made their functions hereditary.[1] As to the private vassals, the recruiting of whom the Carolingians had tried to supervise and who possessed in principle the right to have recourse to the sovereign's support against their *dominus*, they became more involved in this evolution than the first Carolingians would have desired.

There remains the case of the *vassi dominici* not invested with *honores*, that is, the nobles of minor or average wealth. As the king was too remote and was growing weaker, they

[1] The counts, having become vassals, obey the king only in as far as he respects his engagements. Since homage is paid, the duties are reciprocal, and the king is no longer obeyed by his agents as sovereign. The weaker he grows, the more can his 'vassal-agents' impose on him heavy engagements which still further ruin his power.

found it better to yield to the pressure of the local magnate, very often the count. Finally, towards the year 900, royal vassals were found only in the vicinity of the Court.

Was the failure of the Carolingians really total? It was not. Vassalage was far from being the chief cause of the dynasty's decline; it was in fact to contribute largely, from the tenth century to the time of the 'feudal monarchies', to safeguarding the monarchical principle.

B. The Crumbling of the Central Power, and the Attempt to Create Local Centres of Authority

In Francia and in Germany the ruin of the 'State' was at once the cause and consequence of what Marc Bloch has called a 'splitting up of public authority into small groupings under the command of individuals'. Certain countries disintegrated, and henceforward the basic unit was the castle and what was later to be called the castellany. But there was also a movement in the opposite direction, a 'regrouping of regional powers in the hands of one man'.

These contrary movements were no new thing after the Treaty of Verdun. 'Principalities' had been made and unmade as early as the Merovingian age, for example in Austrasia and in Burgundy, apart from Aquitaine and the beginnings of national duchies in Germany, like Tassilon's Bavaria; while smaller units may have disappeared. The new situation emerging was for several regional formations to retain their geographical limits for a very long time to come: not only in Germany where the duchies, except in Lorraine, were national and possessed therefore a certain ethnic, linguistic and juridical individuality, but even in Italy and in Francia. Certain countries were thus united under the *dominium* of one aristocrat.

It was in western Francia, where individualism was less marked than in Germany and the old political divisions less ingrained than in Italy, that the disappearance of royal authority was most serious and that the rise of principalities was a general phenomenon, although earlier ages had done comparatively little to prepare the way for it.

The final disappearance of the Carolingians in 987 was

due neither to chance nor ill-luck. 'The accession to the throne of the Robertians does not constitute a rupture; it consecrates a fact.' J. Dhondt has definitely shown that the disappearance of royal power in western France was due to the 'progressive geographical and territorial shrinkage of the taxable area'. Like the first Merovingians, the first Carolingians had established their power over a vast domain composed of many large fiscal regions disseminated throughout the country. These sources of great wealth were the principal support of the Palace, which conferred benefices in order to ensure new loyalties or consolidate old ones. If the kings had found it possible for many years to ensure an 'equilibrium' (Perroy) between their fiscal region (that is, the ensemble of the individual fiscs) and the magnates' domains, this situation had no longer obtained after Louis the Pious. The Empire became stabilized territorially at the moment when the rivalry between the king's sons, and later between the candidates for the throne – Robertians against Carolingians – obliged them to pay more and more for the always uncertain loyalty of the magnates, who were disposed to 'raise the stakes' even higher. At the end of the tenth century the result was clear; the landed property of the Carolingians had shrunk like a *peau de chagrin*,[1] and its owner was king only in name.

This took place at a time when the principalities were taking shape, regions where the sovereign could no longer intervene except through the intermediary of the prince; that is, very rarely and without much success. The Carolingians had perceived the danger and made a rather half-hearted and ineffectual effort to forge a principality for themselves. The final victory of the Robertians in the person of Hugues Capet (987) had a parallel in the earlier replacement of the Merovingians by Pepin and his dynasty. The latter were richly provided with landed property, while the last of the *rois fainéants* were practically landless. Hugues headed a group of homogeneous counties between the Seine and the

[1] A reference to Balzac's novel. Raphael possesses a piece of shagreen leather which has the magic property of fulfilling every wish he forms; but it shrinks with each fulfilment until its final disappearance coincides with the death of its owner (Translators).

middle waters of the Loire at a time when the last of the Carolingians held little more than Laon and some score of fiscal units along the Aisne and Oise.

The year 987 was marked by the triumph of the territorial principalities, or at least of one of them and of its master. Military, judicial and economic functions (such as *tonlieux*[1] and the minting of money), protection of churches, as also authority over landowners and vassals, were attributed to the duke or the count who might be lord of one or several counties; and not to the king. In short, by the end of the tenth century the first Capetians were little more than 'dukes in their kingdom', their only source of real authority being their own principality.

The 'movement of usurpation' which had begun soon after 850 had proceeded most quickly in the time of Eudes (898). It was at the end of the ninth century that Baudouin II established the county of Flanders, that Richard the Justicer built up the duchy of Burgundy and that the first duchy of Aquitaine and the march of Toulouse were born of the 'incongruous amalgam' of Bernard Plantevelue's counties. It was also about the year 900 that the Neustrian principality of the Robertians appeared, as also Normandy, the latter an entirely 'original formation', being due to the occupation of the land by the Vikings before Charles the Simple ceded it in 911 to their chieftain Rollo. If all public authority inside each principality was not, after 900, concentrated in the hands of the prince, the latter possessed the greater part of it and would not have to wait very long before seizing the rest.

The principalities of western Francia had three main features. Only a few of them had retained their original form; their boundaries were ill-defined; and if their princes encouraged regional traditions, none of these principalities contained a really homogeneous population.

Among the fairly coherent ones which were to preserve, on the whole, their original boundaries – some of them even as late as 1789 – we may count the duchies of Normandy and Brittany, the county of Flanders and even the Robertian

[1] *Tonlieu:* a tax levied for the right of holding a stall in the market for the sale of produce or merchandise (Translators).

domain, the cradle of the future Ile-de-France. They have been called 'giants with feet of clay', since they suffered from the same ills as the kingdoms – in so far as they were too vast and as the circulation of men and of orders was particularly difficult, and as their princes 'were not able to impose rules of succession to put a brake on fragmentation'. Several were therefore divided up as early as the tenth century into units, such as Aquitaine, better adapted to the conditions of the time. One cannot draw a general map for the tenth century because the boundaries remained so uncertain. Towards the year 1000 the duke of Burgundy exercised effective control only in the centre of his duchy (between Autun, Avallon, Dijon and Beaune), while the 'peripheral courts' (from Nevers to Langres and from Troyes to Mâcon) recognized his authority only intermittently.

Despite their fragility, the duchies and counties of western France were sometimes destined to endure for centuries. And yet their populations were never very homogeneous. Neither the Burgundians nor the Aquitanians, nor the dwellers in the ancient province of Neustria, were ever all united in a 'national' principality. After their boundaries were roughly fixed in the year 1000, the duchies of Burgundy and Aquitaine were to contain only a reduced portion of the one-time Burgundia and Aquitania. The county of Flanders contained Romance-speaking[1] people and Thiois.[2] In Brittany, Celtic for the greater part, the centre of gravity was on the eastern fringe of the duchy, in the Romance-speaking regions of Nantes and Rennes. And in Normandy the real 'Normans' – the Vikings – were never more than a minority.

Conditions were quite different in Germany. On the death of Louis the Child (911) the Germans discontinued the custom of recognizing another Carolingian in the person of Charles the Simple, king of western Francia. The recognition of a new sovereign was thwarted by the 'individualism of the ethnic and political groups', that of the national duchies (*Stammesherzogtum*) which went back to a remote past and had survived the Merovingian and Carolingian conquest.

[1] That is, Gallo-Romans who spoke a French dialect (Translator).
[2] Presumably Flemings.

Although the ancient 'laws' of the Alamans, Bavarians and Saxons had fallen into disuse, common memories, languages and customs gave each duchy a possible basis for effective unity. Moreover, the *Stammes* of Bavaria and Alemania had retained their national dukes after becoming part of the Frankish kingdom. But though, at the beginning of the tenth century, each *Stamm* still had a duke, he was no longer a descendant of an ancient dynasty, but the heir of an official appointed by one of the first Carolingians, who had ended by adopting the title of *dux*. At the end of the ninth century the weakness of royal power, and also the Norman, Slavonic and Hungarian incursions, had the effect of renewing the individualism of the *Stammes*, which put themselves under the protection of the *dux*. Towards the year 900 four *Stammes* were thus established: the duchies of Saxony, Franconia, Bavaria and Suabia. In addition to these, Lotharingia, devoid of any ethnic unity because it was occupied by French-speaking people, by Alamans, Friesians, etc., experienced changes of fortune which gave rise to a peculiar individualism of its own. From 925 it was to form the fifth duchy of Germany.

From 911 onwards, two of these duchies, Franconia and Saxony, saw the rise of monarchies. In Germany, at an earlier date than in western Francia, the Carolingians had been definitely supplanted by territorial princes. Conrad I, who became king in 911, was a Franconian. He was succeeded by the Duke of Saxony, Henry I, whose dynasty occupied the throne until its extinction in 1024. The great *Salian* dynasty then began to reign with Conrad II. The Dukes of Saxony claimed that they and their men descended from the Salian Franks, and this charismatic belief led them to revive the tradition of the Carolingians.

Opposition between these German duchies was stronger than in France, because of their individualism. It was to be prolonged even after the Middle Ages. The choice of a new king implied agreement between the various national groups; hence the principle of election was maintained, whereas in France after 987 this principle was soon replaced by a *de facto*, and then a *de jure* heredity. As to the German magnates, the partial independence of the duchies gave them exceptional powers, which were lacking in the French and English magnates when at variance with their sovereigns. If, however, under Conrad I and Henry I, that is from 911 to 936, struggles against the dukes, followed by agreements concluded with them, greatly weakened the monarchy, a very definite recovery of royal power took place under Otto I, who succeeded in bridling them by limiting their rights and treating them as officials. This was a return to Carolingian procedure. The dukes were the king's vassals from the beginning of the new emperor's reign; he could deprive them of office and he did not in principle recognize the son's right to succeed his father in his titles and functions. Such was the position towards the year 1000; but how long was it to last?

For the time being, then, the king of Germany seemed to be in a stronger position than the king of western France. The latter no longer appeared in person in regions distant from his place of residence; while south of the Loire most of the princes did not even pay him homage. It was only north of the river that the princes, for the most part, commended themselves to him and became his *fideles*. But they might break with the sovereign and then again renew contact, attend the sessions of the Curia or not, share or not share in his expeditions, according as they were in rebellion or at peace, at the time of the disturbances occasioned by the rivalry between Robertians and Carolingians. In short, the number of counts and territorial princes really faithful to the king was not great and it constantly varied with the state of general disorder. The king was little more than a territorial prince, and that only if he was a Robertian. All the counts and princes, however, recognized, at least ostensibly, the king's supreme authority, derived both from his consecration by the archbishop and from tradition. They related their acts to the year of his reign; in circumstances of great peril they sometimes even appealed for his help (cf. the case of Borel, count of the Spanish March). Such developments offered a hope for the future.

But such hopes scarcely existed in Italy. Here the process of territorial disintegration was accelerated by the political divisions already existing. In north Italy the bishops exercised the power of counts and created ecclesiastical principalities at Bergamo, Piacenza, Cremona, Parma and elsewere, while marquisates were established in Friuli and at Ivrea. The states of the Church were sandwiched between the marquisate of Tuscany and the Lombard or Byzantine duchies of the south. Royal authority had in fact disappeared, or at most operated only on rare occasions; and since it was exterior to the country, it seemed to offer little hope for the future.

II. FROM THE *VILLA*[1] TO THE RURAL LORDSHIP

The evolution or transformation – opinions are divided as to its nature – which led from the *villa* to the lordship was mainly due to the change that affected an old institution, that of immunity, and to the appropriation by the potentates of the right of *ban*.[2] How far did this process modify the life of the country folk?

A. Immunity

Since the end of the Merovingian era, the estates of the Church had been distinguished from those of laymen by an advantage from which the latter were soon desirous of profiting. It was a question of the immunity which the Carolingians granted even more liberally that their predecessors.

The origin of immunity, which has given rise to much discussion, goes back to the last days of the Roman Empire. The *fisc*, or fiscal domain of the State, was exempted as such from direct or indirect taxation, and the rural workers who lived on it did not pay a poll-tax. Under the Merovingians the domain continued to enjoy fiscal exemption, to which judicial exemption was added as a corollary. The steward of a royal *villa* collected from the inhabitants all the revenue which the king reserved for his own use and acted as the king's delegate in the courts. The inhabitants, as exempt from the jurisdiction of the public tribunals, were subject only to the control of the steward.

[1] The *villa* was a great landed estate dating from Roman times (Translators).

[2] i.e. the right to summon by proclamation all the adult males to render military service. Other duties were also usually required (Translators).

If the king alienated a part of the domain, this part had logically to lose the right of immunity. But, as early perhaps as the sixth century, the connection between the domain and immunity was regarded as indissoluble, immunity being attached to the domain for ever. When alienating land, the king therefore *ipso facto* alienated the privilege. The consequences of this indissoluble connection were to be immense, in transforming the *villa* into the lordship.

In the course of the sixth and seventh centuries the kings squandered their huge landed capital (more vast than the emperor's because their possessions had been swollen by spoliation and conquest) mainly to the advantage of the Church; so that Charles Martel was often only recovering from the Church the donations granted by the Merovingians. Thus, in general, the temporalities of bishops and abbots, which had been mostly constituted under the barbarian kings, were derived from the lands of the domain and, unless clearly stated to the contrary, enjoyed immunity. Now, on the pretext of simplifying their administration, the holders of immunized *villae*, clerics for the greater part, obtained the extension of this privilege to all their other properties. Thus diplomas and formulae conceded immunity to the whole of certain temporalities of the Church. Finally, the last major change in immunity before the Carolingians was that of the judiciary, and this had become the most important, since the right to raise taxes had been abrogated at a greater rate than the decline of the State. Fustel de Coulanges wrote: 'There is no immunity unless the royal judges are excluded.' The latter could no longer hold their courts, condemn, seize, arrest men, or even benefit from the right of shelter in the territory which had been set apart from the jurisdiction of the State institutions. For the person enjoying immunity the advantages were notable. He collected the judicial fees, except that he had – though not always – to pay over part of the fines to the sovereign. Thus the administration of justice was beginning to secure considerable profits to the owners of *villae*, profits which undoubtedly formed a notable percentage of the revenues of their domains.

The Carolingian age saw fewer changes than the Merovingian in immunity, of which the new features, scarcely modified, simply became more clearly marked. But immunity became more general. Vast numbers of diplomas conceded, and not merely confirmed it, so that nearly all the ecclesiastical lands were in possession of it. But immunity was no longer conceded to laymen (this had always been rare), which meant that henceforward immunity was the normal system for Church estates and for them only. The count and his subordinates were excluded from the temporalities of bishoprics and abbeys, and nearly all their powers, even that of raising military levies, passed over to the prelates who became the chief representatives of the king in their many vast domains.

In matters of finance, exemption – *immunis* means exempt – was as complete as in military matters. From all his vassals and tenants the prelate raised, on the king's behalf, not only the *tonlieux* but the contributions levied whether for the army (the *hostilicium*, a tax to replace the obligation of military service); or to deal with the Norman incursions (the Carolingians had raised taxes for the payment of tribute exacted by the invaders); or for the exercise of justice (the 'immunist' was required to pay a third part of the fines to the sovereign). In judicial matters, however, immunity was not complete. The prelate and the count shared between them the power of judging and condemning, Charlemagne having probably insisted that the count should continue to exercise some part of this authority. In penal matters a distinction was made between *causae minores* (misdemeanors), involving a fine of less than 60s. under the jurisdiction of the 'immunist' (and no longer that of the *centenier*, a subordinate of the count), and *causae majores*. These were the gravest offences, such as crimes, involving a fine of 60s. (reserved for the *bannum dominicum*), prison, or corporal punishment, including death. For such offences the count's tribunal had sole jurisdiction, and the immunist was required to bring delinquents to this court under penalty of heavy sanctions, including confiscation of property or loss of immunity.

The effects of immunity were very great, and not only on

ecclesiastical lands; but they were not the effects hoped for by the sovereigns, who had thought they were bringing the immunized territories under their immediate control and consolidating their own power by weakening the counts, who were thus opposed to the immunists. For the loyalty of the counts was a good deal more uncertain than that of the prelates, since the latter were appointed by the king and it was easier to ensure their allegiance. But the Carolingians had deluded themselves, and their control over the immunized domains rapidly deteriorated. This was the fault of the kings, of Charlemagne in the first instance, in conferring new privileges on the churches, financial privileges such as abandonment by the king of his share in the fines, exemption from *tonlieu* for the prelate and his *familia,* and even complete relegation of this tax to the advantage of the prelate; military privileges, too, as limitations of the number of troops which he was required to supply for the army.

Hence the laymen, notably the counts, coveted similar privileges. The Carolingians promulgated heavy penalties against such efforts as well as against the eventual rebellion of the immunists. But it is significant that the sovereigns quickly recognized that their calculations had failed.

They had failed even more than appeared. The immunized lands did not long remain in immediate dependence on the Crown. A new kind of division soon appeared between the king and his subjects in the ecclesiastical estates. The immunist had had, in effect, to form an embryonic civil service, recruiting judges, tax assessors of *tonlieu* etc., whom he often chose from among the clerics of his household. But churchmen could not administer criminal justice, as in cases of flagrant offences, nor could they lead their troops in battle. They were therefore obliged to delegate these lay functions to a subordinate, a member of the local aristocracy. From the beginning of the ninth century this layman was called an *avoué* (*advocatus*) or *vidame* (*vice-dominus*), this last title being used only in episcopal domains. There were two means of paying for his services; to hand over to him a share in the profits which the king had yielded to the immunist, or else to concede certain of the Church's *villae*; or to use both means of payment. Now as the 'advocate' exercised almost the same functions as the count, he very soon revealed himself as intransigent in regard to the prelate, as the count in regard to the king. Just as the count had been, so to speak, making inroads on the king's authority, so the advocate quickly assured himself of a hold over part of the Church property. This, even on a short-term prospect, posed a serious threat to the temporalities. From being intermediaries between the State and the immunized lands, the advocates were beginning to assume the rôle of 'necessary but heavy-handed protectors' as early as the tenth century.

The documents, though rare for the tenth century, are fairly numerous for the eleventh. In the former period advocacy presents features 'radically different' from those of the ninth century. These features probably took clearer shape before the year 1000 and they show that in the interval advocacy had changed from the Carolingian form to something very new (Perrin).

As early as the tenth century the advocate no longer had to act as an intermediary between the immunist and the State in countries where the latter had diminished authority, mainly in western Francia. The collapse of the king's authority led the churches, especially the abbeys, to seek someone who would both defend them against the disturbances and anarchy of the times and act as an agent who could oblige the Church's tenants to fulfil their obligations. Having now no possibility of recourse to their natural protector, the king, the clerics either vested these functions in their advocates, or – as must frequently have happened – unwillingly agreed to accept very powerful laymen as advocates. Contrary to the rules promulgated by Charlemagne, advocates were chosen among the *potentes* (counts or viscounts). Moreover, there was now only one advocate for each immunized house,[1] instead of one for each of the counties which contained the *villae* of a temporality. This, when the properties were widely dispersed, led the advocate to enfeoff[2] his functions to sub-advocates for the most distant domains. In a large part of western Francia

[1] Bishopric or abbey.
[2] i.e. delegate as a fief.

the advocates had nearly all changed into oppressors between the end of the ninth century and the year 1000.

The function was exercised less gratuitously than ever. In the ninth century the advocate would receive, in return for his services, a benefice for life. In the course of time this benefice was changed into a fief, *de facto* hereditary. It could be alienated because it was from the benefice that an advocate 'detached fiefs which he conceded to the sub-advocates.' This fief was a very peculiar kind because it created 'purely unilateral obligations', consisting in the protection of the lord by the vassal without reciprocal service. Contrary to the practice of his predecessors in Carolingian times, the advocate now levied a due of *hospitalitas* every time he visited the immunised land in order to fulfil his duties; and, when he presided over the 'seigneurial courts' (usually three times a year), he received a portion of the fines. This is in the obscure period when private jurisdictions were arising, but of a surety certain immunists were not content with judging *causae minores* only, but were also judging *causae majores,* to the detriment of the counts. The causes pleaded before the 'seigneurial courts' thus increased in number, but the increase in revenue consequent on the greater number of fines brought no advantage to the clerics. Only their advocates profited from it, having consigned the judging of cases under the lower jurisdiction to the agents of the clerics who sat in courts not described as 'general' because their revenue was very small.

Many bishoprics may have escaped the 'constraint of advocacy', but very few abbeys. This advocacy represented a heavy burden. In return for the protection they afforded, the advocates imposed 'exactions' on the members of the abbey, and this tended 'to substitute the lordship of the advocates for that of the abbeys'. Hence, at the end of the century, when the Gregorian reforms took place, the monks acted vigorously to limit all these 'exactions'.

Of the geographical distribution of advocacy one can as yet distinguish only the essential features. In the tenth century and later, advocacy should theoretically have prospered in regions where royal power was weak; but this was not always so. It is true that post-Carolingian advocacy was scarcely able to develop in Normandy, the duke himself having acted as protector of the churches. The new advocacy – the *seigneurial* kind as C. E. Perrin has called it – succeeded the Carolingian east of a line joining the eastern limits of Normandy, Chartres, Orléans, Bourges and Lyon. Now this region contained both strong princes and weak princes. Even stranger is the fact that in the south, which was often rather anarchical, advocacy retained its Carolingian form, described as 'humble' because the advocate acted only as the modest legal representative of the immunist. In any case the Capetian monarchy was to recover strength in the twelfth century and to absorb the functions of advocacy. The latter often disappeared before the 1200s, and it was the king who now assured the protection of the churches. But in the Empire the situation evolved in an almost contrary direction. During the early Middle Ages the king of Germany had remained strong enough to assure the protection of religious houses and prevent an extension of the advocates' powers. This 'Carolingian' advocacy was to survive longer in Germany than elsewhere, disappearing only on the eve of the revolutionary era.

Immunity and advocacy are regarded as among the first causes which explain why the *villa* changed into the rural lordship, mainly because the extension of immunity to the *villae* possessed by laymen had greatly increased in the course of time. Although only one diploma of immunity in favour of a layman (888) has been preserved, it is certain that within the bounds of their estates, laymen exercised a jurisdiction similar to that of clerics in their immunized lands. In the capitulary of Pîtres (864) Charles the Bald places the immunized domain in the same category as that of a lay *potens*, which means that at that time every lay *potens*[1] was assimilated, from the point of view of immunity, to the ecclesiastical *potens*. Thus laymen enjoyed on their estates a *de facto* immunity which had the willing (at first) or unwilling acquiescence of the king. The count extended to his own freeholds the rights he exercised within the limits of his county. Many laymen built up whole or part of their fortune

[1] i.e. a territorial magnate.

by means of benefices derived from the royal domains or from the temporalities of churches, and these lands continued to enjoy their previous immunity. Later, the king consented perforce. It was certainly by usurpation, without any tacit agreement by the king, and even contrary to his will, that many laymen assumed immunity over their own lands.

Immunity, origin of the private jurisdictions which were completely established towards the year 1000, was partly the consequence of the decline of royal power, like the rural lordship or the 'bannal' lordship which derived from it. Powers originally belonging to the State were added to the old rights belonging to the domain, and they caused the already ancient power of the landowner to weigh more heavily on his peasant dependants. As early as the tenth century the immunized lords or the advocates became the judges of nearly all these peasants.

B. The Right of Ban

Under the Carolingians the symbol of public authority was the King's *bannus* or ban. Its significance was as rudimentary and imperfect as the royal power itself. Since the king's primary mission was to maintain peace between the 'Francs', the ban was a general power to issue commands, to control and to punish free men.

In respect of the sovereign, free men thus had a double duty, that of obedience (the king 'constrains and punishes') and of military service (the king 'commands'). In respect of the local representative of authority, the count, this double duty took the form of an obligation to join the contingents of the county every time the Frankish army was called up, and also to take part in the judicial assemblies which judged crimes and misdemeanours and were entrusted with maintaining peace among the 'Francs' (free men). This was what in feudal times was to be called the *service d'ost* and the *service de plaid* or *de cour*.

Between about 850 and 1000 the counts and their delegates continued, in as much as they possessed public authority, to exact fulfilment of these obligations; but this was, henceforward, and with some exceptions, to their own advantage;

which means that the great landowners now disposed of the ban over all the men on their estates and thus strengthened their power over the peasants, since this ban was evidently more effective than immunity. It comprised military powers, judicial powers, and also economic. Its application was very wide. All the *homines* (dependants) would now have to agree to new services and new dues, or accept the renewed application of old charges which had fallen into disuse. It was in the name of the right of ban that the source of profits for the master of the former *villa* were to be swollen towards 1000 on the Continent; and, at the end of the eleventh century, in England where the manorial system was rendered more severe by the Norman conquest.

The right of ban gave its holder such power over his tenants that bannal lordship became the kind of rural lordship which weighed most heavily on the peasants. But what was the position of owners of *villae* who did not possess it? One may suppose that the vague authority which, according to certain historians, the *dominus* had for long past exercised over all the men on his lands was by extension gradually reinforced, and that the *dominus* became a landowning lord.

Lastly, the ban – whether it were the superior ban or the inferior, according as its possessor held it wholly or in part – was not to be acquired at once by all the *potentes*. It is supposed that at first only the counts and castellans enjoyed this right. But it was to be extended little by little to the lower members of the landowning hierarchy. In the Mâconnais the 'extension of justice and powers of command and the confusion between bannal lordship and lordship over land' were to be completed only after 1200. Thus the evolution was sometimes fairly slow.

C. Dependence of the Rural Masses: Numerical Strength and Social Weakness

During the early Middle Ages the rural dependants constituted the vast majority of the population. Apart from them, there were only, as against the landed aristocracy, small freeholders in decreasing numbers, and town dwellers, merchants and others, also not numerous.

To observe that the peasants' standard of living remained miserable explains why they were never able to resist the will of the aristocrats, whose exigencies could only lower that standard, since the age was one of economic depression. The decline in the economic situation of the rustics was almost continuous.

For the Merovingian era, sources of information are very sparse; they are still insufficient, despite great progress in research, for the Carolingian age. One cannot count on the capitularies, which pay little attention even to the free peasants; for centuries the kings left the rural masses to the discretion of the aristocrats. The other sources of information (for example, the land-registers[1]) are also to be treated with caution. They recognise little more than one line of demarcation, that which separated the free from the unfree. One recalls Charlemagne's reply to one of his *missi dominici*: 'There exist only two conditions, that of the *liber* and that of the *servus*.' But in spite of this juridical distinction, if the free and the unfree both worked on a tenure, they were strictly dependent on the *dominus* of the *villa*. The conditions of life were equalising the differing personal statuses. That is why it would be difficult to speak of rural classes – a class of the free and one of the unfree – because the concept of class can never rest on merely juridical criteria.

In the law governing persons, as in the judicial system, Roman Law and barbarian laws clearly distinguished between free men and slaves. Now in the course of the early Middle Ages this distinction became, in reality, progressively attenuated; so that the distinctions between the status of individuals tended to lose their force, the peasants becoming fused in a single stratum of dependants.[2]

[1] *Les polypiques.*

[2] One must not forget the free men who, being small landowners, were not dependants. But their numbers steadily diminished during the later years of the Empire and in barbarian and Carolingian times. The monarchy played a part in this decline. Independence and full liberty carried disadvantages, because the military and judicial obligations of small landowners were very heavy. The *potentes* of the region, especially if they exercised some public function or enjoyed a privilege of immunity, did not lack the means to force the

1. *From the Gallo-Roman Land-Worker to the Land-Worker of the Early Middle Ages.* In the last years of the Empire, the term *colonus,* which had previously meant any kind of husbandman, had acquired a sense both limited and exact – that of a man attached to the land. The peasants who were tenants of a great landowner were involved in a movement which aimed at making many professions hereditary, with a view to palliating the social difficulties and the material decadence which followed the depopulation of the countryside. The institution of the *colonat* was therefore part of a general plan. Just as the aristocrat was fixed by heredity to his municipal function, so the tenant of a land which had been tilled by his family for at least thirty years, was attached to the property, nor could his descendants leave it. If the *colon* remained theoretically free, since unlike the slave, he had no master, he none the less became the slave of his land. On the other hand, the landowner could not remove him from it, and the régime of this new kind of colonat assured in principle to those subject to it security for the morrow. But in reality the system was far more favourable for the aristocrat. Its principal *raison d'être* was to prevent the magnates from being short of labour to work on their domains, the more so as legislation stipulated that the *colon* should owe his 'landlord' the dues and 'customary' services; as the latter went further by imposing the conditions of work he required. The real situation of the *colon* thus came near to that of the slave who had received a tenure. The aristocrat levied the land tax on his *colons,* while he was required to pay over the proceeds to the State; hence frequent abuses.

How far was the legislation of the later Empire applied? The emperor did not dispose of means of coercion sufficient to hold all the *colons* to the land, and in the West a certain amount of mobility persisted in the rural population.

This mobility increased greatly with the Germanic invasions. One can hardly see how the Merovingian or Lombard

francs to hand over the ownership of their lands and take it back as a tenure. When his smallholding thus became part of a *villa* the 'franc' at the same time lost part of his liberty.

'functionaries' could have pursued and recaptured the fugitives. One can therefore be certain that the old obligation fell into disuse, even though some of the aristocrats may have tried to fight against what later ages were to call the 'decampings'.

Thus the Carolingian *colon* was not quite the same as the colon of the later Empire. If one can believe the land-registers, the word was still the preferred term; but the men whom it now designated were evidently not all descended from their Roman namesakes. Even in the relative mixing of peoples due to the great Germanic invasions, there must have been, as at all times, transfers of population from one region to another, the extinction of certain families, etc. Among the *colons* of a Carolingian *villa,* descendants of primitive *colons* must have figured, as well as immigrants – who would be simply men who cleared the ground for agriculture – and especially perhaps former small freeholders.

The Carolingians clearly defined the new status of the *colons*: they were free tenants whose dependence on the master of the *villa* had been supported by the King. 'Let every dominus', Charlemagne ordered in a capitulary of 810, 'exercise pressure on his *juniores* (dependants) so that they become more and more obedient and accept the imperial orders and prescripts'. In short, the first Carolingians worked to consolidate and extend the bonds of dependence from the lowest tier in the social 'pyramid', as they did for the other tiers, and always under the same delusion. They thought to control the masses of the peasantry by the intermediary of the magnates, the latter being their immediate vassals. So true it is that the march towards vassalage and the march towards rural lordship proceeded side by side.

This movement towards rural lordship can be very clearly discerned in respect of the judicial powers of the *dominus,* even if he was not an immunist or – later – in possession of the ban. The Roman landowners had assumed the power of constraining and punishing any of their tenants, even those who, like the *colons,* were free in principle. Justinian whose laws were applied in Byzantine Italy, recognised the aristocrats as having the right to punish their *colons* '*in moderation*';

without appealing to the public courts. The Carolingians were to go further. One knows what happened to the tenants of immunists; but even the others had to follow the lead of their lords, if called on to give army service. It was the same *a fortiori*, in the fiscs (groups of royal domains) where the *judices* (stéwards), probably recruited from the aristocracy, deputized for the lords. A bar was everywhere placed between the *colons* and public authority; and in the case of an impotent monarchy, the public lawcourts were simply not resorted to by those free men, or 'francs', who were in fact all *colons*. More or less prevented by the great landowners from attending the public tribunals, they fell under the judicial control of their masters – except for criminal cases, when the *dominus* was still obliged to produce the guilty person before the tribunal of the count.

By the ninth century the *colon* was in effect treated as unfree, the more so as he had now ceased to be summoned to serve in the army, the master having redeemed the military obligations of his *colons* and assessed them individually for payment due to the king in lieu of service. Carolingian society, like the feudal society that was to follow it, was predominantly warlike. Individuals who did not serve in the army were despised; and so, in spite of repeated declarations that the *colon* was theoretically free, he sometimes ended by being treated like a slave. By the edict of Pîtres (864), Charles the Bald decided to punish *colons* who infringed the royal ban, not now with a fine, but with sixty lashes of the whip, just as if they were slaves.

As these men undoubtedly formed the greater part of the rural population at the end of the early Middle Ages, one can see how greatly the liberty of individuals had been reduced. The *colons* were now no more than 'half-free', their lot had deteriorated, whereas the condition of the slaves had evolved in the opposite direction.

One should not, however, forget that, if the *colon* no longer enjoyed in principle more than the usufruct of his land, of which the full ownership in Roman law had been willingly or forcibly abandoned by his ancestors, when they were small landholders, he could still no doubt dispose of it freely, or even on terms. It will be seen much later that this right, deriving from the rupture of the ancient bond which attached the *colon* to his land, could lead to amelioration of his lot, and even to a genuine social 'promotion'.

2. *From Ancient Slavery to Medieval Serfdom.* The Carolingian slaves, who were less numerous than the *colons*, were very different from the slaves of the ancient world, which explains why historians now prefer to speak of *serfs* and not of slaves.

The bands of slaves who worked on the great Roman domains had steadily dwindled in numbers, so much so that from the eighth century onward they were no longer more than a residual group. This term, however, is hardly exact, because the condition of the *servi* had definitely improved in the course of ages. The slaves of antiquity were a kind of merchandise which the owner could sell and sometimes even destroy. If they were not always ill-treated, their Carolingian descendants (if these were indeed part of their posterity) led a far less painful sort of life. This was partly due to Christianity. The *servi* of the ninth and tenth centuries certainly remained very poor folk, but their life was less precarious. Only a small proportion of them had to lodge in cabins near the master of the *villa's* house and remain at his disposal, their work directed by the steward who provided their subsistence. While these *servi* appear to have had no personal property, they had some commercial value; they were no longer merchandise.

There were many causes for this partial disappearance of slavery. There were still slave-markets before the seventh century. Gregory of Tours indicates that in the sixth century the society of Gaul remained 'very largely a slave-owning society' (Perroy). In the seventh century the picture had changed. This may have been due to a deepening of religious feeling, to the irregularity of the food supply (especially abroad), and to the competition of Moslem slave-merchants; or again, to the long economic depression together with the decay in estate-management in the hands of ignorant stewards. These men urged the *domini* to get rid of slaves who were difficult to manage and to supervise the others in groups by giving them tenures.[1] It was easier to exact the services of a tenant on certain days and in certain periods than to supervise, every day, a whole crowd of *servi* whose needs would have to be provided for. The granting of tenures[2] to the *servi* is to be compared with the transformation of those vassals recruited into the class of vassals *chasés*, that is, provided with a benefice. However, the transformation of the *servi* into tenants cannot be explained solely by a desire to simplify the management of the aristocrat's household.

One must now ask how far the real condition of the *servi* at the end of the early Middle Ages corresponded with their juridical status.

i. *Juridical status.* The *servus* – a term meaning slave before being translated into old French *serf* – had an hereditary disability transmitted by the mother. If the parents were both unfree, the children would be *servi*, and they would be *servi* if a free man married a slave. It was to be said in later years that the unfree was *homme de corps*, belonging entirely to the *dominus* of the *villa*.

Under the Carolingians, as in subsequent centuries, there were no burdens or duties characteristic of *servage*. If in some land-registers one encounters the word *chevage* – a light tax – as a 'servile' obligation, it was probably not a tax everywhere applicable. Servitude was founded only on birth, *chevage* being only the counterpart of some special protection, notably that of the church.

A bond between the two men united the *servus* to his proprietor. The latter could, whenever he wanted, require his slave to resume work on the land conceded to him in tenure and reduce him to his former condition of 'domestic'. But the master also had the imperative duty of protecting and defending him against everything and everyone. On the other hand, the master could have a fugitive serf pursued, since the bond between them was not broken by the flight of the unfree. This bond gave rise to a problem in cases of exogamy (*formariage*). If a slave-woman married the slave of

[1] *en les chasant*

[2] *Chasement.*

another master, she had to go and live on the land of this master, who thus obtained additional labour (that of the wife and of any children born to her). But this master acquired only the labour, and not the property, of the wife and children, which remained the property of the owner of the wife. This difficulty could be solved only by agreement between the two owners. They usually shared the children between them or made a pecuniary arrangement. In any event, in order to control this migration of labour and dissociation of the right of property and the right to labour, the *domini* assumed the right to approve, or not approve, of *formariage*. It is possible that as early as the ninth century a form of monetary compensation had appeared, namely the tax for *formariage* to be paid by the serf or the serve.

Even when given a tenure, the *servus* was not completely associated with the rural population. He suffered from serious incapacities, such as being forbidden to become a cleric and being excluded from the public tribunals where he could neither testify nor take the oath. He was subject to the arbitrary control of his master who had the power to punish him in case of misdemeanour and even of crime.

ii. *Economic Condition.* The housing of slaves on 'servile' *manses*[1], which were smaller than those called *ingénuiles*[2], greatly improved the condition of the unfree. If the master sold a *servus,* he would now sell him with the tenure, and the man would not change his way of life. The unfree simply owed more services than the *colon* and those services were not always clearly defined; this could give rise to grave difficulties.

From the fact that population was relatively mobile, and doubtless for other reasons, there was no longer a necessary correlation between the status of the worker on the estate and the class of estate-owner on whose *manse* he worked. Slaves could thus work on serf-free estates and *colons* on servile ones.

[1] A *manse* (from Latin *mansio*) was a manor of moderate size (Translators).

[2] *Ingénuiles* (from Latin *ingenuus* = free from any taint of servitude) referred to estates entirely free from serfdom (Translators).

Household slaves had become far less numerous, except in Mediterranean countries like Italy. Their lot also had greatly improved. As they were those dwellers on the *villa* with whom the *dominus* was best acquainted, it was probably to some of them that he confided trustworthy functions, such as management of the mill, the oven, the brewery or the wine-press, or the duties of mayor or steward, as well as overseeing the artisans. On very great estates the important offices, those for example in the lord's mansion, were also confided to them. In the tenth century these members of the household (*familia*) had become indispensable. They were called *ministeriales* in France and in the Empire they were to constitute the powerful group known as *chevaliers-serfs*.

In spite of juridical obstacles, a levelling down of economic conditions brought the unfree nearer to the free. But did this relative fusion between the two take place from the bottom to the top? From the bottom, according to Marc Bloch, in whose opinion the *colons* (a name which disappeared towards A.D. 1000) had become unfree in status between the end of the Carolingian era and the beginning of the eleventh century. L. Verriest, on the other hand, thought that this assimilation proceeded from the top. Legally, the dividing line between free men and serfs was not destined to change during the above period, since it was based on birth and not on supposedly characteristic charges (*chevage, mainmorte* and *formariage*, according to Marc Bloch). In fact the unfree gained a little by comparison with former *colons*, according to L. Verriest, since all the peasants had become 'half-free'. From the social point of view, one must not suppose there was any great contrast between the domanial system and the seigneurial. Many distinct features of rural lordship already existed in the Carolingian *villa*, where there was evolution far more than transformation.

III. FROM VASSALAGE TO FEUDALISM

The passage between the two appears to have been generally effected in the course of the confused period between the mid-ninth century and about the year 1000. It was not directly and solely due to the disintegration of the state or of a wider distribution of the bonds of vassalage, but to other circumstances associated with them.

A. Growth of a Hierarchy[1] *of Landed Property; Different Degrees in Authority Over Men*

At the end of the early medieval age, the hierarchy of property in the landed aristocracy corresponded with the degree of power they enjoyed; which is not surprising. The basis of this power depended on land-ownership and varied accordingly.

1. *The Hierarchy of Landed Property.* This hierarchy, of which one can discern the main features, is really known in detail only in a few privileged regions. The strata of this semi-vassal, semi-feudal society are too often known only indirectly, from ecclesiastical records, and there are too few regional studies of these. In default of documentation which is often sparse or obscure, it is by no means certain that one will ever be able to cover the whole field in the West from the few works of social history on this period.

Instead of imprudently generalising, it is better to dwell on what facts are known, because the best examples of these can be studied in Burgundy, and in particular in the Mâconnais towards 950. It is not certain whether this was a typical case, because here the temporalities seem of much less importance. The ancient monasteries had been very much despoiled by laymen, and in the mid-tenth century the new ones were still only in the first stage of building up their fortunes. Thus Burgundy laymen possessed by far the greater part of the land, whether in freehold or in tenure (as benefices, or alternatively, temporary tenures).

During the period of transition from vassalage to feudalism, there was, according to Perroy, 'a time-lag between personal relationships and the system of landholding'. Nearly all the aristocrats were lords or vassals, a system of multiple vassalage being already well established. Very often the vassal held from the *dominus* a benefice (conceded or restored); but this

[1] *étagement* = arrangement in tiers.

benefice formed only a portion of his landed property, greater or less according to his rank in the social hierarchy. Thus freeholds still played a great part in moderately-sized and small patrimonies, and a minor role even in the more wealthy. This fact cannot be solely related to the tardy penetration of vassalage and benefice into the centre and south of Francia; because towards 1000 there were often important freeholdings between the Loire and the Rhine. 'Feudalization' everywhere rose from the bottom upwards, and in the tenth century the 'feudal pyramid' was still incomplete. There must have arisen many fraudulent freeholds. As a result of forgetfulness of ancient contracts of vassalage, negligence by the lord, and bad faith on the part of the vassal, former benefices and former temporary holdings (especially when the man in possession was a *potens* against whom the Church was helpless) became part of the freehold patrimony – an effect of the *de facto* right of inheritance of 'tenures of vassalage'.

One cannot speak of an aristocratic class and hardly even of a group, because the aristocracy was divided into numerous strata. Too many shades of difference and degree, a range of fortunes too wide, could not but deprive it of any real coherence. New patrimonies might extend over vast areas, or they might comprise only part of a lordship. At one end of the scale stood the *potentes, nobiles* or *optimates,* very rich and few in number. At the other extreme were the holders of a 'rump-lordship', whose way of life or standard of living was very near that of their peasant neighbours, from whom they were not perhaps separated as yet by any very clear juridical distinction.

At the head of the *potentes* came the dukes, margraves, marquises and counts, some of whom were turning their lands into principalities. Others had acquired or retained only one county; such, in Burgundy, were the counts of Chalon and Mâcon. All these *potentes* might – but only in name – be the direct vassals of the king, or of some prince, or else they might perhaps sometimes call themselves independent, even by right (that is, in law). But all had brought into their patrimonies the *comitatus,* that is, the ensemble of royal prerogatives which their predecessors had exercised in the king's name. These were an ensemble of powers and profits belonging to the rank of count.

The *powers* were judicial (presiding over the courts, collecting fines, etc.), military (protecting certain castles within the county, this term being geographical: the right to require all free men to serve in the guard; command of the contingents to be sent to the army, whether of the prince or of the count himself, in default of the king's army); finally, economic (levying the *tonlieux*, tolls, etc. for the profit of the count himself).

The *profits*: these were numerous in addition to the judicial dues and to the taxes on the movement and sale of merchandise, as indicated above. Under the Carolingians, these had been called *honores*, a term which was going out of use in the tenth century. These *res de comitatu* had passed, without the king's assent, into the patrimony of the count, who was now even able to enfeoff parts of them by conceding them to men who became his own vassals. This was the essential part of a count's wealth in the tenth century. In the cases most favourable to them, the counts had been able to take possession of the 'desert' lands (forests, moors, and marshes). This had been achieved, for example by Baudouin II, who had founded the power of the count of Flanders. In due course – at the time of the great clearing of forest-lands – this was to give the dynasty a remarkable increase in wealth and power.

The count was often the stronger if his family was allied with some of the very great families of the region. In the Mâconnais the existence has been recorded of three or four powerful families who were not counts. The wealth of these *potentes* increased from generation to generation. Being the only possible supporters for the king, the prince or the count, they had received new concessions, including the office of viscount (a delegation of the count's powers which had become hereditary) and also the defence or possession of a number of castles. The Church had been obliged to grant them rich holdings of a temporary kind, but these were soon transformed into freeholds. Here then was a group of a score or more persons, the heads of the count's family and of those allied with him, and this became the sole governing body which, after the year 1000, was to possess the castellanies and bannal lordships.

Far more numerous were the lords of average wealth. Some of their revenue was of ecclesiastical origin; the family had appropriated at least one parish church and its tithes. The other patrimonies derived from lands received as benefices or in freehold, hence from one or several rural lordships. As the lords in question had not been able to appropriate much of the considerable 'desert' lands, the next wave of forest-clearing was not generally to bring them extra wealth. As to the very humble lords, whose numbers had greatly varied from region to region, their lands were reduced in extent, as was the number of their tenants.

It was an apparent paradox that the patrimonies of the majority of the smaller lords and those of moderate importance consisted of one or several freeholdings. They had not been strong enough to extort temporary holdings from the Church, and once they had of necessity put themselves under the protection of a magnate, they had received only unimportant benefices, the right to levy dues on a peasant tenure, or a part of the tithes, or a small piece of land as a personal domain. The lord had no need to pay much for the loyalty of these lesser men (whom he did not fear but who, for their part, had an urgent need of his protection) as they could not have rendered costly services. The results were clear. In Burgundy at any rate, before 1000, this vassal society remained loosely and incompletely organised, since most of the vassals owed little of their land to concessions from their overlord, and therefore very few services, the latter being more and more linked with the fief and its importance, and less and less with the act of homage. It would be an error to imagine that at the end of the tenth century this society formed a complete 'pyramid'.

Since the tenth century experienced no doubt a certain economic stagnation, and since commerce was relatively inactive, the size and hierarchy of personal fortunes could scarcely have been reduced or modified by economic causes. If there were modifications, these were mainly due to the subdivision of estates on the death of the owner (*partages successoraux*), which the brevity of human life then rendered all the more frequent. An era of under-population like the early Middle Ages is not necessarily an era of small families. Restriction of marriages and births, which was often effective, did not completely prevent the dividing up of aristocratic estates. The daughters had to receive dowries, and the children who entered the Church did not abandon their share, which might return to their nephews, unless donated to the Church. The customs which, at a later time, were devised to limit subdivision (e.g. the *droit d'aînesse*) had not yet come into being. Almost everywhere, no doubt, in tenth-century Francia the children divided up among themselves in equal shares the paternal or maternal estate. The consent of the family was not yet needed in the case of a transfer of property, free or on terms, or of a legacy by one of its members. Hence each generation saw a fresh sub-dividing of the estate, so much so that, in the small estates which were originally composed of one or two lordships, these sub-divisions led to a state of near-poverty for the heirs who found it impossible to obtain a new benefice. They could only, as a poor temporary palliative, maintain the estate undivided and in joint ownership (*fraternitas, frereschc*).

Another cause leading to the impoverishment of the estates is to be found in the donations and pious legacies made by a number of lords, which are fairly well known from the archives of monasteries, cathedrals and colleges. But was there, as some historians persist in asserting, a very large transfer of property to the clerics? One should not exaggerate its extent, although it was very real in the tenth century and much more considerable than towards the end of the Middle Ages. This transfer was justified by the mental and moral outlook of the aristocracy. The best means of securing God's protection here below and one's salvation hereafter was to gave alms to His saints, hence to the patrons of the Church. This donation was the means of obtaining redemption for a sin, even an abominable one. The clergy skilfully contributed to the idea of such donations as a moral necessity. Contributions to the church, renewed by each generation, deprived the heirs of their inheritance and increased the impoverishments of the estates already reduced by the dividing-up of the patrimony.

Those families whose estates were not extensive certainly suffered more than the others, the more so as the lords of middle and inferior means were mainly possessors of freeholds, whereas the magnates possessed, for the most part, benefices and temporary holdings of which only a certain number had been fraudulently converted into freeholds. Now if a freehold, as a lord's sole property, was susceptible of being divided up into as many parts as he wished, and could be freely given away, a vassal could not yet in principle either share out or give away his tenure.

Is one justified in applying to the greater part of the West what Duby has observed in the Mâconnais? – namely, that in the tenth century a certain number of families of the lower aristocracy grew so poor that they finally disappeared, whether by dying out or by being reduced to the state of peasants. For Duby the year 1000 was the 'age of the *déclassés*'. Yet one cannot really generalize. In other provinces the decay of the poorer families may have been less frequent. One fact, however, seems to have been general: faced with the dwindling of their landed property, the freeholders of the tenth century must have abandoned any freedom of action and more often sought a closer contact with the class of more powerful lords, who were to be henceforth possessors of the 'royal' ban.

2. *The Hierarchy of Powers.* Despite the appearance of principalities, it was in the count's field of action that the institutions of the Carolingians state lingered on. In spite of a decline (less marked north of the Somme), they subsisted to the end of the tenth century, particularly in the northern part of the West. But the count was not, or was no longer, in sole possession of power.

(a). The count who formerly represented the sovereign and would be henceforth his 'substitute' under various titles, still exercised his *ban* over all the free men of the county or *pagus*, and this continued towards the year 1000. Despite the sparseness of documentary sources, one can clearly see that the counts remained the military leaders of the free men, but the latter had become *their* soldiers and not the king's, as shown by the many rebellions of counts and dukes, themselves counts in several *pagi*. Now a *de facto* distinction, already perceptible in the time of the great Carolingian sovereigns, became more clearly marked. On the one hand, the free peasants and the very small landholders, who were too poor to arm themselves and leave their lands, were freed by the count from their obligation in return for payment of a tax or a military vehicle. Conversely, there were those who were later to be called the *milites*; these were the aristocrats wealthy enough to arm themselves and own a war-horse, knights who acquitted themselves in person of the military service which they owed the count.

These aristocrats, the *fideles*, had become the count's vassals. They were turning the old *mallus publicus* into a 'court' of vassalage. For if the old judicial institutions survived, they had undergone a major transformation. The free tenants and small freeholders found themselves more or less excluded from the count's tribunal, and were now coming under the jurisdiction of a lower public court, that of the *centenier*; and only the powerful landowners and those of the middle orders continued to bring their legal business before the count's tribunal. To sum up, the magnates had begun to submit their disputes to their peers, since the count administered justice along with his *fideles*, in particular the *seniores*, his richest vassals.

In war, in legal matters, in all important circumstances, one sees the counts surrounded by their companions, who had become as it were the best trump card in their hands.

(b). The *viguiers* or *centeniers*.[1] The courts of the *vigueries* or hundreds, which divided among themselves the jurisdiction of each county, found their judicial powers increased, since all the free men continued to have recourse to them (every district being quite small) and the poorest folk had fallen exclusively under their jurisdiction. This explains the

[1] Apparently synonymous terms, with no exact English equivalent, except that they were judges in what was called 'hundreds', very small subdivisions of the county. They were delegates ('vicars') of the count (Translators).

name of *placitum generale* given to the sessions presided over by the *vicarius* or *centenarius*, who was assisted by scriveners recruited from among the humbler folk.

Although the count's delegates had been entrusted with an important share in public affairs – the poor free men being more numerous than other free men – this did not alter the fact that the *viguiers* or *centeniers* scarcely had any political power. For many of them, as for those under their jurisdiction, the future appeared barren of any hope of change. The economic distinction between poor free men and rich or fairly well-to-do free men bade fair to be transmuted one day into a juridical distinction.

(c). The *castellans* defended the 'public' fortresses whose business it was to maintain the security of the surrounding countryside. Their origin and especially their numbers have been subject to exaggeration. People have imagined a regular 'flowering' of castles; they were in fact spaced out at an average of twenty kilometres from each other. As to their origin they belonged to two eras. The oldest belonged to the ninth century at a time of general disturbance, particularly during the Norman raids. Henri Pirenne thought that they had given rise to the *bourgs* and had served, in cases of general alert, as refuges for the local population. The most recent castles had been built in the tenth century in the most disturbed periods of 'feudal anarchy'. In general they had been built by the kings; or later on by the counts after the king had agreed; later still by the counts who had become independent.

Even a count of only moderate power, like the count of Mâcon, possessed half a dozen castles. It had therefore been necessary to provide for the defence of these castles, and the counts had confided the task to the most powerful of their *fideles*, to those whose principal rural lordships were situated in these regions. The 'guardians' had evidently, in their turn, become hereditary in the tenth century, but had not yet contrived to free themselves from the count's control. They were still in principle only the representatives of public authority, and not yet in possession of it. Already, however, they were actually holders of the power of *ban*, and they commanded the contingent of small and middle-rank rural lords in their district (which extended over a radius of some ten kilometres) after summoning them themselves, for service in the count's army.[1] On the poor free men they imposed services in lieu of military obligations, such as furnishing the castle with food, fodder, etc., and repairing it when needed. Finally, they saw to the execution of the decisions of the local court – that of the 'hundred'.

Guardians of the peace the castellans certainly were; but guardians greedy and onerous. Towards the year 1000 the future would soon be theirs. They often acted as a barrier between the count and the dwellers in their district and, at least in Francia, during the first 'classical' feudal period,[2] many of them were to succeed in becoming truly independent.

B. From Aristocracy to Nobility: Continuity, Rupture or Evolution?

During the later Middle Ages, and even until the eighteenth century, the nobles claimed descent from a very remote past. Even in the modern era many regard themselves as descendants of the Frankish conquerors, the Third Estate having arisen in the Gallo-Roman era. Reacting against the obviously fanciful character of certain genealogies, Marc Bloch, followed by most French historians, has thought that the great families of the Gallo-Frankish aristocracy had become extinct before 1000, and that an 'entirely new nobility' must have come into being in feudal times on the basis of a minimum degree of landed property, of the exclusive right to serve in the cavalry, and of a life distinct from that of the commonalty. On this point as on others, Marc Bloch's ideas, so exciting for the researcher, have not been entirely accepted in the last few decades.

In other words, it is now believed that there was continuity in certain aristocratic families, which later became families of knights. Up to this point in the present study, the terms

[1] '*Ost*'.

[2] '*Du premier âge féodal classique*'. The author is referring to the period from 1000 to 1160 A.D. See Chapter 2, Section A below.

"aristocracy' and 'aristocrat' have been preferred deliberately so as not to pre-judge the explanations that will now follow. It is time to ask whether, before 1000, it would not be possible already to speak of a 'nobility'.

Were the aristocrats of the Frankish period themselves new men? No, reply the 'Germanists', a nobility had existed east of the Rhine from ancient times and it presumably continued as such during the early Middle Ages. The *principes* or *nobiles* spoken of by Tacitus were not merely aristocrats because they made a distinction between themselves and the other Germans, by claiming an ancestry of illustrious and even divine origin. They had the right to a company of *fideles,* the *comitatus,* composed of several hundred men whom they maintained with the resources of their own lands and with gifts from other dwellers in the region, the latter being protected by the fortress of the *nobilis.* But does not this mean taking very far back into the past the ideas of 'bannal lordship' and fortified site? However that may be, H. Dannenbauer, one of the most recent protagonists of the 'Germanist' thesis, thinks that in *Innendeutschland* (Bavaria, Thuringia, etc.) this nobility, small in number, maintained itself, without any great transformation, into the very heart of the Middle Ages. And after the great invasions it presumably installed itself in the Empire and opened its ranks the more readily to the descendants of senatorial families, as these *potentes* of the later Empire had usurped the functions normally belonging to the State, in judicial and fiscal matters. The 'Romanists' for their part insist a good deal more on the permanence of certain families of *potentes* after about 400. According to H. Mitteis, the Franks must have received into the ranks of their own 'nobility' many members of the native 'nobility'.

For many historians then, there was an evolution and not a rupture between Roman and Germanic antiquity on the one hand and the early Middle Ages on the other, even if they see nuances and believe that the 'nobility' of the Germanic tribes may have come into being more slowly and have for long been characterized by merit as much as by birth.

For others, including some German historians, the nobles were on the contrary new men, and there was no 'biological continuity'. It was service to the king that assured these men of receiving privileges and wealth. The Merovingian age would have recognized only one noble family, the king's (*stirps nobilium*), whereas the aristocrats (again according to these historians) formed themselves only in the second half of the ninth century into families independent of the royal lineage and only then became nobles. It would thus be in post-Carolingian times that economic inequalities caused it to be recognized in law that all the 'Francs' – that is, all the free men – were not equal. Only the powerful – the nobles – exercised the right to judge and sometimes the right of ban. There was therefore at least a certain continuity in the idea of class distinctions.

Did there exist a *nobilitas* in the first medieval age,[1] and, if so, what were its features? 'As soon as he opens the documents (even those of the *Haut Moyen Age*) the medievalist encounters *nobiles*', writes L. Genicot. This is clearly shown in narrative and diplomatic sources, whether in Gregory of Tours who speaks of *nobiles*, a *nobile genus*, etc., or in the capitularies when decreeing some measures applicable to *homines laici, tan nobiles quam ignobiles*. The *nobiles* always play the great parts, but this criterion is adequate only to define an aristocracy, not a nobility, which is something more precise. It is true that the term *nobilis* is ambiguous; it may even be synonymous with 'free'. Its bearing may be individual, social or juridical; it may be applied to men of great personal merit, or to a group socially and politically superior, benefiting from an exceptional status. In fact, the writings of the first medieval period use the word to describe a man who belongs to a group of which all the members present an identity of outlook and behaviour; they feel the pride of belonging to the upper and privileged social stratum. Now this seems to precede by at least five hundred years the age of 'classical feudalism' and chivalry. And if the nobles had

[1] '*Dès le premier Moyen Age*'. The author is referring to the sixth and seventh centuries, as the reference to Gregory of Tours makes clear.

never been the only free men, they had none the less been free men *par excellence*. This had been the case with the *potentes* of the Roman Empire, with the *principes* of the Germanic tribes, and later with the principal auxiliaries of the barbarian kings and of the Carolingians.

It is impossible to know whether there was really, from the beginning of our era until the eighth century, a continuity of descent in the nobility or even a 'continuity of ideas' (although it may be possible to discover the latter). For the Carolingian and post-Carolingian eras we are on firmer ground. A continuity of descent from the aristocrats of the ninth and tenth centuries to the nobles of the first feudal age is now admitted, at least in part, by French historians themselves. 'There was transmission by blood from the Carolingian nobility to an abundant feudal posterity' (Duby). One can indeed say *nobility* since this aristocracy was a privileged one, privileges being one of the best criteria of nobility. Pride – which was not new – was not the only bond among its members, because they benefited from a status exceptional in law and in fact. The Carolingian nobles were perhaps new men; all the nobles of the eleventh century were certainly not.

Take the example of Neustria, where a *nobilitas* either first took root or appeared well established in the Carolingian age. Here is the possible explanation of why every noble 'referred to himself in the first place as *de nobilibus ortus* . . ., that is to say that he did not appeal, in the first instance, to his power and his wealth, but to his ancestors' (Duby). If it was long believed that there was an hiatus between the aristocracy of the first medieval age and the nobility of feudal times, this has been largely due to the sparseness of documentary evidence in the tenth century. K. F. Werner has been able to rediscover the links so often broken, notably for Touraine. Here, in spite of the Norman incursions, of which the effect has been exaggerated, the powerful families were already well installed towards 845, forming a solid network of vassalage under Robert the Strong, much to his advantage; and they were still there in the tenth century. This proves the continuity of the nobility in question between at least the reign of Louis the Pious and the age of the last Carolingians in western Francia, as well as the following period, the mid-tenth century, the point after which we have a fairly reliable record of genealogies. But Werner distinguishes between two levels:

(a). At the top, the *Reicharistocratie*, formed of a few groups of families entrusted with the highest functions and scattered over the whole Carolingian Empire. Robert the Strong who came from eastern Francia and was part of this group, had relatives in Touraine. Here then is an élite small in numbers and very mobile;

(b). *The regional aristocracy*, static, and divided into two distinct categories: first, the counts and viscounts, then the *vassi dominici* who, here as elsewhere, towards the second quarter of the tenth century, had become subordinate to the counts and sometimes to the viscounts. They were often members of collateral branches of the counts' families.

If the two levels were clearly distinct, they none the less together formed the body of the 'nobles', separated by a deep gap from the simple free men. In the ninth and tenth centuries they figure in the lists of witnesses who subscribe to the acts of the Robertians. One can conclude with Duby that:

'from the High Middle Ages there existed a *nobility* which had a share in public authority; which was first connected with the Royal House but which gradually detached itself; conscious of its position and the honour of its descent and, as a consequence, closed in principle to parvenus. This nobility was so to speak the foundation of the upper aristocracy of feudal times–the *vassi dominici* of the ninth century were the ancestors of the Castellans of the eleventh century and the barons of the twelfth century. They kept at a distance from the families of the middle group of aristocrats, those who later became knights, but who from this time onward enjoyed juridical liberty.'

Nobility was therefore anterior to *chevalerie*[1] and independent of it: it was a status derived from its ancestors (L.

[1] The 'class' known as knights (Translators).

Verriest). But from what ancestry, paternal, maternal, or both? It appears that at first it was from both branches, which reveals a marked difference between the attitude of the early medieval nobles and the outlook of their descendants in feudal times. Before 1000 the nobles did not ascribe to descent on the male side[1] the superiority which would belong to it in later centuries; in principle they ascribed the same validity to both *agnati* (of male descent) and *cognati* (of female); as witness the most ancient genealogical tree which traces the ancestry of Count Arnoul of Flanders and was composed between 951 and 959. This document lays stress above all on the women and the illustrious character of her lineage, and the only dates mentioned are those of marriages. The object is to affirm the high nobility of the count by connecting him with the Carolingians through his grandmother. In the scribe's view, the important lineage is on the distaff side. *Agnati* and *cognati* are not even on the same level, since the *cognati* take precedence.

This is confirmed by a general study of the nobility of the Rhineland: one such study, in this field, is K. Schmid's enquiry into the nobles of Alemania. In the twelfth century the concept of the family was dynastic. Members of the family traced their ancestry through the males, and the collateral branches of the lineage preserved the memory of this 'agnatic' origin. 'The *race* will present itself as a house'. The line will bear the name of the residence its members occupy in common, the cradle of the family, transmitted from father to son. But nothing of this kind exists before the year 1000. There were no family names, only individual names (a fact which renders so arduous any research into genealogies at the end of the first medieval period). All that existed was the *Sippe*, 'a loose-knit group of allied families', and there was as yet no *Geschlecht*, a line or family uniting all those descended from the same male ancestor. In Alemania, for example, descendants on the distaff side did not take precedence as in the families of the Flemish counts; but they were at least on a footing of equality with the *agnati*. In family life the relationship with the mother thus consciously played a great part,

[1] *'filiations agnatiques'.*

and children usually received names taken from the mother's family. In truth, 'of the two sides of descent', writes Duby, 'it was the one of which the nobility was the most brilliant, the prestige the greatest and the ancestors the most glorious, that took first place'. But there was as yet no *race*, because the nobles were doubtless not yet installed in fixed abodes. There was no *house* but 'multiple shelters', since families possessed lordships widely scattered, and were often on the move owing to alliances and heritages.

The appearance of the *house* and the *race*, and therefore the very notion of nobility, was connected with the evolution of political power. Under the Carolingians a single *house*, the king's, was the first to show itself as a *race* and to recognize the superiority of male descent. It was by associating himself with this house as 'sustained' by it, and later by receiving *honores* and *benefices* from it, that a noble could make his fortune. Nobility was therefore 'domestic' (*Hausadel*), it could not organise independent *houses* for itself, and in the distribution of royal benefits those descended by the female line were on the same footing as those of male descent. Later, after about the mid-ninth century, the 'noble' families freed themselves from royal domesticity, took possession of political power, and thus passed from the *Sippe* to the *Geschlecht*. The noble's *house* became 'the independent and permanent centre and crystallising point of a race on which it conferred power'. From these origins the line of male descent grew little by little stronger and reserved to itself the transmission of ancestral glory, of landed wealth, of authority – of, in short, nobility. This was 'one of the aspects of the advent of feudalism' (Duby). But had this point been reached towards the year 1000? The rhythm of change was not the same from region to region; but on the whole, autonomy had already been won by the great houses, notably by the counts; it was won successively by the lower ranks of the nobility. Before the early eleventh century the families of the castellans and other holders of the power of ban, in the Mâconnais, were already organized in formal lineages, whereas the smaller nobles were to reach this position only in the eleventh or even the twelfth century.

Genicot's studies[1] have led us to ask whether there was continuity, rupture or evolution. The reply appears almost certain: there was no rupture in the passage from aristocracy to nobility, but continuity at the same time as evolution.

[1] See the Bibliography at the beginning of Chapter 1, p. 16 above.

Bibliography

GANSHOF, F.-L., L'origine des rapports féodo-vassaliques (I problemi della Civiltà Carolingia, *Iª Settimana di Studio del Centro di studi sull' alto medioevo*, Spoleto 1954, pp. 27–69. Pp. 71–157: exposé on Italy by P. S. Leicht and on Spain by C. S. Albornoz); Les relations féodo-vassaliques aux temps postcarolingiens (*IIª Settimana . . .*, Spoleto, 1955, pp. 67–114; L'échec de Charlemagne (*C. R. de l'Acad. des Inscript. et Belles-Lettres*, 1947, p. 251); L'immunité dans la monarchie franque (*Rec. Soc. Jean-Bodin*, Vol. I, pp. 171–216).

DÉLÉAGE, A., *La vie rurale en Bourgogne jusqu'au début du XIᵉ siècle*, Paris 1941.

DHONDT, J., *Etude sur la naissance des principautés territoriales en France* (*IXᵉ–Xᵉ s.*), Bruges, 1948.

LEMARIGNIER, J. F., Les fidèles du roi de France, 936–987 (*Rec. Clovis Brunel*, 1955, pp. 138–62); De l'immunité à la seigneurie ecclésiastique . . . (977–1108) in *Etudes* dédiées a G. le Bras, pp. 619–30.

PLATELLE, H., *La justice seigneuriale de Saint-Amand*, Louvain 1965.

VERRIEST, L., *Institutions médiévales*, Mons-Frameries, 1946.

On the nobility:

DUBY, G., Une enquête à poursuivre; la noblesse dans la France médiévale (Rev. Hist., 1961, pp. 1–22.

GENICOT, L., La Noblesse . . . dans l'ancienne 'Francie' (*Annales Moyen Age*, 1965, pp. 539–60); Naissance, fonction et richesse . . . ; le cas de la noblesse du nord-ouest du continent (*Prob. de stratif. sociale*, 1966, pp. 83–100).

PERROY, E., La noblesse des Pays-Bas (*Revue du Nord*, 1961, pp. 53–9).

PART TWO

THE CLASSICAL AGES

From the Early Eleventh Century to the End of the Thirteenth Century

Chapter 2

GENERAL FEATURES OF THE AGE

Towards the year 1000 there appeared what is called 'classical' feudalism. But for some historians this was a second feudal period, for others only the first experienced by the West. The period it occupied and the various features it assumed raise many problems.

We know that in F. L. Ganshof's view it was a question of a new feudalism. After the Carolingian feudalism[1] a second

[1] The Carolingian period was of great importance in the history of the bonds of vassalage and of the great domains, and still more in the history of the relations between vassalage and the *villa*. The development of bonds of dependence under the Merovingians helps to explain the first expansion of the *villae*, but the *benefice* in lands was not yet 'the normal and almost obligatory consequence' of vassalage. With the Carolingian era 'the two institutions . . . of vassalage and benefice were united in large measure in such a way as to constitute a system of institutions' (F. L. Ganshof). But it was as yet only a question of fact, not of law.

If there is general agreement as to the importance of Carolingian times from these points of view, it does not extend to all the other aspects presented by vassalage and benefice and by the *villa*. Even on the vocabulary there is no agreement. If the connection between the bonds of man to man on the one hand and tenure to payment on the other, is believed to be general and systematic from the early ninth century, one will not hesitate to speak of a *Carolingian feudalism*, as Ganshof does. If, as others think, including the present writer, the combination of the essential elements which define feudalism had at that time remained imperfect, not general and not systematic, one will speak rather of a *Carolingian vassalage*, although this term is not a very happy one because it appears to ignore what was already often bound up with the problems of social hierarchy, of the land, considered as a frequent consequence of vassalage and as a means of enabling the vassal to perform his service.

feudal age appeared, genuinely 'classical'. It began towards the end of the tenth century and was to subsist, without major changes, until the 1300s. Classical feudalism would therefore have subsisted for about three centuries, an era marked by a fundamental unity. But Ganshof deliberately limited himself to the juridical aspects of this system. Now even if the legal structures did not undergo profound changes during these three hundred years, it is improbable – if one takes the word feudalism in its widest sense, if one envisages its social and political structures and way of life – it is improbable that one could discern two or several distinct phases in this long period, supposing that one accepts the limits *a quo* and *ad quem* proposed by Ganshof. One will continue to connect as far as possible the study of feudalism with the study of lordship – of the land which supported feudalism – which was itself subject to all kinds of economic and social forces. These were very changeable in the three centuries in question because of the great material improvement in rural economy. But the exact chronological periods are very difficult to determine in economic and social life, and much more so in the juridical domain.

It was from a point of view different from Ganshof's that Marc Bloch had attacked the problem in 1940 in his *Société féodale*. He had examined the ways of life then obtaining in connection with the economic changes and the changes in mental outlook which are still so difficult to discern. The West, in his view, experienced two feudal ages. The first arose presumably from the ruins of the Carolingian Empire, from the ruins of the State, partially restored; ruined in a material sense also as a result of the Norman incursions, the effects of which he was tempted to exaggerate. The first feudal age would then have appeared towards the end of the ninth century and have lasted until about the beginning of the twelfth century. It would have been an era very poor economically, with each region subsisting almost on its own resources, with virtually no commerce. These conditions were in Bloch's view responsible for the social structure, especially of the aristocratic society. As to the second feudal age, which arose about 1100, this lasted two centuries. The feudal world was then profoundly modified by the 'economic revolution', that is by the great clearing of forests and marshes, and by the renewal of urban and commercial life. This second feudal age was the result of economic expansion, as the first had been due to economic depression.

This distinction between the two feudal ages, associated with two opposite phases of economic history, is of the greatest importance. But Bloch's assignment of the dates at which these ages flourished no longer seems quite satisfactory. Since 1940 the study of the economic history of the middle ages has made great progress, and the present tendency has been partially to fill in the gap between the tenth century and those which followed. Towns and commerce had not disappeared at the end of the ninth century and in the tenth; hence, instead of speaking of a 'revolution', it would be better to speak of a more rapid evolution of the economy. Even had there been a 'revolution', this would have taken place in the eleventh century; if there were a break, it took place before 1100. One might, it is true, reply that the economic changes could have affected the feudal system only after a certain delay. And there is another objection to Marc Bloch's argument: were the feudal 'periods' the same in all the countries of the West, which was so fragmented? One may feel doubtful.

The Mâconnais, certainly not an extensive region since it contained only 150 parishes, has benefited from two advantages. It has preserved archives so rich that they have permitted a study in depth, and it has been the subject of Georges Duby's excellent book, *La société aux XIe et XIIe siècles dans la région mâconnaise* (1953). But in fact this work covers a longer period, from 950 to 1240, that is, nearly three centuries.

Duby distinguishes a succession of three kinds of social structure – hence the division of his book into three parts – the changes having occurred towards 1000 and about 1150. There is no need to go over the ground of the first phase, the phase preceding 1000 during which a society of feudal-vassalage was formed and when the bonds and obligations of vassalage were still incomplete, sometimes vague; while Carolingian institutions had not yet lost all their efficacy. There remain the second and third phases, in other words the two feudal ages.

1. THE FIRST FEUDAL AGE

This age, covering the period 1000 to 1160, was in Duby's view 'the age of the independent castellans'. In the Mâconnais, as in many parts of France, the power of the duke or count underwent a decline, sometimes temporary, sometimes final, and this last was the case in the region of Mâcon. It then befell the duke or count what had befallen the Carolingians at the end of the ninth century. Public authority had almost ceased to operate and the magnates were powerful only in proportion to their wealth. The *comitatus*, or power of the count, followed the power of the king into the world of illusory appearances, and much more than of old, authority was measured by the number of great rural lordships, and the number of vassals, possessed by an aristocrat. The difference had grown very small between the *potentes* who were counts and those who were not. The *potentes* were all castellans; they possessed a lordship of a different kind, namely a group of rights and prerogatives connected with the possession of a castle. Round this fortress was grouped the little company of the castellan's vassals: they were all warriors, hence a clearly defined equivalence between *vassal* and *miles*. A common mentality, a common way of life, and a 'code of chivalry' were taking shape.

Was this really a time of 'feudal anarchy', as is so often repeated? It was rather, one feels, an attempt to establish a new order, but now in a very limited rural framework, each castle controlling a small territory. Hence arose the institutions for maintaining peace, the strengthening of bonds of lineage, and the strictest definition of feudal duties. Hence also arose a more rigorous control of the peasantry by the castellans. The overriding influence of the castellan's power over the rural lordships and their inhabitants was considerable, and never perhaps were the bonds between lordship and feudalism to be as numerous and as close. Above rural lordship stood *bannal* lordship, at first almost synonymous with that of the castellans. In exchange for the protection, more or less effective, furnished by the castle, the peasants had to grant the holder of the right of ban, who would not always be the only castellan, returns in money, merchandise and labour, charges weighing equally upon the free and the unfree, and tending to render uniform the status of all the peasants.

The paradox is obvious. These local centres of authority, which were often new, were born of an age of extreme fragmentation in country life, connected with the economic depression at the end of the early Middle Ages. But the eleventh century benefited from a remarkable economic recovery. The material expansion which took place in the eleventh century – and which had its counterpart in artistic and intellectual activity – and also the increase in population, affected by the organisation of disorder, or rather of order, were apparently on the local level. At the same time the economic expansion and the increasing material activity were to cause the disappearance of a social organization which rested on such frail foundations. But the decay of this social system was slow and, in Duby's view, the age of the castellans was to end only towards 1160.

Is it enough to recall that the technical and economic changes and the rise in population took place slowly, and that the period of great expansion – corresponding with the second phase of forest-clearing – occurred only in the twelfth century? And is it also enough to say that the social structure generally lagged behind the economic? These questions have not yet been completely answered.

Lastly, may one apply to other parts of France this picture of the first feudal age in the Mâconnais? Probably, at least for those regions where the power of the duke or the count suffered a long eclipse. For Germany, this is much more doubtful, since royal power enjoyed there a rebirth, albeit temporary. And, because of the battle of Hastings, England experienced a quite different evolution.

II. THE SECOND FEUDAL AGE

This, in Duby's view, covered the period between 1160 and

1240, and was marked by the passage 'from castellany to principality' and to 'feudal monarchy' (Petit-Dutaillis).

The land was no longer to be the only source of wealth and power, although it remained the principal one. It was now bringing in much more than formerly, owing to the increased yield of the soil, the extension of those areas of the domain under cultivation, and the rise in the number of tenures. It was the rival lords, even the simple *milites*, who often benefited from economic upheavals, from the greater volume of currency and the more rapid circulation of money. To meet new needs, new resources were found in the sale, on a greatly increased scale, of agricultural produce.

Local authorities were none the less in danger and castellany was threatened with extinction, the more so as royal power was strong in England from the time of William the Conqueror and later, after an eclipse, from 1154 and the reign of Henry II, and as the French monarchy awoke from its lethargy during the twelfth century.

The rebirth of royal power had, however, no immediate effects. The narrow framework of the castellans did not give place to the vast framework of the kingdom until the territorial divisions of the country had been simplified. At the outset, the great lords, counts or dukes, gained from this simplification. They established a hierarchy in 'feudal society' by imposing more precise obligations on the castellans, who were already their vassals, or were obliged to accept vassalage. It was now that the 'feudal pyramid' was really completed; leaving no place for the small vassal lordships which had been almost autonomous with no definite bonds to link them together. From this work of concentrating authority the kings profited, especially in France, by taking over from the princes, or bringing the latter under control. One can describe this second phase as 'feudal monarchy'. But political evolution did not always reach this stage, as witness the example of Germany. Here the great princes thwarted the efforts of the kings, who, unlike the Capetians, had no domain of their own, that is, no personal principality save for some short-lived exceptions.

The rise of the princes, and later of the kings, was made possible only by a certain revolution in the hierarchy of feudal wealth on the local level. It has been said with Marc Bloch that, in face of the 'rise of the bourgeoisie', the nobility had been impoverished and had declined, and that this brought about a hardening of its attitude and a more clearly asserted feeling of 'caste'. But matters were not as simple as this. One may say that all the nobles had not been able to profit from the larger areas brought under cultivation; that the very high birth-rate was leading to the sharing out of estates, and that wars and crusades often cost more than they brought in. Historians have also dwelt, though with some exaggeration, on the prodigality and administrative incompetence of the knights. More and more there came to be two very different groups, the 'plebeian nobility' and the wealthy nobility. Hence the desire among the former to find other sources of income and the need to enter permanently into the prince's service, for example into the corps of his 'officers', administrators and judges. But the other group often took the lion's share. In any case, 'the transformation was complete' in the middle of the thirteenth century.

III. DIVERSITY OF THE WEST

The chronological divisions proposed by Duby cannot be applied to the whole of the West, which was broken up. Neither in time nor geographically was the development entirely uniform, as will appear from a comparative study of several large regions.

a. *The regions between the middle waters of the Loire and the Rhine.* As with the early Middle Ages, any study should start from this region and centre upon it. It was here that there appeared, earlier and more deeply rooted than elsewhere, a 'classical' lordship, a society of vassalage, better contrived social forms and also an organization of the land in lordships and a feudalization of society more complete. It was here too, despite the importance of the castellans, that the Carolingian state institutions maintained themselves with more success and longer, and served as a 'support' (Perroy) for the counties or duchies which were able to escape dissolution during the first feudal age.

b. *The French sectors west of the Paris basin and south of the Loire*. The further one moves south-west or south-east, the more do lordship and feudalism seem late in development, imperfect and sparsely scattered. Freehold lordships were to subsist here in great numbers, for example around Bordeaux.[1] And regional authorities which had gone to pieces in the tenth century had little success in recovering strength. Aquitaine was in a state of complete anarchy and the Plantagenets were never to succeed in really controlling it; witness the death of Richard Cœur de Lion while besieging the castle of a rebellious vassal. It was not until after the Albigensian Crusade and the time of Alphonse de Poitiers that order was restored in Languedoc, mainly achieved by the immigration of feudal barons from north of the Loire. Lack of precision in the vocabulary, which still persisted in 1789, shows that the southerners were ignorant of the characteristics of lordship and feudalism.

c. *The kingdom of Germany* (*east of the Rhine*). Perrin has observed that 'for the countries lying beyond the Rhine, it was in the first instance their incorporation into the Frankish Monarchy that had decided their readiness to accept institutions' of vassalage, and later of feudalism. The old 'national' duchies which had been strictly subject to the Franks in the eighth and ninth centuries experienced a more rapid development of vassalage and later of feudalism. This was the case in Alemania, Franconia, Thuringia and still more in Bavaria, where vassalage had been introduced in the time of Pepin the Short and where, in after years, freeholds became rare.

The situation was different in Frisia and Saxony, because these countries had entered the Frankish kingdom only under Charlemagne and the delay of half a century was never made good. But this argument, based on chronology, does not fully explain the situation: there were others reasons.

[1] R. Boutruche, *Une société . . . en lutte centre le régime féodal: l'alleu en Bordelais et en Bazardais due XIe au XVIIIe siècle*. Rodez, 1943.

The peculiarity of Frisia is as obvious as it is difficult to elucidate. The country had no seigneurial régime, and so no feudal system. As there were no rural lordships, it was impossible for a real feudalism to appear. 'It is undeniable', writes Perrin, 'that feudal institutions took root preferably in regions where a seigneurial system made it possible to allot (to vassals), out of vast lordships, numerous important benefices. On the other hand, in regions where freeholds were numerous, while lordships were sparsely scattered and of no great size (cf. south of the Loire), feudalism did not find ground favourable for its development.' This was the situation, *a fortiori*, in the few countries where lordship did not prevail, as in Frisia.

The situation in Saxony is generally explained by the social structure of the country, a structure which had persisted on the whole after the Carolingian conquest. Divided into many social groups, strictly separated from one another, Saxony could not readily accept a contract of vassalage which supposes, in theory, a certain equality between the vassal and his lord. Only in the last quarter of the eleventh century did relations of feudal vassalage undergo certain changes, because the struggle against Henry IV was to force the Saxons to regroup themselves. But the failure of Henry the Lion in his attempt to transplant into Saxony the solid feudal organisation with which he had been familiar in Bavaria, reveals the persistent backwardness of Saxony in relation to other Germanic countries.

In any event, when the institutions of feudal vassalage infiltrated into German lands, they became modified and acquired peculiar features. Of this development contemporaries were well aware. In the twelfth and thirteenth centuries the Germans thought that there existed a German law, different from French or Italian law. This is explained by the fact that in the regions first brought under Frankish law, institutions developed more slowly than in Francia, doubtless because up to the eleventh century cavalry had not been largely substituted for infantry, a substitution which was in fact effected only at the time of the first two Crusades. Apart from this, lordship and feudalism had not covered

Germany with a net as finely meshed as in France. Many 'sunfiefs' (*Sonnenlehen*), that is freeholds, were to maintain themselves intact. The control that might have been exercised by lordship and feudalism remained incomplete, just as it was south of the Loire, though for partly different reasons. Aside from these two features – anachronism and incompleteness – there is a third and important one. Still more than in France, the land element (the fief) predominated over the personal (vassalage), and this marked German law (and also Italian) more deeply than French law, so much so that in Germany investiture was regarded as sufficient to confirm the contract. In the thirteenth century the Italians went even further, since investiture, here and there in the peninsula, sometimes even preceded the paying of homage. It is evident that the growing weakness of royal power in Germany in the late Middle Ages did not fail to influence the feudal system. It was, for example, an obligation for the sovereign to renew the feudal status of a princely fief when there was no direct heir; whereas the king of France could reunite it to the royal domain and did not fail to do so.

d. *Italy*. The present writer has been obliged by lack of space to sacrifice the study of Italy, but also by lack of works as numerous and as thorough as those which exist on France, Germany and England. Only the major characteristics can be indicated.[1]

First, the country districts were not, as they were north of the Alps, centres of economic, social and even 'political' life. The cities, though smaller than heretofore, retained this role; so that the *potentes*, both counts and warriors, continued to live in towns and not in country castles. It was from their fortified mansions, in the heart of the city, that they commanded their *fideles* and very soon engaged in commerce. These city-dwelling nobles brought the surrounding countryside, both peasants and rural lords, into subjection; at least the nobles in great cities like Florence did so.

This obtained principally in central and northern Italy,

[1] C.-E. Perrin, *L'Allemagne, l'Italie et la Papauté de 1125 à 1250*. Paris, C.D.U., 1956. E. Pontieri, *Tra i Normanni nell' Italia meridionale*. Naples, 1948.

which had undergone the Lombard domination before the Frankish conquest, and later the influence, sometimes eclipsed, of the German monarchy. But beside this urban nobility there were great lordships, especially on the frontiers or 'marches'. Marquises, counts or bishops had built fortresses on the lower ground, but had not generally managed to over-rule the nobles of the great cities. The law in this part of Italy, known as *Jus Langobardorum,* which was put in writing at an early date, scarcely recognised the connection between fief and military service.

Southern Italy presented different features, consequent on the long Byzantine occupation and the slightness of German influence. The main characteristic was the persistence of Roman Law. Unfragmented and hereditary landed property continued to comprise the greater part of it; so that, in spite of the strength and large numbers of bonds of dependence, there was never to be a real feudalism. Despite these differences, two features were common to the two halves of Italy: regular military service was rare and, with exceptions, the nobles in the South as in the North lived in the towns. The Norman conquest did not cause the appearance here, as it did in England, of a real imported feudal system.

e. *The imported feudalisms.* These existed mainly in England and in the Latin principalities in the East where the conquerors (Normans and 'Franks') imported[1] the system to which they had been accustomed. Lack of space compels the writer to omit the Eastern feudalism and discuss only the English.[2]

In the great island, the 'natural' evolution was modified in 1066. What is known of the Anglo-Saxon and Anglo-Danish societies leads one to think that before the conquest they were characterised by bonds between man and man, which, however, were neither as definite nor as widespread as in Carolingian lands. The aristocrats (Saxon *thegns,* Danish *iarls*) none the less used for their profit, in a certain measure, the bonds of personal dependence. The battle of Hastings

[1] Whence the expression, which is Marc Bloch's.

[2] F. M. Stenton, *The First Century of English Feudalism, 1066–1166.* 2nd edition, Oxford, 1961.

did not perhaps mark the complete rupture which historians have imagined.

After the Norman Conquest came the installation of William the Conqueror's men in the domains taken from the Anglo-Saxon or Anglo-Danish aristocrats. The new king immediately established a system of vassal-feudal relationships like those in Normandy. That is to say, the system was imposed from above instead of developing from below, and it was the monarchy that imposed it. Hence the great originality of this Anglo-Norman feudalism which was not formed against the State and the Crown but, on the contrary, at their bidding. Where Charlemagne, in the times of vassalage, had failed, the kings of England largely succeeded. For a long time feudalism was to be the ally, the foundation, of royal power, and not its adversary.

Chapter 3

THE RE-ESTABLISHMENT OF AUTHORITY FROM BELOW UPWARDS

Society in the classical ages of feudalism, especially in the first, was a society strongly marked by hierarchy. The theory of the *ordines* of the Carolingian age was revived but modified by the clerics, who elaborated two types of orders, these being three in number. One of these interpretations was inspired by social conditions. It distinguished between those who pray (*oratores*), those who fight (*bellatores*) and the peasants (*agricultores*). This was, for example, the interpretation adopted by Rathier of Verona (d. 974) and Adalbéron of Laon (d. 1030). In his *Poème au roi Robert* Adalbéron expressed himself as follows: 'The City of God, which is believed to be one, is divided into three. Some pray, others fight, others again work. These three co-existing orders could not suffer separation. The services rendered by one permit the work of the other two. Each in its turn undertakes to succour the whole.'

In the twelfth century St Bernard expressed the same view; like so many others, he insisted on the three orders being complementary. This theory 'permitted the social system to be regarded as integrated by an act of providence', the hierarchy became sacred, and to every man was assigned a task by the will of God. To ensure his salvation, and to contribute to social harmony, everyone should therefore submit to the vocation (*obedientia*) of his order.

It was imagined that these orders had been determined from the beginning, conceived by God at the creation of the world and for the duration of the earthly city. In this theory, therefore, there was no place for evolution. 'In a fixed world, everyone performs the same services indefinitely. There is no place for new functions'. (A. Chélini). In reality the theory corresponded only to a short period in the evolution of society, to the first feudal age and, perhaps, the beginning of the second. The bourgeois[1] had no place in this vision of the world, so it was necessary to remedy the defect, because none of the orders were able to ignore the bourgeois for long, not even the *bellatores,* from the time when burgesses began to lend them funds and even purchase fiefs. Hence in the thirteenth century the notion of 'status' or 'estate' was to became current, beside that of *ordo*; a new notion, social and professional in character. 'The whole concept of the social structure was disappearing and new groups were now recognized (for example, bourgeois and artisans) as having a specialized duty, on the analogy of the urban crafts.' But the concept of *ordo* subsisted because the desire to maintain Christian unity remained very much alive, and no other notion could have better answered to it. St Bernard himself had succeeded in including the bourgeois and artisans by regarding the third *ordo* as no longer consisting only of peasants but of all *laboratores.* Thus modified, the theory of *ordines* was to play a very great part at the end of the Middle Ages and in modern times. In France as late as 1789, men were to speak of the Third 'Estate', this word being almost synonymous with 'order'.

I. THE DOMINANT SOCIAL GROUPS: THE KNIGHTS

Towards the year 1000, and doubtless after a certain time-lag, the men who could write – the clerics (clerks, because in the main only clerics could write) – modified their vocabulary for the purpose of describing aristocrats. Thus *vassus,* for example, replaced *fidelis,* and the word *nobilis* fell into disuse especially, except in certain countries like Poitou. This word *nobilis* was vague, designating in principle 'a group without

[1] That is, townsmen of all kinds, artisans, craftsmen, merchants and manufacturers (Translators).

fixed limits, or privileges, or titles' (Perroy). Little by little it was replaced in some areas by the word *miles,* which applied like its predecessor, but in a manner more exact, to the noble's way of life. And curiously enough, the aristocrats who had rarely troubled to adorn themselves with the title of *noble* were very soon to glory in a new term, because we shall find many acts beginning 'I, X, Knight' (=*miles*).

Miles was not synonymous with *free,*[1] because the word was not used to describe the free men who had no military vocation. It was not identical, either, with *vassus* or *fidelis.* Limiting this study to France, which (with Lotharingia) was the region where these problems have been best disentangled, one finds that certain vassals (domestic and ministerial officials) had not adopted a military career. The *milites* as a group formed a *militia,* the terrestrial as distinct from the divine militia formed by the order of clerics (cf Saint Benoît de Nursie).

Was the substitution of *miles* for *nobilis* simply a tardy adaptation of the vocabulary, towards the year 1000, to a situation that was really old, the capacity to arm oneself for fighting on horseback having for centuries past been limited to the more well-to-do? As this does not appear to have been so, an important circumstance must be stressed. Thus the noblemen were at that time engaged in acquiring accepted privileges; that is, they were on the way to becoming crystallized, very largely, under the collective name of *chevalerie* (the class of knights).

In fact the eleventh century saw the conclusion of an evolutionary change which had begun at least in the eighth century. In the armies of the West the troops of heavy armed knights no longer enjoyed a simple primacy; they had an exclusive privilege. The knights were organized in small homogeneous groups, the *conrois,* each composed of knights of the same castellan, *milites castri,* all vassals of this castellan and accustomed to living, training and fighting together. In

[1] In Germany, Lotharingia, Berry and the Paris basin, there were *chevalier-serfs.* Beaumanoir simplified the matter over much by a rigid contrast between *chevalerie* (knighthood) and servitude (P. Petot, in *Revue Hist. de Droit fr. et étr.,* 1960).

the Forez and the Mâconnais, and generally in central France, the knights of the eleventh century belonged to fairly well-to-do families, claiming descent from the same ancestors as the castellans, their lords. From this time onwards, 'accomplishment of the same functions of knighthood seems to have been . . . a strictly hereditary function'. On the other hand, in northern and north-western France, even in the twelfth century, many knights were living on a prebend, that is in a domestic situation, in their lord's castle (Duby). And where the *droit d'aînesse* was to take root, the younger brothers – the *juvenes* – were obliged, in order to live, to join the companies of vassals in the houses of the very 'powerful'.

This said, the problems surrounding knighthood remain the most controversial, and are now continually giving rise to new research. In default of being able to discuss them all in detail, an attempt will be made to note the principal points of agreement or disagreement, particularly in French-speaking countries.

The central problem is to define the composition of this social group as exactly as possible; and another problem, bound up with it, is to discover whether it was open to newcomers, and if so, whether it was completely open or not, and until what period.

Vassal dependence and decree of wealth are not sufficient criteria – knights might be freeholders; the lordships belonging to them were numerous and of varying extent, and this was to become more common owing to heritages and purchases. A military way of life seems to be the best criterion, but this operated less decisively from about the thirteenth century, when the knights were to become officers of the king or of a prince, than it had done in the preceding centuries. One must also ask whether there was a 'juridical barrier', 'a social partition', and whether this existed or not between the knights and other free men.

In his *Essai sur l'origine de la noblesse en France au Moyen Age*, a work of 1902 which is still authoritative, Guilhiermoz saw in the French *chevalerie* a noble 'class', very easy of access to newcomers at the outset, but which later became closed –

towards the thirteenth century – although not completely. This theory was confirmed though slightly modified by Marc Bloch, first in certain articles and then in his excellent *Société féodale* (1940), a work which French historians have followed for many years, and which is still a classic. Conscious of having a way of life and a code of life different from those of other men, conscious therefore of their superiority, and avoiding marriage outside their own milieu, the nobles first formed a social 'class'. From the second half of the twelfth century they slowly turned into a 'juridical class', endowed henceforth with hereditary privileges, a new phenomenon, under the double influence of knighthood and of feudal hierarchy. Dazzled by the prestige of the dubbing of a knight, 'powerful' men had themselves regularly dubbed and then had this ceremony reserved for their sons. The 'class' of knights next presumably closed its ranks and became a 'caste'. As a consequence of this, dubbing was no longer necessary, and the sons soon ended by inheriting the father's position without even having undergone the ceremony. Hence a 'caste', evidently a closed one in the thirteenth century, in reaction against the material and political advance of the bourgeoisie, which was buying fiefs put up for sale by needy knights. The closing of the nobility's ranks would then be the defensive reaction of a 'class' threatened in its interests and its power. Many French historians had appeared to accept these views, for example as regards the Mâconnais, the north of France or Alsace. Georges Duby himself seemed at first to take a more radical line by thinking that as early as the 1100s, the nobility of Mâcon was a closed 'caste' which new men could no longer enter. The closing of ranks in this region would – in his view – have been as complete as it was advanced in date.

Léopold Genicot has opportunely recalled the danger of extending Marc Bloch's conclusions to the whole of the West. Like Verriest, he has pointed out that the lands north of the Somme had, 'both in the matter of judicial institutions and of the status of individuals, for long preserved the old Frankish structures. . . They stood out in obvious contrast to the other regions of France where institutions, being less old and less well-established, evolved more quickly under the influence of feudalism and adapted themselves with less difficulty to social changes'. It is in these words that Perroy, who has partly accepted the above views, summarizes Léopold Genicot's position. In the region of Namur there existed until the end of the thirteenth century an hereditary nobility, closed to newcomers, and distinct from the knights, who were a military group defined by its way of life. So in Lotharingia for several centuries it was unusual to regard *chevalerie* as equivalent to *noblesse*.

There was therefore a time-lag in 'the prestige attaching to the status of knight', which was more advanced in France (except north of the Somme) and in England than in Lotharingia and Germany. As early as the eleventh century, in the greater part of France the knights asserted themselves as a social group. Earlier still, under the Carolingians, the clergy had worked out the concept of the *miles Christi*, but this idea was not really adopted until the tenth century. The *miles* wins salvation by protecting the people of God, hence he deserves to enjoy legal privileges. The regulations governing law and order thus conferred on the *milites* a particular status, very much higher than that of other laymen. Now, at the same time, authority was vested in other groups, and the magnates who had the right of ban began to exact various services from which the knights were exempt, even before this right of ban ceased to be a monopoly of the castellans, and before most knights had acquired such rights for themselves. Thus in the eleventh century the knights formed 'a body privileged in temporal as in spiritual matters', although the idea of a nobility of blood enjoyed more prestige than 'chivalry' or knighthood, and was long to survive in France, both in literature and in social customs. In any event, the knight is 'at once priest, soldier and judge' (Genicot).

In the Empire, on the contrary, the influence of the Church scarcely affected the notion of knighthood. In the eleventh century, royal or princely authority, in the maintenance of peace, supported the idea of *libertas*, which here meant nobility. It was the noble who, in the Empire, was priest, soldier and judge, three vocations held in principle or in fact by the king. This means that in the whole of western Europe, in spite of very marked regional differences, certain men, knights or nobles, had the same vocations, enveloped in a semi-mystical prestige, vocations modelled on that of the king; and this, with or without the sovereign's assent, and varying according to the age and the region.

Within the Empire and in several neighbouring provinces, it was only in the thirteenth century that nobility and knighthood were equated in word and concept. Was this due to the tardy recognition here of the greater prestige of knighthood, or to the material difficulties of the nobles, difficulties which have been readily exaggerated and which scarcely offer a satisfactory explanation? Or was it rather due to the 'increasing strength of the princes', who levelled out the 'aristocratic strata'? This last supposition is very probably the most valid. The power of the castellans was reduced, while the village knights appropriated a part of the ban – the lower ban – and changed their dwellings into strongholds. Next, the ordinary knights took advantage of the 'widespread arrogation of the right of ban' and raised themselves to the level of the old nobility.

Almost everywhere in the thirteenth century the reconstitution of the 'states' – royal states in France and England, princely states in the Empire – was soon to modify the privileges of nobles or knights. For long years ahead, to be a noble was to escape taxation. Hence the prince was compelled to 'control the membership of this free class of men'. There were in general to be two criteria, which, when necessary, treated nobility and knighthood on the same footing. A knight (or noble) had to prove that he was descended from a knight, and that his ancestor had been dubbed knight. This control exercised by the State was to lead rapidly to the notion of derogation. Nobles would now have to prove their right to the title.

To decide whether knighthood was, or was not, a class more or less closed to newcomers, and from what date, one must first try to answer two questions: what was the numerical strength of this class, and how far was it subject to change?

In the Mâconnais at the beginning of the eleventh century the knights were few in number, and their numbers decreased in the course of the century. This was because a knight's equipment was costly and because his way of life involved the need for many periods of leisure; he had to guard the lord's castle and there were expeditions to places near or far, while the length of this military service was fixed only in the thirteenth century. There were also family wars, tournaments and training in general. A man had therefore to be in possession of a good rural lordship of at least a hundred and fifty hectares,[1] it is thought, in which the domain was profitably worked under the direction of a steward. Hence many small nobles were not able to reach the status of knight or maintain themselves in it. This was the situation in the Mâconnais in the early eleventh century. A total of seven rural lords with the title of knight were then living in five parishes. Towards 1100 there were no more than four; and of the three families which had ceased to rank as knights, one had become extinct, while the two others had been so impoverished that they had agreed to work as provosts or stewards of the castellan. From this example it seems that one can generalize, when one considers the small number of knights whom the princes themselves were able to assemble during the early feudal period. There were not then, towards 1100, as many families of knightly rank as there were parishes.

The knights did not however constitute a caste. They often gained by an infusion of new blood from the increasing population and from parvenu intrusions. The relative numbers in the several aristocratic families are still little known, but Genicot has shown that the few families of the 'nobility' in the region of Namur first proliferated, then divided up into smaller branches, before decreasing in numbers after the thirteenth century, owing to the extinction of certain branches. This decrease in numbers cannot be explained simply by the dangers inherent in military life; the practices designed to prevent the sub-division of estates were also largely responsible. The younger sons entered the Church or

[1] 360 acres.

refrained from marrying. Perroy's research in the Forez bears witness to the same phenomenon. A fairly large number of families of this rank became extinct in a relatively short space of time; but not all such families, and not everywhere. Duby has noted an 'astonishing permanence' of several families of knights in the Mâconnais in the eleventh and twelfth centuries. There are still living in the West, today, families which 'go back to the time of the Crusades'.

The extinction of ancient families was constantly and largely made good 'by the accession of new families honoured by reason of their alliances, their functions or their wealth' (Duby), but in very unequal proportions from one region to another, and in different periods. Almost everywhere at the outset this small élite was open to those who were sufficiently well off to buy arms and horses, to give most of their time to training, and to delegate the management of their domains to stewards. In many *milites* of the twelfth century Marc Bloch saw the descendants of successful adventurers or of peasants who had grown rich by dint of economies. Such men in fact led the same kind of military life as the knights and possessed similar landed property. The best proof of these statements is no doubt to be found in the literature of the twelfth century, which depicts many professional horsemen hiring out their services to great lords, the latter fairly often seeking the support of mercenaries, new men who had sometimes come from far away.

However, during the first feudal age these newcomers did not everywhere encounter the same facilities. The mercenary had first to find a lord fairly well-to-do and able to assign from his estates a new fief for his new vassal. This was not possible in the case of a castellan or a count of no great importance, a remark valid for the whole of the West. The geographical conditions were not the same everywhere, as witness the contrasts between central and southern France on the one hand and north-western France and part of Lotharingia on the other. In central and southern France the military obligations of vassals, during the first feudal age, had been light and vaguely defined. A lord therefore granted only small fiefs, and one could become a knight only if one possessed some freeholds in addition. There was nothing here to attract adventurers. In the nature of things the ranks of *chevaliers* could, at best, only be partly open to newcomers, for example in the Mâconnais. Things were different in the rich and vigorous principalities of north-western France, of lower Lotharingia, and of England which followed the example of Normandy. These countries were reservoirs of professional fighting men who swarmed abroad as far as the East. Contrary to a widespread opinion, Perroy thinks that the high birth-rate in these countries, even if one could prove that it was high, could not be the sole cause of this expansion. As early as the eleventh century Flanders and Normandy were held by princes who disposed of both authority and riches. This was why they could attract to a military career a greater number of men whom they would provide with fiefs, fiefs which in Normandy might contain as many as four or five hundred hectares[1] (including the domain), that is to say, that they were much larger than the fiefs in southern or central France. Towards 1100 the duke of Normandy could call a thousand knights to arms, while in 1172 there were to be 2,800 fiefs, which no doubt covered half the cultivated area of Normandy. Among the holders of these fiefs were the sons of knights, and also new men, though in what proportion one does not know. But it had not been possible to provide fiefs for all the new men, either in Normandy or in England or in Lotharingia. In England in 1166 certain professional soldiers with no houses of their own were supported by their lord in his own mansion or castle: they were *milites de dominio*. In the district of Namur they were called *milites de familia* or 'knights of the (count's) household'. It is certain that in the first feudal age the knights in all these countries were an open and not a closed social group.

On the other hand, during the second feudal age, this social group, while never completely closing its ranks, generally tended to be far less receptive to newcomers. This was because only the descendants of knights were regarded as knights. The social group had therefore become hereditary.

[1] Over 1,000 acres.

This is not to say that a new man might not contrive to enter, but that the number of newcomers could not be great, owing to the lack of available places. The old families, which had often been impoverished by the Crusades and the wars of the thirteenth century, viewed these newcomers with no friendly eye, the more so as wealthy burgesses were now trying to acquire fiefs, a fact which obliged customary law to rule that the purchase of a 'noble land' – that is, a fief – did not make the purchaser a noble. If the 'knighthood-nobility',[1] had not completely closed its ranks as Marc Bloch thought, they were at least only partially open, owing to the material hardships, and to a lesser extent the economic difficulties suffered by some of its members, although the property of the nobles did not suffer a general collapse.

II. CASTELLANS AND CASTELLANIES

A. The Castles

There had been castles in the West before the year 1100, without speaking of the restored fortifications surrounding cities of Roman origin or the defences hurriedly built against the Normans, defences which then sometimes fell into ruin. It was after 900 and especially after 950 that men began to build fortresses in considerable numbers, designed no longer to protect a township or a monastery but to control the surrounding country against anyone fomenting disorder. It was a question of a new type of fortification (*castrum, castellum, munitio, turris, firmitas* – hence the word *ferté*) nearly always independent of a township, set apart from certain *vici*.

It consisted of a surrounding wall or fence – a wooden palisade at the outset – protected by its situation on a natural hilltop or an artificial hillock (called a *motte*), or on the bank of a stream. A moat was dug around this *enceinte*. Inside, at the point easiest to defend, stood a *tower*, later called a *donjon* (*dungio* derives from *dominus*) which often gave its name to the whole fortress (turris = tower, but also

[1] For the thirteenth century it seems better to use the term 'nobility', since all sons of knights no longer had themselves dubbed, without losing their privileged status.

fortress, castle) and was the key building. The situation of the fort was dictated by its geographical and strategic advantages, the object being to watch and control roads and navigable rivers. A distinction was drawn between the 'hill-top castle', built on high ground which commanded a good view over the surrounding country, for example in the area between mountains and plain (as in the Forez), and the 'road castle', built by a cross-roads or near a river, to defend its valley, as were the fortresses on the plains. In Flanders the castles of Douai, Aire, Ypres, Bruges and others were older than the cities which now bear those names.

Neither before nor after 1000 could castles be built in principle by any but the local or regional possessors of the right of ban. Even weak sovereigns like the first Capetians built castles, at least in their personal domain, just as did the counts and princes of France; and it was generally agreed by historians, before M. de Boüard's archaeological researches, that an adventurer was not able to build himself a 'tower'. To do so would have been materially difficult, for lack of money or service, because a castle even of timber cost a great deal to construct, maintain and protect.

It was the counts who built the greater number of castles. One of the principal builders was Foulque Nerra, count of Anjou, who caused some fifteen fortresses to be constructed in his county and in neighbouring regions, at Loudun, Mirebeau, Moncontour and elsewhere. Or it was the viscounts like those of Thouars and Châtellerault who were in principle dependent on the great county of Poitou. This was between 950 and 1050. The prelates also built castles. And if in theory the counts had to authorize any new buildings in their district, one may well suppose that this did not invariably apply in practice. They could not always control the operations of their delegates, the viscounts and castellans. Finally, during the first feudal age, the more official kind of fortresses gave those who owned or guarded them a keen sense of independence, and this independence was often real; which explains why Duby has described this age in France as the era of 'independent castellans'. Such was the situation in central and southern France, but not in Normandy where, in the eleventh century, the duke kept a firm hold on nearly all the castles, as did the count of Flanders in his domains. But control was by no means complete in a country as vast as Anjou, even though the counts were men of uncommon energy. From the tenth century onwards they had been great castle-builders, Foulque Nerra in particular; but they were obliged to confide the charge of many castles to vassals who soon turned disobedient. In the second quarter of the twelfth century when Geoffrey Plantagenet set out to restore authority in his county, where it had suffered a decline, he had to spend some years in recapturing and demolishing the castles of his most rebellious vassals, much as, a little earlier, Philippe I and Louis VI had done in the Ile-de-France.

It has been generally held that castles were few in number before the year 1000. This theory was advanced by way of reaction against the opposite theory, according to which feudalism arose in an age of anarchy when castles were very numerous. M. de Boüard, however, has just pointed out that historians have believed fortresses were comparatively rare, because they were influenced by a 'legal conception' of the origin of feudal buildings. Now aerial photography and excavations on the ground reveal 'a considerable number of fortified sites of an archaic kind'. As this piece of research is by no means complete, it appears prudent to distinguish, with reservations, between real fortresses and simple 'mottes'.

It still seems true that in many regions the number of real castles, which were few in the tenth century, did not increase very greatly after the year 1000. However, in the Mâconnais, where the count's power was on the wane, the number of castles increased from about six at the end of the tenth century to only ten or eleven toward 1150. Similarly, fortifications were not numerous in the Forez and the Roannais (Perroy). There were two reasons for this: first, the progressive replacement of wood by stone, so that building became more and more costly in spite of the increase in the seigneurs' income. Secondly, the masters of ancient castles, if not the count, the prince or the king, frequently opposed such new constructions. Hence the many local wars in which the *potentes* leagued together to destroy the 'adulterous' fortresses, wars in which they were supported by the peasants whose interest was obviously to oppose an increase in the holders of the right of ban, and therefore an increase in exactions.

According to J. Boussard's calculations, England in 1154, on the accession of Henry II, scarcely contained as many as 250 castles, each controlling from thirty to forty parishes. The building of 'towers' had just been finished by about this time; seventy-five were in the king's hands, the remainder being guarded by prelates or vassals, direct or indirect, of the Crown. Castles were of course almost absent from certain regions, but they were particularly numerous in the marches (for example on the borders of Wales, which was still practically independent except in the south) or in regions not completely conquered, like South Wales.

These two observations – the small number of real fortresses and the relative abundance of 'frontier castles' – would also hold good for the greater part of France, and notably for all western France, from Normandy to the Pyrenees, which was held by the Plantagenets. Hence a very loose 'network', each fortress controlling the countryside within a radius of from about five to ten kilometres, which was sufficient in respect of the military techniques of the age. There were also good examples of 'frontier castles' on the disputed borders of the Plantagenets' Normandy and the Capetians' Ile-de-France, for example in Vexin.

Perroy distinguishes two kinds of castle: frontier castles, the most numerous in principle, standing in regions of insecurity and maintained only at the cost of incessant warfare; and 'defensive' castles, the normal type, although not always the most widespread. They maintained a semblance of order and provided tolerable dwellings for the knights of the district where they exercised a fairly strong economic and political influence over the peasants. These were the fortresses which it is most important to study.

Castles built of timber had been formidable enough, though much less so than those of stone, which first appeared in the Loire valley about 1000 and then spread over the whole of the West between that date and the twelve hundreds. A stone castle could not be captured except by surprise or at the cost of a very long siege. Strongholds impossible or very difficult to take were numerous. Philippe I and Louis VI had unheard-of difficulties in capturing those marvellous fortresses of the Ile-de-France which had increased their owners' sense of independence and encouraged them in rebellion, as in the affair of Le Puiset.

If the true castles were residences of great lords, the *motte*, or mound, was from the eleventh century onwards 'the typical dwelling of lords of minor or only moderate importance' and it was doubtless regarded 'as the symbol of seigneurial authority' (Boüard). *Dungio* was a synonym of *motta*, a term which came into use later. It was a question of 'a fortified seigneurial dwelling', and very many examples of such have been discovered from Anjou as far as the Scheldt, passing through Normandy, and even in Norman Italy. This kind of habitat 'was within the reach of lords of minor or moderate status, not particularly well-to-do'. The peasants could work at raising the mound and building the timber house which was to surmount it, and which may not have actually been called a castle. In Anjou, Touraine, Normandy and Flanders these mounds 'do not seem to have been erected according to a plan which would suggest the intervention of an authority higher than that of the builder. . . On the contrary, in England, where after the Norman conquest feudalism was organized on the initiative of the kings and was very strict from the outset, it has been observed, in Shropshire, that the mounds and the small circular earthworks were carefully distributed so as to assure the defence of the three great castles of the Montgomerys: Shrewsbury, Caus Castle and Hen Domen' (Boüard). It appears, then, that when the 'mounds' were not surmounted by a small 'castle', they were subordinate to the real castles. In short, the 'mounds' belong rather to the history of rural lordship and were not the real fortresses of feudal lords. It is to these that we shall now return.

B. Castellans, Castellanies, and Castellan Lordships

The true castle was not simply the basis of a military system.

It had become the centre of actual power and it was within its framework, the most important during the first feudal age in France, that the three *orders* of society were organized, willingly on the part of the knights, perforce in the case of the clergy and the peasants.

The power of the castellan extended over a definite *territory*, hence the administrative divisions of the country were greatly modified. The fundamental unit had become the *pagus* (*pays*, country) a word which had been substituted in Carolingian times for *comitatus*. This *pagus* or county, was subdivided into *hundreds*, a word often replaced in the tenth century by *viguerie* or *voierie*, which derive from *vicaria*. But during the first feudal age certain viscounts (delegates of the counts) had taken advantage of the decline of the counts' power to carve out a territory for themselves whereas, formerly, their own power had only been delegated and had had no territorial basis. There were no viscounties. There was therefore no continuity between the viscounts of the ninth century and those of the first feudal age, who had often become the hereditary lords of a territory over which they exercised all the rights of ban, as did, for example, the viscounts of Thouars, Châtellerault and Béziers. Meanwhile most of the *vigueries* disappeared, the word serving now only to describe the function of a minor agent of the lord.

The former powers of the viguier[1] had fallen into the hands of the castellan, while the *vigueries* – in the geographical sense – were replaced by new sub-divisions known as *territories*. The territory was the judicial area within which the castellan exercised the right of ban, in principle exclusively. A viguerie did not coincide with a *territory*. *Territorium castri* was the expression first used in northern France. As it was vague, people more often preferred the words *districtus castri*, which meant that the castle exercised its power of constraint (*districtus* = Fr. *détroit* = constraint in the legal sense) over a geographical area. *Mandement*, a word which was to appear only in the twelfth century in central and south-eastern France, is an equivalent, since *manda-*

[1] Many legal terms of the feudal era have no English equivalents. The *viguier* might be described as a provost (Translators).

mentum and *districtus* are synonymous. Burgundy and eastern France used two precise terms: one, *pôté* (*potestas*), is equivalent to *mandement* and *détroit*; the other, *sauvement* (*salvamentum*), has a moral bearing, because it was the area in which the inhabitants were under the safeguard of the castle, whose lord could, in return for his protection, impose duties on them. After 1150 these various words were to be replaced by a new one, and in the end one hears only of the castellany (*castellania*).

All this did not happen in a day, but in the course of the eleventh century new administrative regions were taking shape in France. These areas were changing, confused, sometimes obscure, with many *enclaves* and frontiers deliberately left vague; they consisted rather of zones disputed between neighbouring barons. To picture these regions on a map would be hazardous unless one had at one's disposal, as Duby had for the Mâconnais, an exceptional abundance of archives. But all this was peculiar to France. In Norman England there were no castellan lordships, because the king was strong. The castle of a vassal was, perhaps like the 'mottes' on the Continent, only the administrative centre for the manors of the *honour*, that is, of the great fief held by the vassal. There were therefore no castellanies, military and judicial districts, but only *liberties* or *franchises*. Each *honour* constituted a *franchise*, and its possessor, whether cleric or layman, exercised various rights over the population in the place of the king's agents; but in terms of money it brought in far less than was exacted by the French castellans. It simply gave the incumbent great prestige and social influence over the peasants, similar in certain respects to those of the French castellans, and that is important. But there ends the similarity.

The situation in Germany was different from the situations in France and in England. In the twelfth century the castles were still in the hands of the counts, the right to build fortresses having early escaped from the control of the monarchy. But the counts, when they had enfeoffed some of their castles, still reserved a right of control over them, just as the princes did over the castles of their vassals. The castle was said to be 'liable to be handed over to any garrison great or small', and the vassal was required to guard it at all times (service of Burghut). It seems then that there were no independent castellanies as in France. And whereas the Norman kings of England had brought the castles into subjection and the kings of France were to do the same, in a large measure in the twelfth and thirteenth centuries, never were the German monarchs to recover a right of control over the fortresses, save on their own lands and in the counties directly dependent on their authority, where they had not lost that right. It was the territorial princes of Germany who were to profit from this concentration of power and not, as in France and England, the kings.

Of the powers and resources which the French castellans derived from their right of ban, two kinds of authority can be distinguished, setting aside the purely military aspect of the question.

a. *Powers of police.* These powers were the most justifiable, though often the least profitable. Their object was to protect the movement of travellers and merchandise. Care of the highroads had passed from the king and then from the duke or count, into the hands of the castellan. It was called *conduit* (*conductus*). Except where the castellan was merely a brigand, this *conductus* was efficacious; this, and of course many other factors, help to explain why the commercial expansion of the eleventh and twelfth centuries became possible. Sometimes the lord provided an escort for merchants, pilgrims or notables; sometimes he gave them a 'safe-conduct' or assurance of protection in return for a fee. Or again, and this was the most lasting and profitable method, he imposed a toll, an *ad valorem* tax payable on all merchandise which passed through a given point. In this way tolls became more and more numerous after about 1050, at least in France. If these tolls, or safe-conducts, were not prohibitively high and if the protection they afforded was genuine, they facilitated a much greater circulation of travellers and goods. But the proliferation of tolls, which continued until the end of the Middle Ages, might oblige traffic to take routes through regions where peace was better assured. In any case, in proportion as economic growth expanded in the West, the tolls, which had not brought in much at the outset, ended by becoming one of the major resources of the castellans. Meanwhile, the right of *conductus* gradually lost its importance, because the count, and then the king, were to grant their own protection over a far wider and pacified territory. In the twelfth and thirteenth centuries the *conductus* granted by the counts of Champagne, and later by the kings of France, afforded a remarkable protection for merchants visiting the fairs of Champagne.

b. *Other powers: bannal lordship and castellan lordship.* Whether one should distinguish between two kinds of lordship held by the castellan is open to discussion. It seems preferable, however, to make a distinction because the right of ban did not remain an exclusive privilege of the castellans but, on the contrary, especially in its economic features, was shared between them and other rural lords, and doubtless, in early days, with those who owned a *motte*. Even on those dwellers in the region who were not his tenants, a bannal lord could impose various obligations, including that of using his mill, oven, winepress and brewery, in return for a tax which represented both the value of the service and an 'exaction'. The economic rôle of these rights of ban, in the French countryside, was of the greatest importance. But at different times, which are still not well known, many other rural lords contrived to obtain this right, which appears largely to have represented the 'lower' ban.

After the economic ban came the military ban, which this time was exercised exclusively by the castellan. After the end of the tenth century the military chiefs in possession of a castle arrogated to themselves the 'higher' ban over all the peasants. The profits of the right, in addition to those of an economic kind which have just been mentioned, consisted for the castellan:

i. in requiring the villagers to bear all the military expenses: to build or maintain the castle, to contribute to its defence, to take part in the castellan's wars as foot-soldiers or by providing food and fodder, or again by furnishing waggons for transport;

ii. in punishing the peasants for infraction of the rules, and in arrogating to himself the expenses of administering against them, for any cause whatsoever, civil or criminal justice.

The ban was certainly 'a marvellous instrument of domination' (Perrin), especially when in the hands of the lord of a 'ferté'.[1]

The churches in the castellany did not completely escape the ban, but by right of their immunities they contrived to obtain either a share in its prerogatives, or a more or less light 'tariffing'[2] of the bannal rights. As *guardian* of the religious houses in his territory, the castellan was not generally able to impose or maintain any arbitrary power over the clergy or over the men dependent on them.

It goes without saying that the castellan could not have established nor could he have maintained his power and wealth if he had not managed to bring effectively under his control all the knights or minor nobles of his territory. The *milites castri*, not at all well-to-do (except in northern France and in England), men connected by family alliances but whose properties were subdivided with every new generation, could not have lived, maintained their rank and provided themselves with arms, without the assistance and generosity of the castellan. Economic dependence and bonds of vassalage were strengthened reciprocally in this way, to the greater advantage of the master of the 'tower'.

But if the heyday of 'independent castellanies' can be situated towards the early eleven hundreds, the twelfth century was to see their decline, and the rise in France, and elsewhere, of other territorial authorities with a usually wider sphere of action.

III. NEW TERRITORIAL GROUPINGS: THE PRINCIPALITIES

Though the problem here is of the greatest importance, treatment will be brief, both for want of space and because there is no lack of available works which deal thoroughly with the question.

As the Christian regions in the Iberian peninsula have

[1] From *firmitas*, equivalent to *castellum*, a strong 'tower' or fortress.
[2] i.e. they paid at a much lower rate (Translators).

not been studied and as England is not concerned in this matter, it remains only to indicate the essentials as they affected France, Germany and Italy, or at least northern and central Italy.

A. France

One cannot describe the French principalities of the eleventh, twelfth and thirteenth centuries as 'states' in the same way as one could describe the Burgundian 'state' at the end of the Middle Ages. For a long time indeed, except in the Plantagenet dominions of the West, the authority of the counts and dukes rested on the importance of their personal fiefs and of the vassals dependent on them. Little by little, however, they contrived to take over the rights properly belonging to the monarch, for example the right to mint coinage, and also, to the detriment of the castellans, the right of ban. If the twelfth century witnessed the decay of the castellanies, it was also the age when many principalities first rose to power. The princes' task was to be twofold: to bring their rebellious vassals to order and to establish an administrative service within their principalities.

There exist many maps of the 'great fiefs' in the twelfth and thirteenth centuries, whereas it would be hazardous to attempt to draw such a map for the tenth and eleventh. This is significant, because it shows that the geographical limits of the principalities were being to some extent established – although one must not exaggerate here – and that these limits were acquiring a certain degree of permanence. A relatively great number of principalities date from the first medieval age. They were not at the outset, as in Germany, held together by any individual peculiarity, such as that of a tribe or race; but the habit of living together ended by creating, in the population, a kind of individuality which it would obviously be an anachronism to describe as 'provincial'. Certain great fiefs preserved in general the same form as at the end of the early Middle Ages. The best examples are those of Normandy, of which the frontiers remained exceptionally stable, or Brittany and Flanders. Some princes, however, tried to extend their boundaries, like the enterprising Foulque

Nerra (987–1040), count of Anjou, who did more than encroach on the neighbouring principalities. The trend of the times, in short, especially in the twelfth century and later, was towards a simplifying of the political map, an indisputable sign that the princes were succeeding. One example in particular shows clearly that the age no longer favoured a fragmenting of the country, but larger regroupings: this was the expansion of the Plantagenets who, from the time of Henry II, ended by controlling the whole western half of the kingdom.

The best example of the unification of a principality is, of course, that of the royal domain, the more so as it partly explains how the Capetians were to succeed in increasing the power of the Crown, which had grown so weak, in limiting the independence of the other princes, and finally in taking possession of a large number of great fiefs. According to J. F. Lemarignier, Hughes Capet and Robert the Pious, in spite of the political dislocation of the kingdom, always took their stand on the Carolingian tradition, without concentrating their efforts on unifying and strengthening their domain. Henri I (1031–1060) was the first Capetian to understand that the only, or almost the only, foundation of his power lay in the possession of the principality of the 'Ile-de-France', the more so as the counts and bishops were increasingly abstaining from attendance at Court. Henceforward the royal palace was no longer to contain the council of the 'fideles' but only of the great families in the royal domain, families often united to the Crown by bonds of kinship; it was also attended by the castellans and knights, to whom were added the humble mayors of villages. This involved a geographical contraction, but it also enabled the king to strengthen his authority and judicial powers, without which one can hardly understand how Philippe I (1060–1108) and his successor Louis VI (1108–1137) could, as they did, master the robber lords and bring back order into the domain. The latter was rich but of only moderate extent, and before the reign of Philip-Augustus the administration was rather primitive by comparison with those of several great fiefs. But it was at least firmly held in hand by the king who, being a powerful feudal lord, thanks to his domain, could for the same reason start his attack on the great fiefs, of which he imitated the administrations. In the end the Capetians were to benefit from the work accomplished by the dukes and counts (R. Fawtier).

B. Germany

As royal power in Germany, between the eleventh century and the early fourteenth, followed a curve opposite to the upward curve of the Capetians, so the 'Germanic' principalities continued to rise in power much longer than the French. Thus the territorial fragmentation of Germany survived until quite recent times. And while the 'feudal' map of France tended to greater and greater simplification, the map of Germany became more and more complicated. In Germany there was a territorial regrouping in certain instances and also a greater degree of fragmentation in others.

The formation of principalities was connected with the feudalizing of public functions, and this affected all the dukes and counts. The feudalization of lay princes goes back to the tenth century, but that of ecclesiastical princes, bishops and abbots of royal monasteries, dates only from the end of the twelfth century. These princes then ceased to be regarded as functionaries. At the beginning of the thirteenth century, the king remained the supreme judicial authority in the kingdom as a whole; but somewhat later, Frederick II, wishing to obtain the support of the princes for his great design, the close union between the kingdom of Sicily and the Empire, was to grant them exorbitant privileges in 1220 and 1232. He confirmed them in the royal rights which they enjoyed, and in so doing, he hastened the process by which the *Fürsten* were advancing from *Landesherrlichkeit* (territorial lordship) to *Landeshoheit* (territorial sovereignty), and notably to the possession, at the expense of the Crown, of superior judicial authority. This process was completed after 1250 and the final collapse of royal authority.

Western Germany, or 'Old Germany' as confined within the limits of the early Middle Ages, is to be contrasted with Germany east of the Elbe, a land recently colonized. The western part became extremely fragmented, whereas to the east the map was definitely less complicated, because there was no lack there of powerful principalities, none of which had an uncertain future. One should also observe that the continued fragmentation did not entirely weaken the jurisdiction of the princes, and that a whole hierarchy of principalities was established.

The principalities of the first rank were held by the *Fürsten*. Under Frederick II there were sixteen lay and ninety ecclesiastical princes, the formation of great religious principalities being one of the characteristic features of medieval Germany. The princes were dukes and those counts who enjoyed exceptional power and authority: margraves, landgraves and counts palatine. Other counts were later to be raised to the dignity of princes, so that in the fifteenth century there were to be some forty lay *Fürsten*.

The senior principality was the duchy. At the end of the early medieval age there were five: Lorraine, Saxony, Franconia, Suabia and Bavaria; but Lorraine was divided at an early date, Brabant being substituted for Lower Lorraine. Then the duchy of Bohemia became part of the Empire (its duke was later to acquire the title of King). Under Barbarossa other duchies were created: Brabant, Austria, Styria, Carinthia, Westphalia and Moravia. Certain margravates, namely Brandenburg, Lusatia and Misnia, are to be counted among the senior principalities. It was these principalities of the highest rank which, in the thirteenth century, were truly States, possessed of administrative machinery. And it was mainly from among the lay and ecclesiastical holders of senior principalities that the Golden Bull of 1356 was to choose the Electors to the Imperial title.

The second rank among the principalities consisted in counties which were still important and whose incumbents sometimes bore the title of Landgrave or Count Palatine: such were Thuringia and the County Palatine of the Rhine. Others were dependent on princes or on the king, like the county of Tyrol. The lay or religious lordships, occupying the lowest rank, were still fairly extensive.

Germany was, however, more than a conglomeration of

entirely sovereign, if not truly independent, States. What maintained a minimum of cohesion was less the monarchy than the nobility, which was beginning to organize itself as an order (*Stand*). The memory of past glories, of the struggle against the Hungarians and then against the Slavs; the feeling, above all, of belonging to the same civilization, distinct from that of the 'Latin' peoples of the West and the South; finally, the maintenance of the imperial idea – all these things prevented Germany being no more than a meaningless word.

C. Northern and Central Italy

It is not proposed to consider the States of the Church, which as early as the twelfth century had become a sovereign entity. The Pope was faced here by the anarchy maintained by local lords, but his territories were not feudal.

Though there still existed a 'kingdom of Italy', the king – that is the Emperor – was only master of Italy and then very incompletely, when he brought in an army. One of the effects of this collapse of power was the extreme fragmentation of the land and the large number of autonomous regions. There were, roughly speaking, two kinds of territory, in the general sense of the word. The counties had been split up even more than in Germany, and many lordships and localities had profited from this, more or less with the Emperor's assent. In addition to the duchies and marquisates which often comprised several counties, there were the great cities. Thanks to the communal movement, the cities were to free themselves from the feudal system, after which all, or almost all, would seek to take possession of the surrounding country and establish a *contado*. The *contado* was not a feudal principality; and so northern and central Italy witnessed the coexistence of feudal principalities – duchies and marquisates – and 'territories' which, at least on the higher level, had nothing feudal about them.

IV. THE FEUDAL MONARCHIES

The expression 'feudal monarchy', invented by Petit-Dutaillis, represents a phenomenon of great importance. A monarchy was feudal when the king derived the essence of his power from his feudal prerogatives.

Whether the German monarchy was feudal is a question on which German historians are divided, notably as regards the tenth century. It is true that Otto I reduced the dukes to their function as officials in the Carolingian fashion. But the 'Carolingian' aspect of the monarchy finally grew blurred. In the twelfth century it was completely feudalized, as the Concordat of Worms turned the ecclesiastical principalities into royal fiefs, while Frederick Barbarossa tried to restore royal authority by taking his stand on feudal law. One can say in conclusion that the German monarchy, and not simply because it remained elective, did not succeed in recovering any strength with the help of feudal law.

Quite different is the example afforded by the kingdoms of France and England. The Anglo-Norman kings had at once taken their stand on feudal law; but the reason why this operated for so long was probably because feudalism had been 'imported' and imposed by the king. Royal authority drew great strength from it, but there came a time when the Crown went too far in exploiting the system. This proved to be one of the great causes for the reaction of the barons, which led to Magna Carta and to much disorder during the thirteenth century. It was not a question of establishing a 'parliamentary monarchy' – the expression is an anachronism – but simply of tempering the power of the king and the prerogatives which imported feudal customs had given him. There was nothing in this movement that was not very conservative.

The best example of a great feudal monarchy is certainly that of the Capetians because it is in France that one sees most clearly how a spontaneous and not imported feudalism could in the end prove beneficial to royal power.

The Capetian was not, as is too often repeated, a 'small lord', the Count of the Ile-de-France. Other princes, in their domains, could be more powerful than he; but none, except when in temporary rebellion, really 'refused to recognize the theoretical supremacy of the king'. For this there were two reasons: first because he was the *king*, a sacred personage, the heir to the title of Charlemagne, of whom the legend long remained a living force. Thus kingship endured and eventually, at least from the twelfth century onward, the king was able to strengthen his position. He was a being apart, representative of God and guarantor, in principle, of public peace. Hence an obvious prestige even in the eyes of great laymen, and still more of the clergy. At the height of the Gregorian reforms there was never any marked friction between the Capetians and the Popes. 'This does not mean that (great lords) will not make war (on the king) and that he will not be beaten. Few sovereigns have been defeated as often as the Capetians down to the time of Philip Augustus. But the king will never be crushed; because, in spite of his weaknesses, he remains the king, the anointed of the Lord' (R. Fawtier).

Little by little the feudal pyramid was built up. It is now thought that it was completed in the time of Suger[1] – that is, in the first half of the century – under the influence of the Gregorian hierarchies, which had been inspired by the work of Cluny (J. F. Lemarignier). Henceforth the king 'is to be the supreme suzerain and all the feudal lords will be, directly or indirectly, his men' (R. Fawtier). The 'survival' of the Capetian monarchy is, in the second place, due to the fact that after the eleventh century most of the great lords were feudatories of the king; later, they all were, from the time of Suger onwards. This second reason is the more important for our purpose.

Taking advantage of his dual role as sovereign and suzerain, the king did not at first allow the prerogatives which feudal custom granted him to be clearly defined; it was only at a later stage that he used them to extend his domain and increase his power.

In the eleventh century and during the first half of the twelfth the kings rarely hesitated to assert their position as suzerains, and without too much difficulty. In 1002, the duke of Burgundy having died without heir, Hugues Capet refused

[1] Suger, an important authority for the history of the eleventh and early twelfth centuries, was abbot of Saint Denis and minister of Louis VI and Louis VII (Translators).

to recognize Otte-Guillaume, who had been chosen by the magnates. At the cost of several campaigns waged over a period of thirteen years, he succeeded in imposing on them his own candidate, who was Robert, his second son. It is true that the Capetian did not always attain his object, as for example in Flanders in 1127 where the *principes* had accepted Guillaume Cliton; but at least the principle did not fall into oblivion. It was not only a question of the right to intervene in the choice of a prince in the absence of a direct heir, but also, on great occasions, of obliging the magnates to respect the fealty which they owed the king. In 1078 Philippe I forbade the duke of Aquitaine and the prelates to hold a 'pseudo-council' which had been convened by the legate for reasons hostile to the king – forbade them under pain of violating their pledged word. Guillaume VIII, assisted by the men of Poitiers, molested the Fathers who were to attend the Council. The king was not supported merely by his prestige, but also by the fact that a prince often wished to treat him considerately because he might one day need his help. In 1162 and 1163 the Count of Toulouse, being threatened by Henry II of England, who had just become Duke of Aquitaine, appealed to Louis VII to help him in these words: 'we have lost our land, or rather yours since . . . everything that is ours is yours'.

Many princes betrayed the kings – treason being widespread at every level of feudal society – but they did it with an uneasy conscience and without always pushing treachery to its limits. This was to be true in the thirteenth century, during the Regency of Blanche of Castille, which is no matter for surprise, since the Capetians had by then grown powerful. But it was true even earlier. In 1103 the Count of Flanders allied himself with the king of England against Philippe I, 'saving the fealty due to the king of France'! 'If', he added, 'King Philippe came to England and brought Count Robert[1] with him, the Count would bring as small a contingent as he could, so as not to incur the forfeiture of his fief by the King of France.'

[1] He, himself, the count of Flanders. He would have to make some show of supporting his suzerain (Translators).

Fawtier has shown that 'the vassal who rose in rebellion against the king, even when the latter was as weak as Philippe I, was not exempt from fear. His oath of fealty embarrassed him because, by violating it, he was giving his own vassals a dangerous example.' Even a weak sovereign could seize the fief of a rebel and grant it to a third party, if the latter were strong enough to take possession of it by armed force. It was, moreover, the very weakness of the first six or eight Capetians that prevented the princes 'from realizing the danger to their future as great nobles from the theoretical rights which the political system attributed to the king, rights only occasionally put into practice'. And that was why 'the Capetian dynasty, on the morrow of the day when it acquired an adequate territorial foundation – that is under Philip Augustus – found itself almost at once the master of the feudal system'.

Slowly, and by a process still not clear in detail – because historians have only recently perceived that the 'feudal pyramid' had not been completed at the end of the first medieval age (that is, from 1000 to 1160) – the Capetians ended by making all the princes their vassals. By various means, and thanks to the prestige of the coronation and the anointing with oil, they then asserted their position at the summit of the pyramid, that is, their position as suzerain (supreme lord). If the king acquired a fief of moderate importance, held by some lord, he had not to pay homage to that lord. Suger in 1124 considered it unquestionable that the king, in his kingdom, owed homage to no one: a principle that was always to be reasserted with the greatest vigour. In a decree of 22 October 1314 the Parlement recalled that 'the kings of France are not accustomed to pay homage to their subjects'. Nor to anyone outside the kingdom, not even, and especially not, to the Emperor when claiming supreme temporal power over the 'Latin' countries of the West.

With regard to the barons, the Capetians derived most of their moral authority from their position as suzerains. Little by little, and mainly from the time of Suger, they made a wider use of their right to seek counsel of the great lords: hence the very promising growth of the *Curia Regis*. Here great lawsuits were now to be tried, bishops were to summon counts and dukes to appear, urban communities were to plead their business. At first the great lords acted as judges, but in face of the flow – still relatively limited – of new cases, and in view of the progress of common law, they then agreed that professional judges should assist them and even, in the majority of cases, declare what the law was. But for a feudal lord the duty of giving counsel went beyond the juridical domain. From the reign of Louis VII onwards assemblies of barons were held in the royal palace in Paris which were in effect political. At such assemblies it was decided to go on a Crusade, or to make war on the Plantagenets, or to promulgate ordinances for the maintenance of 'peace', to the great advantage of the Church and the people. The magnates acquired the habit of coming to Paris to wait on the king and then to execute his decisions, because these would have been taken in their presence and with their assent.

From this duty of giving counsel, of which Philip Augustus and his successors were to make much more use and turn to great profit, were to spring all the higher institutions of the monarchy, as well as the expansion of the domain and the authority of the Crown. Philippe II was 'to obtain decisive advantages from his feudal prerogative. By reason of its feudal character, the *Curia* became in his hands a formidable instrument of government' (Petit-Dutaillis).

The power of the Crown was reinforced in an extraordinary manner by the total or partial acquisition of great fiefs, without speaking of a multitude of minor ones. It is not a question here of recalling just the stages in this growth of power, but solely of appreciating the methods practised by the great Capetians. They 'did not make much use of force', preferring 'individual agreements', and exploiting to the maximum, and with at least an appearance of good faith, all the possibilities offered by feudal law. Charles V was certainly not the first king of France to have deserved the surname of the 'Advocate'! The best example of this procedure, and the best known, was the disinheriting of John Lackland; it showed, besides, that one had to add to the weight of feudal law the weight of military power and political genius, which Philip Augustus was by no means lacking in.

'A suzerain who had money, an extensive domain and a good army could make great demands on the duty of his vassals' (Petit-Dutaillis). This is what the Capetians did, beginning with Philip Augustus. The feudal nature of the monarchy proved more and more to be 'a source of strength'. After due enquiry, the obligations of the vassals were set down in writing, as the Plantagenet Henry II had already done in England; the vassals were counted, the number of the king's direct vassals was increased (a return to Charlemagne's policy) and a wide use was made of feudal sureties. It will also be seen how, from Philip Augustus to Philip the Fair (1285–1314), the kings used, if they did not abuse, the rights of *relief*,[1] of ward and of marriage.[2] By exploiting the possibility of making exchanges, recognized by custom, Philip Augustus contrived to acquire the fortresses which were strategically best situated.

More important was the fact that the two services which the vassals owed their lord, the 'service' of counsel and of military and financial aid, enabled the sovereign to assemble armies, numerous for the age, and, without being always himself aware of it, to begin creating real organs of government and administration. It is true that the *service d'ost* was now limited by custom to forty days; after which the vassals were free to leave the army, though the king might retain them by paying them wages. This period of service was not long enough for distant or ambitious undertakings, but it none the less enabled the great Capetians and also Blanche of Castille to extricate themselves from awkward situations. One example may be recalled. Philip Augustus's victory at Bouvines was due as much to the valour and loyalty of his troops as to his own genius. But the consequences of the king's use of the 'service of counsel or of the court' were still more significant, and even immense. From this service, owed by the barons to the Crown, arose the renewal of the

[1] A kind of inheritance duty (Translators).

[2] The king acquired the right of selecting his own candidate as husband for a girl left as heiress to a fief (Translators).

king's 'legislative power', and the birth of the Parlement de Paris, which can be described, with some few reservations, as the most admirable institution of medieval and modern France, as also of the other central organs of the monarchy.

'The essential role of the king of France', writes Fawtier, 'is to be the great justicer. But justice, in its earthly aspect, is never anything but the application of the law, and it is a more delicate question to know how far, in the Middle Ages, the king of France possessed what we call legislative power'. The king, like the dukes and counts, was always in principle able to obtain his vassals' consent to a decree which had been debated and decided in his *Curia,* and which only concerned his domain. But what of general decrees, designed for application in any or every part of the kingdom?

The first two decrees affecting France as a whole date from the reign of Louis VII. In 1144 he banished from the kingdom the Jewish converts who had relapsed; in 1155 he promulgated 'the Peace of God' for ten years. It was a somewhat platonic decision, the 'manifestation of an outburst of piety among the barons present at the session, who had given their approval to it (*ex beneplacito*) rather than an arrangement desired by the king himself'. It was clearly only from the reign of Philip Augustus onwards that there was a real change. Decrees to limit clerical jurisdiction, to regulate the subdivision of fiefs, to forbid usury, etc., were promulgated in his reign and in his son's 'by agreement between the king and the barons'. From the reign of Louis VIII and during the regency of Blanche of Castille, the barons who had been absent from the session of the royal court which had decided on a general measure, had to agree to its being carried out in their fiefs.

During the personal reign of Saint Louis the 'feudal' aspect of royal decrees diminished. Owing to the influence of the jurists who were always more imbued with Roman law, and also owing to the reunion with the crown of Languedoc, where Roman law had experienced a great revival since the twelfth century, the king's power became more and more that of a *sovereign,* and less and less that of a *suzerain.* Under the influence also of the canon lawyers, Saint Louis 'thought that the king has the right to impose his will on everyone, because it is obviously consonant with general usefulness', or 'the common benefit', as Beaumanoir was to say. Philippe III was even more active as a legislator. But this application of Roman and religious ideas had been made possible only 'because the predecessors of Saint Louis had been able gradually to widen the area in which their edicts were obeyed, thanks to the system of feudal consultations'.

More important still was the development of the royal jurisdiction, in matters of justice. It was this which, by tenaciously encroaching on the jurisdiction of the feudal counts, weakened the principalities and prepared the way for their union with the Crown. Everything, at bottom, proceeds from justice, and the king is supreme legislator only because he has asserted himself as supreme justicer.

Here too the king and his court had slowly regained all the ground which had been lost since the Carolingian successors of Charlemagne. Until the reign of Louis VI the Court – in other words the king and his barons present at the session – had had to take cognisance only of disputes between prelates, or between prelates on the one side and neighbouring advocates and lords; or else, after the early twelfth century, of lawsuits affecting the towns; but not criminal cases affecting great lay lords which were settled by their peers in conformity with feudal law. But rarely had the king submitted to his Court any of his personal differences with his great vassals. On the other hand, from the time of Louis VII the judicial activity of the Court developed, in spite of the resistance of the great lords and even of the clergy; this, even though Louis VII was regarded as a weak king. Hence Philip Augustus easily managed to establish the competence of his Court, which now contained a number of professional jurists, to adjudicate on lawsuits between the barons, or between the barons and the king. In 1202–1203 John Lackland was condemned to lose his French fiefs. This was not the first time that a great feudatory had been condemned, but it was the first time that the king was able to get the sentence of his Court executed by force.

It was in the middle of the thirteenth century that the Parlement – or the Parlements, as was said at first – became distinguished as the permanent judicial section of the *Curia Regis,* before becoming, towards 1300, an independent and specialized body, with a structure of its own. The moral prestige of Saint Louis led to a much larger number of cases being brought before the Court. His fame as a good justicer was now added to the prestige of an already powerful monarchy, which had become an effective guarantor of peace and order. There were also many appeals for arbitration. Even the king of England agreed to have recourse to this Court on the occasion of a quarrel with one of his Gascon vassals. *Appeal at law* was the principal instrument in the rising power of the Parlement, and this, Montesquieu has observed, constituted a revolution. The right of appeal was moreover a procedure recognized by many feudal customs; it allowed those subject to the jurisdiction of one lord to have recourse to the lord immediately superior to him, in order to have a sentence revised. Now from about the year 1250 the 'Parlement' contrived to facilitate appeals by organizing the procedure of the *enquiry.* A delegation of the *Curia,* composed of specialists, visited the scene of the dispute in order to investigate it anew. Appeals therefore became more numerous, especially as one could always appeal to the king, he being the supreme lord, and from any part of the kingdom. In the hands of the Parlement de Paris, appeal at law was immensely important for the progress of royal power, not only because it led to a relative unification of procedures, but also because it encroached on, and sometimes destroyed, feudal jurisdictions. Born of a feudal principle, the Parlement, perhaps unconsciously, destroyed the surest foundations of the feudal system from which it had sprung.

It would be too simple and even untrue to say that, since the monarchy strengthened itself at the expense of the nobility, it showed itself deliberately hostile to the nobles. All the gains of the monarchy were not obtained by force. If, like certain princes, the kings 'fomented and exploited the divisions among the nobles'; if they used new and 'rising forces'[1] against them, they also made them an integral part of the monarchical structure. It was from among the nobles that they recruited most of their officials. And the king always considered himself the first among the nobles, and therefore the head of the nobility; and even its defender. With this in view, the king of France reserved to himself the exclusive right of conferring nobility. If, from the time of Philip the Fair, the kings obliged the lords to accept the homage of their vassals who were commoners, they also obliged the latter to pay the due of 'Frank-fee', and they continued to supervise any access to nobility.

[1] The well-to-do merchant class was to be allied very effectively with the Crown. One should add that later kings like Louis XI and Louis XIV used bourgeois as their real ministers and officials (Translators).

Bibliography

BÖUARD, M. de, Quelques données archéologiques concernant le premier age féodal (*Annales du Midi*, No. 89, 1968, pp. 383–404.

BOUSSARD, J., *Le gouvernement d'Henri II Plantagenet*, Paris 1956.

CHELINI, A., *Histoire religieuse de l'Occident médiéval*, Paris 1968.

DUBY, G., *L'an mil*, Paris 1967.

FAWTIER, R., *Les Capétiens et la France*, Paris 1942. Eng. trs. by Butler and Adam, *Capetian Kings of France: Monarchy and Nation*, Macmillan, London, and St Martin's Press, New York, 1960.

FOURQUIN, G., *Les campagnes de la région parisienne*, Paris 1963–4.

LEMARIGNIER, J.-F., *La gouvernement royal aux premier temps capétiens, 987–1108*, Paris 1965.

Oxford History of England, Vol. 3 (From Domesday Book to Magna Carta, 1087–1216, by A. L. Poole), 2nd edn., Oxford 1958; Vol. 4 (The Thirteenth Century, 1216–1307, by M. Powicke), Oxford 1954.

PACAUT, M., *Les structures politiques de l'Occident médiéval*, Paris 1969.

PETIT-DUTAILLIS, C., *Le monarchie féodale en France et en Angleterre (X^e^–XIIIe siécles)*, Paris 1933. Eng. trs. *Feudal Monarchy in France and England; From the 10th to the 13th Century*, Routledge, London, and Harper & Row, New York, 1964.

RICHARD, J., *Les ducs de Bourgogne et la formation du duché du XIe au XIVe s.*, Paris 1954; Châteaux, chatelains et vassaux en Bourgogne aux XIe et XIIe s. (*Cahiers de civil, méd.*, 1960).

PART THREE

HOMAGE, FIEF AND LORDSHIP

From the Eleventh to the Thirteenth Century

Chapter 4

FEUDAL LAW[1]

I. THE CONTRACT OF VASSALAGE

If vassalage was destined little by little to lose its importance and meaning because of the evolution of the fief, the personal element was still to remain indispensable.

The contract sets two men face to face:

a. the man who in the eleventh century is very often called *miles,* and then, from the twelfth century, *homo* or *vassalus.* He is the *vassal,* the *man*; the *Mann* of Germanic texts; and

b. the person who is less and less called *dominus,* and more and more *senior,* whence the terms *seigneur* and *Herr.*

The 'acts imposing obligations on both parties' remain very close to those of the Carolingian *commendatio.* The rites which create this bond between man and man were described in writings that are clearer and more complete than those of earlier times. In many French texts they were to be described as '*foi et hommage*' although the act of homage preceded the oath of fealty. The expression makes clear that the ceremony contained at least two rites.

A. Homage and Fealty

1. *Homage.* In Latin, *hominium,* and then *homagium* (a Latinization of French *hommage*); in German, *Mannschaft.*

[1] There is an up-to-date bibliography in F. L. Ganshof, *Qu'est-ce que la féodalité?* Add the colloquy on the social structure of Aquitaine, Languedoc and Spain in the early feudal age (*Annales du Midi,* No. 89, 1968) for feudalism in the Midi. The best study of a feudal custom remains F. Olivier-Martin's *Histoire de la coutume de . . . Paris,* Paris, Leroux, 1922–30.

All these terms reveal the success of the word *homo* to designate the vassal. To do homage to someone is to recognize oneself as his man.

Homage consisted of two elements:

a. the *immixtio manuum*, the essential part of the ceremony. Unarmed, bare-headed and usually on his knees, the man places his hands together between those of his lord, the lord's hands enclosing the vassal's. This material act, with a physical contact, was an indispensable rite in a civilization where juridical systems had not developed very far and where, at least in the eleventh century, writing was only in limited use. This rite was to persist to the very end of 'feudalism' (in France until 1789), despite the immense development of law and of written documents, especially after the twelfth century.

b. the *volo*, a declaration of will. Though not obligatory, it was in very widespread use. The formula varied, but it always contained an expression like: 'Sire, I become your man.' On the other hand, it was less frequent for the sire to express his acceptance, or willingness.

This homage was an act of *autotradition*, to use Ganshof's word, on the part of the vassal to the lord, symbolized by the rite of the hands. It must be free, hence the declaration of willingness. In principle, the vassal must not have been already subject to the power of another lord; but in fact, as early as the first feudal age, it often happened that the vassal was the man of several lords. At least, however, the formal prohibition was generally maintained in respect of serfs. Serfs, being the property of their master, could not hand themselves over by an act of 'autotradition', since their previous state of dependence was humble and exacting. It was not possible either, at least in principle, for a free peasant to become a vassal, on account of the obligations, which for a long period were exacting, which he owed to his rural lord. In the course of the second feudal age the *ministeriales*, or 'chevaliers – serfs', of Germany were, however, permitted to do homage, their rise in social importance having blurred the servile taint which had previously affected them.

2. *Fealty* (*fides*, *Treue*, *Hulde*). A homage was followed by

an oath of fealty. The new vassal took this oath standing and with his hand on the Gospels or on a relic. The form of the oath varied in time and place, but with a definite tendency to pass from the concision of the Carolingian age to a certain prolixity, such as an enumeration of the many respects in which faith would have to be kept. One need hardly dwell on the strength of an oath sworn in the presence of God. The religious element in the ceremony was not new; it had already existed under the Carolingians; which means that the church had not waited for the age of knighthood before taking a hand in the ceremony of vassalage.

It is usual to question the bearing of this oath, since it might seem superfluous after the preceding rites which had fixed the reciprocal duties of the two parties. In the case of a vassal the handing over of oneself[1] had not for long past involved a subjection analogous to that which would arise from the self-dedication of a dependant of lower rank. The vassal's freedom was not really limited, and hence it was appropriate to explain the engagement he had undertaken (Perroy). On the other hand, the oath involved 'an engagement for the future'. To require the vassal to take this oath, Ganshof thinks, supposed that he remained a free man, and it was for him a guarantee.

There was then no vassalage without an oath, and this conferred on the engagement a character such that any violation of it would be a mortal sin. Hence the oath has immediately to follow the act of homage.

But towards the end of the eleventh century a grave problem arose of which the implications had been nearly forgotten since the time of Hincmar. How far could a cleric engage himself as a vassal? A churchman, a prelate in particular, could not take an oath in the same way as a layman, because his hand, like his whole body, had been consecrated by ordination. Now in the tenth and eleventh centuries the investiture of temporalities and even of ecclesiastical functions, when these had been taken over by the great lords, was effected by the same ritual as for the property

[1] '*La tradition de soi*', something like the Carolingian 'commendation', in brief the act of becoming a vassal (Translators).

of any vassal, whereas the new prelate had previously sworn fealty and done homage to the lay lord. In the last quarter of the eleventh century a reaction took place, because of the Gregorian reform which aimed at freeing the Church from the feudal bonds that constrained it; and the nature of the homage and investiture by laymen, as applied to religious functions, appeared a scandal. This faced the princes with difficulties which seemed insoluble, particularly in Germany where the bishops were still regarded as imperial functionaries. It had been Otto I who had associated them with the government of the country, which was a sufficient reason for keeping a strict control over their recruitment. In addition to their episcopal temporalities, the bishops had received property from the Crown, and even royal rights (*regalia*), for example the rights of a count over an area beyond that of the temporality. These *regalia* were conferred by the handing over of a symbolical object, the crozier, to which was later added the placing of a ring on the finger of the new bishop. In short, the close union between Church and Crown in Germany was for long years the essential principle of royal policy in that country. Hence the desperate resistance of the kings, and also of the princes in so far as they had taken possession of the *regalia*, at the time of the Quarrel of the Investitures. And as investiture was simply the juridical consequence of the homage which had been done, this homage was also attacked by the Gregorians. If the difficulties were less acute outside Germany, they none the less existed in all countries. Compromises were in the end effected almost everywhere and in about the same period, between 1107 and 1123. In Germany it was the Concordat of Worms (1122).

If the necessity of investiture was maintained, since for long past the temporalities had been nearly all held as fiefs, the act of homage was 'sweetened', and one can even say that during the twelfth century it was progressively to disappear in Germany, as in France and England. The ecclesiastical vassal had simply to *promise fealty*, this promise being restricted, since it could not interfere with his duties as a cleric (*salvo ordine suo*, his order being safeguarded). It was a promise to act in good faith, but not supported by an oath.

This was all the more serious as, during the second half of the eleventh century, the oath had apparently become the essential part of the contract. Sometimes the ceremony of the hands was no longer performed; sometimes it was replaced by the kiss. But most often the kiss was added to the rite of the hands, instead of supplanting it. While not indispensable, it was a religious act (cf. the kiss of peace) which rendered the homage an institution of peace. The great use which the Church made of this, in its struggle against the surrounding turbulence, is well known. And it bears witness to the penetration of religious ideas into a contract which had at the outset been merely profane and with which the Church had so long been contaminated.

3. *Peace Homages.* This exceptional kind of homage was in great vogue in the eleventh and twelfth centuries, and afterwards grew less frequent. It was exceptional, since it bound together men of the same rank and did not involve the concession of a fief. This homage was a means of putting an end to a conflict by creating a bond of 'friendship' between two former enemies; and it also enabled an individual guilty of a great injustice to furnish moral damages to his victim.

One can well see that the Church was at the source of this kind of peace-making institution, but it was a quite exorbitant exception to feudal law because it implied no subordination of the vassal as regards the lord.

4. *Homage of the Marches* (march = the confines of a sub-enfeoffed region).[1] This last kind was hybrid because it was a question sometimes of a homage of peace, sometimes of a regular homage. It was not widespread, but in use only on the frontiers of Burgundy, Champagne, the Ile-de-France and Normandy; and it was reserved for the great lords of principalities neighbouring on theirs.

Two examples may be cited. It was on the confines of the

[1] '*Mouvance*'. This legal term was used (1) of the relationship between a fief and the lord who had conceded it, and (2) of the fief itself. Thus (see below, p. 133) Normandy was legally *mouvant* of the kings of France (Translators).

duchy of Normandy, generally after a conflict, that the dukes did homage to the king of France. To the duke's obligation to do homage normally on one occasion, was added this 'peace homage' after a war, with a view to restoring 'friendship' between the prince and the king. In the second place, other 'homages of the marches' were justified by the indeterminate border lands between great fiefs dependent on the Crown[1] and by everyone's desire to encroach on his neighbour's lands. If one lord had built a castle illegally in the no-man's land which was disputed, he could agree to do homage to his neighbour and to receive this fortress from him as a fief. These homages were sometimes reciprocal, if each lord had gained a few acres of land at the expense of the other.

In any event, this kind of homage was to grow rare after the thirteenth century.

In the thirteenth century homage had almost completely disappeared from the kingdom of Italy, that is, from former Lombard Italy, while it remained in vogue in the patrimony of St Peter and also in Norman Italy, where the Norman customs of homage and fealty had of course been imported by the invaders. Certain Popes, like Innocent III, were to profit from the use of homage in their relations with certain sovereigns. One must note, finally, that the use of *servile* homage was to become more common in France after the twelfth century, but less so than in Germany.

Moreover, if the contract of vassalage continued to be executed by word of mouth, it happened more and more often that for great personages a charter was drawn up. This was a method of which Philip Augustus was to make considerable use in respect of his great vassals.

B. *The Effects of the Contract of Vassalage*

The present writer will follow Ganshof, who distinguishes between 'the power of the lord over the person of the vassal' and the reciprocal obligations (the contract being 'synallagmatic', or indented) of the contracting parties.

[1] *'Mouvances féodales'*.

1. *The Lord's Power over the Vassal's Person.* Homage implied a *traditio personae.* 'It is an immediate and direct power over the person of the vassal, a power limited solely by the notion of what was incompatible with the dignity of a free man' and, in principle at least, with the respect due to the king (Ganshof).

That was the appearance. In practice, this power was still further limited, except in a few regions and except as concerned those vassals, now few in number, who, being unprovided with a benefice, were living as the lord's associates. Two terms in use by thirteenth-century jurists summarized the bearing of this power. The vassal owed the *senior* his *subjectio* (submission) and *reverencia* (respect). These were mainly external marks of submission and respect, such as holding his stirrup when the lord mounted on horseback, rendering the 'services of honour', for example escorting him in company with the other vassals on ceremonial and solemn occasions.

2. *The Vassal's Obligations.* In 1020, when Guillaume V, Duke of Aquitaine, desired a better knowledge of the law of feudal vassalage which was still nebulous in southern France, Fulbert, Bishop of Chartres, wrote him a remarkably clear letter on the obligations of the vassal (and of the lord). The vassal, according to Fulbert, must '*faithfully*' furnish 'his lord with *counsel* and *aid*'.

a. *Fealty*: it was mainly a question for the vassal of abstaining, by reason of his pledged word, from any act hostile or dangerous to the lord. He must not cause injury to his body, or put his security in peril (by betraying 'his secret' or his castle). He must not violate his rights as judge, or his 'honour'; and he must do no damage to his possessions. While it was a 'negative' obligation, fealty was also a way of acting. 'For it is not enough to abstain from doing ill . . . , one must do good'. The formulae of oaths of vassalage, a large number of which have been preserved for the thirteenth century, corroborate Bishop Fulbert's explanations.

b. *The obligation of auxilium: Aid* presented itself in two forms, military and material (not always in a pecuniary sense).

In the days of 'classical' feudalism, especially in the early days, *military aid* was of the first importance. It was a question of the military service which was in principle '*the raison d'être* of the contract of vassalage', just as in former times. 'It is to have knights that the lord accepts vassals' (Ganshof).

The modes of service varied, according as the vassal held little land in fief, or as, on the contrary, he was a powerful noble. From the eleventh century onwards the kinds of service required were better proportioned than before to the importance of the fief:

—the vassal could be obliged to serve in person, completely armed or provided only with the most important pieces of armour;

—he may have undertaken not only to serve in person, but also to bring with him a specified number of knights who are his own vassals (and therefore under-vassals of his lord). It is to be noted that in England the principle, which was sometimes transgressed, required the lord to summon his vassals to arms only for the king's service.

Military service could assume varied aspects. In France and England a distinction was made between the *chevauchée* (*cavalcata*), a service as escort, or to take part in a short expedition in one's own neighbourhood; and the *ost* (*hostis, expeditio*), in the event of a real war. From the reign of Frederick Barbarossa a particular kind of service obtained in Germany: the *Römerzug*, an expedition which the king conducted to Rome with a view to being crowned emperor. One was required to take part in this as a vassal or under-vassal of the sovereign, and no longer as a subject. Lastly, almost everywhere in the West, the vassal could be required to perform the service of *guard* in some castle of his lord's; if he himself was a castellan, he had to put his fortress at the disposal of his lord when so required.

The vassals of course never rested until they had obtained a limitation of the length of the service due from them, which was exacted without hope of the least pecuniary compensation. It was in France from about 1050 that they first obtained satisfaction. In England and Germany they had to wait about another century. And it was also in France that the limitation was most clearly fixed, generally at forty days in the year.

Sooner of later, it was permitted to buy out the obligation of service under certain conditions. In England the consequences were considerable, and this proves that feudal institutions could be a source of power for the Crown, notably in financial matters. Under the Plantagenet Henry II, *scutage* (the tax for buying off service) was systematically substituted for service, even for direct vassals, except of course in time of war. At some date before 1200 the same system existed in Germany, though only for the *Römerzug*. But the Capetians did not succeed in developing scutage as widely as the Plantagenets, whether from lack of power at the outset, or later by intention.

The *auxilium* included also the duty of rendering material aid, but not exclusively in money. This kind of *aide* seems to date mainly from the twelfth century, except in Germany. Lords acquired the habit of levying this aid in various circumstances, though custom later fixed the limits to these.

In Normandy, and hence in England, there were three kinds of 'exceptional' *aide* in money: contributions to the ransom for the lord when he had been taken prisoner; on the occasion of his eldest son being dubbed a knight; and when his eldest daughter was married. A fourth case was established in France and spread over nearly all the country in the second half of the twelfth century; this *aide* was due when the lord set out for a crusade. Hence the French expression of '*aide* in the four cases'.

There in fact existed another, though less widespread, namely the *droite-taille*, a direct tax due to the lord when he bought a piece of land. It will be observed that the same word was used for the dues which, from the eleventh century onwards, the villeins owed a bannal lord.[1] Many twelfth-century texts use this word *taille* to describe the whole group of feudal *aides* and exactions from the peasants. These two kinds of *aide* were easily confused in respect of the circumstances and of the rate or incidence of the tax. The parallel between the two is not surprising, since feudal lords acquired

[1] i.e. One with the right of ban (Translators).

little by little the right of *ban*. But there is a lack of detailed studies on various aspects of the relations between rural lordship and feudalism.

By this indirect method of *material aide*, the Capetians, when powerful, and also the Valois kings, on several occasions tried to get certain sections of the population, and not merely the knights, to accept this tax. It was to be an appreciable source of revenue for the Treasury, though necessarily exceptional. There is a good example dating from the fourteenth century: after the French defeat at Poitiers, the *aide* was levied to pay for the ransom of King John; and Charles V had to continue collecting it after his father's death in order to build up and reorganize the French army, with the prospect of a renewal of the war against Edward III.

c. *The obligation of consilium*: On the part of the vassal this consisted in assisting the lord with his counsel, and therefore in attending any assembly convened by the lord when desiring the advice of his vassals. To avoid too many journeys, this obligation was gradually reduced by custom.

As a general rule, the vassal was required to take part with his fellow-vassals in meetings of the *Court* (*curtis, curia*), a deliberative assembly presided over by the lord. One of the first attributes of the *Curia* was to judge the cases brought before it, the lord requiring his vassals to 'declare the law'. The meeting was therefore both a political assembly and a tribunal. In principalities and kingdoms, once the authority of the prince had been established, the *Curia* was to prove a remarkable means of using feudal institutions to strengthen the central power.

3. *The obligations of the lord*. Ganshof has noted the 'very marked parallel' between the lord's obligations and the vassals'. Fulbert of Chartres had written that the lord had *in omnibus vicem reddere*; that is to say, he owed his vassal both fealty and various kinds of assistance.

a. There is little to say about this *fealty*, except that, like the fealty due from the vassal, it had a negative bearing (he was not in any way to hurt his *man*, either in his honour, or his property, or his life), and a positive aspect (to do good).

The assistance was of two kinds, as under the Carolingians: protection and maintenance.

b. *Protection*: in the eleventh and twelfth centuries it was above all a question of protecting the vassal against his enemies by force of arms. Examples of this abound. If the vassal was attacked, the lord had immediately to make war on the vassal's adversaries. This duty of affording protection was gradually to pass into the hands of the princes and kings, who had become the effective guarantors of public peace in respect of all their subjects.

By all these means, including on occasion force of arms, the lord was required to procure for his *man* the peaceful enjoyment of the fief conceded to him. He had also to render him 'good justice' and help him with his counsel. Thus in 1128, according to Galbert of Bruges, the Count of Flanders had to remind his lord, the King of France, that he owed him *consilium et auxilium*, the reciprocal obligations of his own.

c. *Maintenance*: from the eleventh century to the thirteenth the reason which formerly existed for this still held good: that of enabling the lord's *man* to perform the services he owed, military service above all. Later on, the ground for this obligation grew less clearly defined, varying with the region.

As in former times, the lord could proceed in two ways. He could maintain the vassal and his family in his own house; or he could grant him what was henceforth to be called a fief. The changing situation, begun at the end of the early medieval age, continued to develop; there would be fewer and fewer vassals who were not 'housed'. But there were still to remain a fairly considerable number, in England at least until the twelfth century, and still longer in Germany and in France, where they were called *bacheliers*. It none the less remains true that almost everywhere, after the eleventh century, the vassal was usually 'housed'; sooner or later the 'bachelier' had a good chance of obtaining a fief.

C. The End of the Contract of Vassalage

The vassal was nearly always linked to a lord more powerful

than he, and the feudal hierarchy reinforced the hierarchy of wealth in landed property and the hierarchy of military power.

In principle the contract remained, as before, valid up to the death of the first of the contracting parties, and hence indissoluble. In fact it was of still longer duration. In the days of 'classical' feudalism and in spite of individual instability – which Marc Bloch has perhaps exaggerated – men did not conceive of any engagement that was not perpetual. All agreements, for example those establishing 'peace', were concluded in perpetuity, and were binding on the contracting parties. This is the more easily understood in respect of institutions of vassalage, since the possession of a fief had become hereditary.

Yet how many oaths were broken as soon as they were sworn! Especially was this the case when oaths of vassalage, with their wide implications, were in question. One of the great themes of the *Chansons de Geste* and the romances of chivalry is the case of conscience which arises for the good knight out of respect for his obligations to a lord more powerful, and therefore more readily inclined to abuse or violate the contract.

Charlemagne had already foreseen some exceptions to the rule of engagement for life, but these had concerned only cases of personal injury inflicted on a vassal by his *dominus*. One had to go further. Fulbert of Chartres considered that the lord who did not show enough benevolence to his man should be regarded as *malefidus*, of bad faith, hence felonious. Now it had become more and more customary that no vassal was bound to continue serving a lord who had become a felon.

This is what happened when the lord no longer fulfilled his obligations. But the Church went further. When it excommunicated a lord (employing a weapon for years a formidable one) it *ipso facto* or explicitly freed his vassals from their oath of allegiance; for no Christian should serve an excommunicated man or have any dealings with him. The Church used this weapon to chastise brigand barons, and also kings and emperors. But in fact vassals generally continued to respect their obligations despite the prohibition of the Church, a prohibition supported by canon law according to which every oath had a religious character.

When the vassal, either rightly or under the influence of an interest stronger than the maintenance of the bond between man and man, claimed the right to break his engagements, he did it according to an established procedure, that of the *défi*[1] (*diffidatio*, breach of faith). In presence of his lord, he publicly announced his intention of no longer regarding himself as his man. This breach of contract was often marked by a ritual. At the beginning of the twelfth century the vassal would throw down a straw (see the Chronicle of Galbert of Bruges); to throw down the straw (*exfestucare*) was synonymous with 'to defy'. Later one threw down a glove.

This was a very dangerous act, since the lord who had been defied generally took up arms to punish his vassal. This is the origin of such expressions as *take up the defiance, take up the glove*, meaning that the lord accepted the challenge. And if, in law, abandonment of homage had as a consequence abandonment of the fief (even more than the Carolingian *benefice*, which was the counterpart of homage) the vassal in fact would then consider his former fief as a freehold, which he would have to defend by force of arms. Only a very powerful vassal, or group of vassals, could risk taking a decision so full of pitfalls.

The lord, on his side, might sometimes wish to repudiate a vassal, for example, if he performed his services badly: he could then 'defy' this vassal by throwing him a straw or a glove. At the same time he would announce his intention of recovering the fief, either temporarily (*saisimentum*), if he wished only to give a serious warning, or for good. Here again there was the prospect of a war which the vassal would doubtless lose. Definite seizure (*commissum*) of the fief would ruin a vassal who had no freehold. Hence local custom generally decided that a lord could neither pronounce such seizure, nor carry it into effect, without first taking counsel of the other vassals assembled in his Court: this procedure protected a vassal against a transitory fit of rage on the lord's

[1] Hence 'defiance' and even 'challenge' (Translators).

part. The most famous *commissum* was certainly the one pronounced by Philip Augustus in 1202, after hearing a complaint from the Lusignans, his under-vassals, against his vassal John Lackland. All the fiefs held from the king of France by the Plantagenet, that is, the western half of France, were seized, and the king soon set about conquering Normandy. The Capetian considered it his right to keep for himself the lands which he had confiscated, whereas on the contrary the king of Germany, in such circumstances, was required to enfeoff them to another vassal.

Apart from the possible bad faith of one of the contractants, another danger could threaten, not the duration, but the efficacy of the contract. Before the end of the ninth century it had become possible in France for a vassal to be the man of several lords. The 'thirst for benefices', as Ganshof calls it, had given rise to this violation of the foundation of links of vassalage, which in principle is impossible to understand.

To seek to do homage to other lords was to seek other fiefs. It was often the simple, but very widespread, desire to increase his patrimony which was the vassal's motive. But what would happen if a man was a vassal of several lords who were at war with one another? To be the vassal of several was really to be the vassal of none.

From the end of the ninth century an attempt had been made to react against a practice which threatened to deprive homage of any meaning. In spite of initial hesitation, the various solutions had one point in common. One of the lords was to be privileged, the homage done to him taking precedence of the others. In 895 a notice, the first testimony of a double vassalage, deemed that that lord who had conceded the most important benefice was the principal lord. Later, in northern Italy, the custom was based on chronological order: the lord who had received the earliest homage was to be served as a matter of priority.

The 'French' system, finally, was that of *ligesse,* which perhaps arose first in Normandy about 1050. It spread over most of France, and before 1100 reached Lotharingia. It was evidently imported by the Normans into southern Italy and into England. One of the lords had to be served wholly (*integre*), without reservation, 'with all the rigour which was of the very essence of primitive vassalage'. He was the *dominus ligius*, the *liege* lord (no doubt from German *ledig*=free). Then the word was used of the vassal (liege man), of the fief, and obviously of the homage.

How far did this *ligesse*, a kind of super-contract of vassalage, fulfil its object, which was to put a brake on the dissociation caused by multiple vassalage? One must distinguish between the situations in various countries:

In England the remedy was effective because up to the end of the twelfth century custom insisted on the fact that a vassal could have only one liege lord. From the time of Henry I (Beauclerk), *ligesse* tended to become a monopoly to the advantage of the Crown.

In Lotharingia and in France, failure was obvious. From the twelfth century on, one could be the liege man of several lords. However, from this time and still more in the thirteenth century the Capetian kings used their growing power to ensure that the liege homage paid to them was paramount. It took precedence over all other homages, and it was the homage done by the peers, that is the great vassals possessed of a principality.

In Germany, *ligesse* scarcely appeared before 1150. The king and the great lords, lay and ecclesiastical, leaned for support on their *ministeriales* (serf-knights) who were strictly subject to them. But towards the middle of the twelfth century, this social group became less subordinated. Free knights became '*ministeriales*', and the former ministeriales received fiefs from several lords. Frederick Barbarossa then tried, without much success, to imitate the Capetians by demanding that the territorial princes do homage to him, and to him alone.

So there remained many instances, in several parts of the Continent, where the multiplicity of contracts of vassalage concluded by one *man* led to depriving these engagements of the greater part of their value. One should therefore include this kind of multiplicity, not to put too much emphasis on the expression, among those cases where the contract was lapsing from pure ineffectiveness. There were still material consequences, since the various fiefs remained united in the hands of one owner.

II. THE FIEF, A FEUDAL TENURE

The real element in the bonds of feudal vassalage remained in principle what it had been under the Carolingians, 'a tenure freely granted by a lord to his vassal with a view to providing him with the means of maintaining himself legitimately and to enabling him to provide his lord with the required service'.

But this element in vassalage was modified, first in the terms describing it. The word *beneficium* persisted for varying periods according to the region. It was retained until about 1100 in France and Italy, and well into the twelfth century in Germany, a country relatively slow in developing. The word also retained its other meanings, for example in the Church, or to describe tenures granted to agents of the household or the domain. But a little before 900 a new word had appeared, *feudum* or *feodum*, in the sense of a tenure of vassalage, no doubt both in Italy and in southern 'France'. Until then this word, which was perhaps Frankish, described – like German *Vieh* which comes from it and means 'head of cattle' – moveable property. The success of this new meaning was to prove immense, first in Francia and Italy, then in Lotharingia. As early as 1087 a charter of Hainault alludes to a *beneficium quod vulgo dicitur feodum* (a benefice called a fief in everyday language). In the thirteenth century the whole of Germany was to employ this term; the word corresponding to *fief or fieffe* being *lehen*.

But in the districts where feudalism was not to take such deep roots, as north-east of the Loire, its vocabulary was to remain or become vague, even incorrect in strict feudal law. In Brittany and still more in Languedoc, Guyenne, etc., the words *feodum, fief, fieffe,* described almost any kind of tenure. Confusion was to persist in the terminology in use between rural lordship and feudal lordship, between rural tenure and feudal tenure. One means of obtaining a better knowledge of the diversities of feudal law would be to draw a general map of the regions in which certain words were used. This would reveal areas where feudalism was strong, others where it was weak or incomplete.

Norman law, and consequently Anglo-Norman law, constitute a case apart. Here the same confusion reigns as in the southern regions, but the reasons given are not altogether satisfactory. As late as the thirteenth century, people write in England of *tenura* and *tenementum*, often without further detail; we hear that a *liberum tenementum* owed *servitium militis* (the knight's service). The word fief, imported by the Normans, remained synonymous with hereditary free tenure; in the thirteenth century it was to be progressively replaced by an unequivocal expression. The *feudum militis* (*knight's fee*) could only designate the tenure of a vassal.

In Lotharingia and in Germany the word was also applied to other tenures, including those of servants, and an explanation had to be given; the fief in its proper sense was the *feodum militare*. But what is most important to observe about German terminology is, as in other aspects of feudal law, its archaic character. In the twelfth century *beneficium* was still very much in use; it was translated by *lehen*. It was only in the thirteenth century that *fief* became the equivalent of *lehen*.

In relations between vassal and lord the 'real' bond or connection had taken precedence over the personal. This evolution continued. In the twelfth century the ceremony of homage was currently held to be subordinate to the existence of the fief; many texts allude to the *homagium pro feodo* or *de feodo*, that is, homage due for a fief. Little by little this real element in the contract was modified, less in its nature than in the rights which the two parties had over it.

Since the year 1000 the practice of concession of landed property as a fief had been increasing, for in the tenth century, especially in 'France', public institutions, though greatly weakened, were still in existence and could still impose certain duties on the aristocracy. It was often the small freeholders who had most need of protection, and the protection they sought was that of the *potentes*, castellans, territorial princes or powerful churches. This protection they bought by becoming vassals and taking back their freehold properties as fiefs; only rarely receiving supplementary land to round off their possessions. But after 1000 the situation was reversed. The military obligations of the freeholders were falling into disuse because the public institutions had now altogether disappeared in many regions. The lords who held the right of ban were obliged to 'pay' the freeholders to get them to enter into their vassalage, the more so as holders of small or moderate-sized domains no longer had the resources needed to arm themselves completely. Powerful lords therefore had to bid against each other in order to extend, or even preserve, their 'clientèle'. A custom was established, between 1000 and 1030, of compensating a man for becoming a vassal by granting him a fairly substantial domain. Thus, to the 'fief of resumption' (a former freehold) was now added the 'fief of concession'. Examples of this custom will be found in Georges Duby's work. One sees, in short, that from the eleventh century the possession of a fief was to be truly the *raison d'être* of vassalage; and this feature, more clearly marked than of old, was to subsist as long as 'feudalism' lasted; that is, until 1789 in France.

A. The Object of the Concession

This was a piece of land, in principle. The fief had a territorial basis, of variable size. For the early feudal age historians do not yet possess, as they do for the end of the Middle Ages, long lists of fiefs with descriptions of each one; but there are enough isolated examples to establish the widest possible size range. The average fief, hence the 'tenure' of a knight of moderate means, included a landed lordship – often bannal, at a later date – with a reserve domain and peasant tenures. At one end of the scale were the fiefs of the humblest vassals: a small copyhold[1] and a reserve as small. The poorest therefore lived on the proceeds of a 'rump-lordship', of about the same size as many peasant holdings. At the other extreme

[1] '*Censive*': a tenure for rent. This kind of tenure did not come into being in England until the fifteenth century and was called a 'copyhold' (Translators).

were the very great fiefs, composed of vast lordships inhabited by numerous tenants and covering wide wooded areas, ready to be cleared or in course of partial clearing. Such fiefs very often possessed all or part of the right of ban over all the inhabitants of the territory. The largest complexes were of course the principalities, for example the duchy of Normandy under the jurisdiction[1] of the Capetians, or Hainault under that of the Empire. Just below the principalities were the baronies. In the twelfth century this name was applied in Anglo-Norman countries to the 'dominations' which were extensive but still not principalities. The title of baron had not yet acquired the limited sense of a high-ranking vassal, and all the vassals of an important lord had a right to the title. But later on the word was to be reserved for the men coming immediately after the territorial princes.

Two great questions are connected with the nature of the fief: was the basis of landed property always very clear; and was land really indispensable to the existence of a fief?

The income from land varied a great deal and the fief might thus take very variable forms. A copyhold without a reserve domain (quite common, as there were about a thousand or rather more in the south of France) a castle without surrounding lands, a *tonlieu*, a toll-bar, a mayoralty – all these were immovable rights connected with the lordship, whether this were landed, *bannal*, or that of a castellan. But could a fief exist without any local or territorial basis?

This depended on the era and the country in question. The first case was that of fiefs whose vassalage involved only the right of ban. A fief of this kind, in eleventh- and twelfth-century France, was called a *comitatus*, and this, in principle, was what the Capetians enfeoffed to great vassals, for example to the Count of Flanders, who maintained that he possessed most of Flanders and Artois in freehold, and therefore that only his powers as Count had been enfeoffed to him. This enabled the king to maintain the 'sovereign' principle, according to which all public functions were dependent on him. But more generally, except in northern France, the great vassals did homage mainly for the land and hardly at

[1] *Mouvant.*

all for the function. In Germany, on the other hand, the *functional fief* (still called *honor* or *honor publicus* as under the Carolingians) was more common, even in the twelfth century. Dukes, counts, margraves, bishops and abbots of royal monasteries, were always regarded as above all titulars of public functions, and it was as agents of the Crown that they did homage and received their fiefs (both functions and endowments attached to them) which, when held by laymen, had in fact become hereditary. In the twelfth century, however, Frederick Barbarossa was to recognize the relationships of feudal vassalage. Henceforth, only dukes and margraves and ecclesiastical princes would hold their fiefs directly from the king, the counts now holding their counties only as sub-fiefs of the sovereign. In all cases, the old word *honor* was reserved for these 'functional fiefs' which, in Germany, were so distinguished from other kinds.

There was a second sort of fief, without basis in land, but connected in one way or another with the Church. Of these there were two classes quite numerous in the early feudal age, but later much less so. The first kind were the ecclesiastical revenues usurped by laymen who had then sub-enfeoffed a part of them to their own vassals. It was not here a question of the *temporalia* (which had also been usurped but which of course had a territorial basis) but of the *spiritualia*. These were offerings and dues paid to the 'altar' (*altaria* = the whole of the church and its revenues), on the occasion of baptisms, marriages, churching of women, burials and great liturgical festivals. If from the end of the eleventh century, under the influence of the Gregorians, these *spiritualia* were generally returned to the clergy; others, like the tithes, including the *novales* connected with the clearing of forests, were very often to remain in lay hands. But at least the Church was to obtain from the usurpers and their vassals an admission that they held them from the Church as fiefs. The second kind of fiefs under discussion were the *advocacies*. In the eleventh century and especially after the beginning of the Gregorian reform, the monasteries often succeeded in inducing their advocates to take back from them as a fief the judicial, military and financial rights which they were exercising on Church lands. Thus defined, the fief often brought in more revenue than the seigneurial rights which the clergy had retained.

There remains the last kind of fiefs with no basis in land. These were 'purse-fiefs' or 'pension-fiefs' (*Kammerlehen* in German), which would be called *fiefs-rente* in the thirteenth century. If one could somewhat less certainly indicate the regions where the previous kinds of fief were in vogue, it is not possible here. The fief consisted now only in the right to receive at regular intervals a sum of money, described as a *rente*.[1] The institution had been known as early as the eleventh century in the former Carolingian lands, and one of the oldest Flemish examples goes back to 1087. Two brothers received from the abbey of Saint-Bertin a 'benefice' consisting of a pension of four silver marks payable at Michaelmas. The record expressly connects the entry of the two laymen into vassalage with the payment of this sum: 'Having become our vassals by (the ceremony of) the hands, they receive as a fief, every year, each man two silver marks'. But the 'purse-fief' was not always paid in money or by the lord's treasurer, and it was not necessarily an 'annuity on the Treasury'. It might consist of an income to be received from a specified source of seigneurial receipts, for example from a *tonlieu* or a *toll*, which frequently happened in the Netherlands in the twelfth century. The lord's tax- and toll-collector remained his official, but he took from his receipts the *rente* (or pension) due to the vassal and paid it him.

The appearance of purse-fiefs a little before the end of the eleventh century is of great economic significance. As a consequence of the expansion of industry and commerce, of the more rapid circulation of money and the increase in the money supply, land had ceased to be 'everything'. Feudal services were no longer therefore necessarily remunerated by the grant of land, and this fact could offer advantages for the lord. The vassal holding a *fief-rente* was in fact in his pay. If the service was badly rendered or if the vassal was unfaithful, the lord could cut off supplies without having to

[1] An annuity or pension (Translators).

employ the slow and cumbersome procedure of the *défi*, the seizure and the *commissum*.

But serious handicaps limited the development of such fiefs. They were an innovation, and customary procedure displayed a repugnance for 'novelties', especially in Germany where feudal law, always rather archaic, was very slow to admit this kind of practice. Given this opposition, which was fairly general, the *fiefs-rente* were never to be widely diffused. They appeared very late and were then little more than fiefs of expectation, so to speak, the lord making an annual payment while awaiting the time when he could grant a piece of land in place of it. The German 'law-books' of the thirteenth century admitted such fiefs only on condition of their having an appearance of territorial foundation (for example, a pension based on the receipts for a *tonlieu*). They condemned pension-fiefs consisting of an annual pension, 'without special appropriation and assigned from the general revenues supplying the lord's treasury (*camera*)'. In 1222 a decree of Henry VII prohibited the *Kammerlehen*. What was the reason for this opposition? It was not solely due to the late development of German law. The fact was that in the eyes of German jurists a fief offered a full guarantee only if it was a piece of real estate. But the main reason was certainly the slow rate of economic development in parts of Germany in the first half of the twelfth century.

So too in the Netherlands, that is in Flanders and Lower Lotharingia, *fiefs-rente* were, at the end of the twelfth century, regarded only as 'fiefs of expectation'. Another handicap was for a long time unfavourable to their diffusion. The prince or king had to possess a well organized central treasury, his domain had to be well managed, his financial administration properly conducted, and his monetary resources abundant and regular. The country had to be economically rich, and its lord also. During nearly the whole of the twelfth century, the practice was therefore limited for the most part to the Netherlands, to Norman England (where the Crown disposed of a good administrative service and great financial potentialities) and to the Latin principalities in the East (where trade was extremely active, hence the profusion of *fiefs de soudée,* the vassal being *soldé,* that is salaried). If a prince began to make use of this procedure it was a sign of progress, of recent growth in his finances. Such were the cases of the Comte de Champagne (because of the fairs) and of Philip Augustus, towards the years 1180–90.

The political influence of *fiefs-rente* was considerable. They often enabled a sovereign to establish 'foreign clientèles', and obtain outside alliances. This was the policy of the Anglo-Norman and the Angevin kings. Between the end of the eleventh century and the thirteenth, they brought into the orbit of their influence a number of princes and lords, especially in Flanders and Lower Lotharingia. Such contracts of vassalage did not, however, create any bond of subordination between the parties; they simply linked equals and confirmed political alliances. If the kings of France arrived at this practice only during the reign of Philip Augustus, they then made great use of it up to the time of the Hundred Years' War: not only respecting the Count of Flanders (who, by his relations with the Angevins on one side and the Capetians on the other, could raise the bidding), to counterbalance the 'English' influence, but outside the kingdom, east of the Meuse, and sometimes east of the Saône and the Rhône. This was one of the principal measures which, little by little, increased the Capetian influence over the Imperial lands and prepared the way for territorial acquisitions at the expense of the Empire. Without being always very solid, these alliances facilitated the expansion of France eastwards, beyond the frontiers of 843, in the centuries to come.

B. Investiture

Investiture was the successor, so to speak, of the Carolingian *traditio,* and much more is known about it. In this matter the early medieval conception persisted. When a real right was created or transferred, a 'material' act was necessary. This was the *vestitura* or *investitura* (German *Lehnung*), which as a rule immediately followed the homage, except in northern Italy, where it preceded the promise of fealty (homage being rare in that country).

The lord presented his vassal with a symbolical object, in

action or in fact. If it was a 'symbol of action', the object was retained by the lord; it might be a rod, a sceptre, a glove or a ring. According to Galbert of Bruges, the Count of Flanders in 1127 used the same bâton to confer investiture 'on all those who came to do him homage'. If the symbol was an object, then the lord left in the hands of the vassal whom he had just invested, the bâton, the piece of earth, the standard – or the crozier, for the imperial bishoprics of Germany and Italy before the Concordat of Worms.

Once invested, the vassal possessed *seizin* (German, *Gewere*) of his fief, sometimes called *tenure*. He henceforth enjoyed the use of it and was in law protected against any disturbance from outside. This fact is surprising. The Civil Code makes it clear that a man becomes proprietor and possessor of real estate by the sole fact of the signature of the contract of sale by the two parties. It is true that certain contemporary laws, on the contrary, next require a formality to transfer possession and property from the right of the seller to that of the purchaser: this is a souvenir of Roman law which made a clearer distinction between property and possession. And so, when there came a renaissance of ancient law, between the eleventh and twelfth centuries, a not unsuccessful attempt was made, first in Italy and then in other western countries, to assimilate *seizin* to Roman 'possession', which further consolidated the right of the vassal over his fief.

Almost everywhere men very soon thought of drawing up a written statement recording both the act of homage and the investiture with the fief. These documents were not very numerous before the 1200s, but they then proliferated. The vassal had first undertaken to *show* on the spot what his fief was (*ostensio feodi*), a *monstrée* (showing, display) which was replaced by a written enumeration. The stereotyped expression *aveu et dénombrement* intimated that the action contained two operations.

A ceremony in reverse marked the renunciation of the fief. The vassal announced that he was divesting himself of the fief in favour of the lord and that he 'was decamping'. He gave back a symbolical object, the same that had been used for the earlier investiture.

There was not only a link between homage and fief, there had also from ancient times been a bond between the land or the right granted as a fief and the land, itself a fief or freehold, from which it had been detached and which remained the lord's. The French language readily described this bond or link as a *mouvance*, a term also used to describe the relation existing between the fief conceded and the lord who had made, or taken back, the concession. *Mouvance* was also used of an administrative and judicial, and even military, area or province. Kings and princes divided their domains into provostries (*prévôtés*), castellanies, and bailiwicks (*bailliages*), every fief situated in one of these areas being described as *mouvant* or *servant* of the local capital where the ceremonies of homage and investiture took place in principle.

It was mainly the French feudal jurists who used the expression 'fief servant' (of a 'fief dominant') to describe a fief which acknowledged service. Little by little the *service of the fief* replaced, as an expression, that of 'obligations of vassalage', which was older. The latter, owing in principle from the outset, because of the homage paid, came gradually to be attached to the fief itself, during the first age of classical feudalism, and even more frequently during the second. As the fief was bound up with the service of vassalage, it became increasingly the object sought in homage. Thus both by custom and its acceptance by the nobles, service came to be regarded as rent for territory. In other words, the service enjoined by vassalage had turned into the service due from the granting of a fief.

C. Rights of the Two Parties Over the Fief

At the end of the first medieval age the right of property over the benefice – which had become a fief – had been divided into two parts, the vassal's share increasing steadily in importance. The situation had scarcely changed in principle. To the lord belonged the *jus eminens* (= property in Roman Law); to the vassal, the *jus utile* (= usufruct in Roman Law). Both men could therefore say 'my land' when speaking of the fief in question.

But in fact matters were not always so simple. They were

simple only if the vassal held his fief from a freeholder (as the king, a layman, or the church – in the last case, an ecclesiastical freehold, being privileged, was described as '*franche aumône*'). The freeholder had indeed the whole 'bare-ownership'[1]; but apart from those held by the king, freeholds no longer predominated throughout the West. If it is not yet possible to draw a general map of the prevalence of freeholds, the principal zones are fairly well known. By comparison with the end of the tenth century, the number of freeholds had often decreased, at the same time as the feudal pyramid was rising. It appears that freeholds persisted mainly in the south of France, precisely because feudalization there remained incomplete; as also in parts of Lotharingia and Flanders. In customary law, the presumption of freehold was generally admitted, the rule 'no lord without title' being admitted *de facto*, although it was formulated as a rule only after the thirteenth century.

The opposite rule ('no land without a lord') prevailed over the rest of France (see, for example, Beaumanoir). In eleventh-century Normandy freeholds disappeared, and they became rare elsewhere, as in the Ile-de-France. It may of course be a question of illusion on the part of historians, because in the archives freeholds leave fewer traces than fiefs; and fiefs are frequently mentioned after the general use of the practice of 'avowal and enumeration'. Thus it has been ascertained that in England there were only fiefs after the Conquest. The king declared himself the only freeholder, the whole land being divided into fiefs (those of the tenants-in-chief) or sub-fiefs, held directly or indirectly from the king.

In Germany, more often perhaps than elsewhere, kings and princes systematically developed relations of feudal vassalage, by resuming in a certain measure the policy of the first Carolingians. Their efforts – those of the Hohenstaufen, for example – were, however, only partly successful. It has been shown above that this was true of Lotharingia; but it was partly true of the rest of the Empire. Royal or princely attempts to impose feudal vassalage find an echo in the works

[1] '*Nue-propriéte*': meaning without usufruct (Translators).

of thirteenth-century German jurists. 'Wishing to systematize absolutely the relations of feudal vassalage, they described freeholds as *Sonnenlehen* (fiefs of the sun): but such an assimilation was purely a matter of words'. Perrin gives a striking example of the 'persistence and extent of freeholds in the thirteenth century'. In consequence of the lawsuit of 1180, Henry the Lion was dispossessed of the fiefs which he held from the king, but not of his freeholds. Now these were so vast that in 1235 Frederick II was able to turn them, on behalf of Otto the Child, Henry's grandson, into the duchy of Brunswick-Lüneburg, which was to hold 'a place of honour' in the Empire for centuries.

When the lord enfeoffed one of his freeholds to his vassal, he retained the whole of the *jus eminens*; but if he sub-enfeoffed a part of his own fief, the *jus eminens* was shared between him and his own lord; or else this right was divided into three, four, five or more portions, if there were a great number of sub-enfeoffments. The French jurists, however, thought that only the highest of the lords in question disposed of the eminent or 'direct' domain; the inferior lord and the vassals sharing the domain in usufruct; but there is nothing to show that this corresponded with reality.

As early as the eleventh century it was no longer true to say that the vassal's rights over the fief amounted only to those of the Roman usufructuary, in spite of the continued employment of the term *usufructus*. As this fact was realized, an effort was made to find words more conformable to the new state of things. In the twelfth and thirteenth centuries the rights of the lord were described by such words as *dominium* (*feodale, supremum*) or *possessio* (which is strange). The rights of the vassal were called *proprietas* (which was false), *dominatio* or *jus hereditarium*. After the twelfth century progress in the study of Roman law led to a closer analysis. Even in 1228 Accurso, the great authority on Roman law in Bologna, admitted the complete division of property rights into two parts. To the lord (at least in principle, if he was a freeholder) belonged the *dominium directum* (later known as the *eminent domain*); to the vassal the *dominium utile*. This distinction, which many French customary procedures were to adopt, was to be clarified in the fourteenth century, and later also accepted in Germany.

When the vassal was recognized as having only the usufruct, he had only the *jus utendi et fruendi*, the right of enjoying the fief and taking its produce as his own. After the eleventh century he in fact also had the *jus abutendi*, or possibility of disposing of it. This right without becoming quite complete, was conceded more widely between the eleventh and thirteenth centuries, and customary procedure finally confirmed it.

D. Heredity of the Fief

De facto heredity had begun to make its appearance in the second half of the ninth century and in the tenth. The most powerful vassals were the first to succeed in bringing benefices and temporary holdings into their patrimonies. Holders of the *ban* and of *honores*, notably the counts, succeeded in bringing into their personal possession the vast territories which they held as counts. This movement spread when the sovereign was weak, but slowed down whenever a king or a prince asserted his power. Sometimes the movement was reversed. The last Carolingians and the Robertians had often tried, sometimes successfully, to recover a count's *honores* on the occasion of his death. But in any case just before the year 1000, *de facto* heredity had become, with exceptions, a part of general custom, to the disadvantage of the king, the prince and the Church. On the other hand, for less important benefices, those granted by the counts, the castellans and the clerics to vassals of average or lower rank, this kind of heredity was not entirely admitted before 1000. Examples are not lacking of the right being recovered on the death of the vassal.

It was in the eleventh century that *de facto* heredity became really general in France. For this there were various reasons, in addition to that of man's natural tendency to change a property for life into an hereditary possession. There was, first, a social motive. The bonds between relatives in noble families were then growing closer, hence the development of co-partnership among the heirs. To withdraw a concession made for life meant incurring the hatred and rebellion of a whole 'clan'. There was secondly, a political motive. In the eleventh century holders of the ban had a more pressing need to recruit new vassals, and they had to pay more for the loyalty of the vassals they already had; hence a granting of fiefs to their men more frequently than of old, hence too the impossibility of recovering the fief on the death of the vassal, even if the latter had no collateral heirs; and even if the lord had conceded the fief explicitly for life; and even if the feudatory had, on behalf of his heirs, expressly promised restitution when he should die.

This evolution proceeded more slowly in Germany. As early as the period 850–1000 there were certainly many examples of *de facto* heredity. But two forces militated against its success: the Church and the Saxon monarchy. They only retarded it, however, because many fiefs had become hereditary even before the reign of Conrad II, the founder of the Salian dynasty. It was he who, in the first half of the eleventh century, was to hasten the movement towards heredity.

The measures decreed by this sovereign were less generally applied in north Italy than in Germany. In north Italy the *capitanei* (royal vassals) were in opposition to the *vavasseurs,* who were their own vassals and therefore under-vassals of the king. The vavasseurs wanted to transmit their fiefs to their heirs, but this the 'Captains' opposed. By the constitution of 1037 Conrad II legalized the heredity of benefices held by the *capitanei* and recognized in the vavasseurs' fiefs the same hereditary nature. This attitude is not explained simply by Conrad's hostility to Aribert, Archbishop of Milan, one of the most powerful captains in Lombardy. The fiefs of lay or ecclesiastical captains were already in fact hereditary, but not those of vavasseurs, and the monarchy must have wished to lean on the latter for support against the captains. In Germany, on the other hand, no general measure was decreed by Conrad, but his desire was identical. His biographer, Wipo, affirms that he did not wish to see fiefs which had been held by the father withdrawn from the descendants. His object was to establish closer relations with his under-vassals. When his son-in-law, the Duke of Suabia, rebelled, the counts in that duchy supported the king against their duke: 'an almost unique example of an attempt at direct contact between a German king and his under-vassals', writes Perrin. Finally, in the twelfth century, heredity really became part of social customs, first in the direct line and, after 1150, also in the collateral. However, even in the thirteenth century (see the *Sachsenspiegel*) there remained a certain number of life-fiefs, conceded *non ratione feodali . . . . sed pro beneficio temporali*.

England constituted a case apart because, at the time of the Conquest, heredity was already a principle practically undisputed in Normandy. Hence, when consulting *Domesday Book* one is not surprised to see that all the tenants-in-chief had been established by the Conqueror on an hereditary basis; although those of the Normans who had rebelled against William had evidently been dispossessed. It is thought, however, that the situation was rather different in the case of sub-enfeoffment when this had been agreed to by the churches at the instance of the sovereign or of very powerful laymen. Even so, two texts of 1083, relating to Westminster Abbey, and of 1085, concerning the Bishopric of Hereford, which created 'knights' fiefs' simply for life, do not permit the supposition that such concessions for life only, on the part of ecclesiastical lords, or *a fortiori* on the part of lay lords, were at all general. In the twelfth century all the knights' tenures were hereditary, to the great detriment of the temporalities.

Affirmation of the rule that a fief was hereditary was therefore, in the eleventh century, a general phenomenon in the West. It was henceforth a question, with exceptions, of an heredity of right, still subject to a few limitations.

Once this right was admitted, it was still necessary that it should not be too prejudicial to the lord. Everywhere the lords were able to impose conditions, for a definite or indefinite time, which really meant that the fiefs had not turned into freeholds and that the eminent rights of the lord, if limited, were nevertheless maintained – a proof of seigneurial power. In the eleventh century these conditions were as follows:

(a) that the heir should recognize the enfeoffed character of the tenure;

(b) that he should be in a position to fulfil the service of the fief, as its holder, in default of which the lord could withdraw the fief for a time or concede it to another man;

(c) that the fief should not be shared among several co-heirs, which would make it impossible for each of them to render the service that was due.

a. *Investiture and succession-due.*[1] Despite the political and social upheavals of the eleventh century, the memory that a feudal tenure was for life was not lost in law, and rarely in fact. All the customary procedures admitted that in theory the fief returned to the lord on the death of the vassal. And since the bond of vassalage, and so the grant of the fief, came to an end with the death of one or other of the contracting parties, the fief, on the disappearance of the lord, returned in principle, in the same way, into the patrimony of his heirs.

In both instances, on the death of the vassal (German, *Mannfall*), as on that of the lord (*Herrenfall, Thronfall*), this return into the lord's patrimony was entirely theoretical. If the lord died first, the vassal remained in effective possession. If the vassal died first, even the severest customs decided that if he left a son who was a major, and therefore in a position to do homage and render the service due from the fief, this son should take possession of the fief, although he was then obliged to address a request to the lord that he might be admitted to do homage and receive investiture. It was generally admitted at the outset that, during this lapse of time, the new vassal (or the same, if it was the lord who had just died) did not have *seizin*. But later certain procedures, with a view to turning feudal tenures into patrimonies, admitted that he was already seized of the fief.

Often, as early as the eleventh century, the lord could refuse neither homage nor investiture of an heir who was direct and legitimate and of age, nor could he prevent him, by laying down conditions, from having the immediate enjoyment of the fief. Before 1150 English custom already admitted only one pretext for refusal: namely, if the demander was not the legitimate son of the dead vassal, in which case a lawsuit for 'death of ancestor' would be pleaded before the

[1] '*Relief*', corresponding to modern estate duty (Translators).

lord's court or the king's. In the opposite case, if the vassal wished to retain his fief, he would do homage to the new lord even if he had no confidence in his fealty: this shows how far the bond based on land-tenure had taken precedence of the human relationship symbolized by homage. Homage was still needed, but was now accessory.

If one now considers the thirteenth century, one notes that in many French provinces, customary procedure had strictly limited the period of delay within which a man had to present himself at the lord's court in order to do homage and receive investiture (generally forty days), in default of which, and unless he had obtained *souffrance* (=respite= *respectum homagii*) he would be guilty of 'default of homage' and his fief would be liable to seizure. But this was something fairly new, owing to the progress of royal or princely power. Until the twelfth century, no delay had been prescribed.[1] In the absence of good will on the part of vassals, or if the great lord had been repeatedly negligent, it had been possible to change fiefs into freeholds. It was to palliate this danger that kings and princes had acquired the habit of proceeding to periodical enquiries with a view to tracking down cases of fraud.

Even when fiefs had been officially recognized as hereditary, the lord had not always been completely the loser. In various parts of the feudal West succession to a fief gave rise to the collection of a lucrative due – generally called a *relief* – which seems to have originated in at least two ways. In several barbarian kingdoms, including the Anglo-Saxon countries, the *dominus* had been able, on the death of the dependant whom he had 'sustained' and equipped, to demand the restitution of his armour and weapons. This was the *heriot* (German *heri*=army). This right had probably been maintained and even extended to the succession to a fief of vassals provided with benefices. An enquiry of 1133 concerning the Bishop of Bayeux' knights stipulates that, on the death of the father, the son owes the prelate the harness of his father's horse and coat of mail, which then represented a very substantial sum. At the end of the thirteenth century Beaumanoir

[1] Meaning that there was no definite time limit (Translators).

records that in his time *relief* still involved, in northern France, surrendering the dead man's war-horse.

A second source from which this succession-due originated has been clearly brought out by Olivier-Martin in respect of Parisian law, and by Ganshof for the Netherlands. When 'the hereditary nature of the fief had not yet been completely fixed, the lord could lay down conditions before he admitted the heir of a vassal to swear fealty and render homage, and before investing him'. He could, in short, 'get payment for his consent', as indeed the rural lords were doing in respect of succession to rural tenures which were also, here and there, on the way to becoming hereditary. In the origin of many practices, one should recognize that bargaining had its place. But sometimes the assimilation of the feudal tenure with the rural was pushed too far by those who used an old feudal term for rural tenures, or else who employed the same term, in both cases, to describe succession-dues. Thus after 1066 in England the term *heriot* described the taxes for conveyance of tenure,[1] to be paid by the peasants (the best head of cattle; or one of the agricultural implements). In Lotharingia and the north-eastern part of the French kingdom the word *relief* (*relevium*) served for both kinds of tenure. It was the same principle as that defined by the great Parisian jurist of the fourteenth century, Jacques d'Ableiges, and which he quite clearly described. On the death of its holder, the tenure *chiet et gist* on the ground, and the lord – rural or feudal – must 'take it up'[2] in order that the heir may have seizin, and therefore enjoyment of it. Other words were used in France, as for example *redemption* which intimated that the heir must *redeem*, or repurchase, the land in question. The identical term of *Lehnware* was used in Germany.

At the outset it was a (forced) gift offered to the lord. The oldest example of this goes back to the time of Hincmar, who represents this offering as a gift (*exemium*), although, despite the rarity of its mention in Carolingian times, one may suppose that it was already in fairly wide vogue. Like many 'gifts', this one, at least in France and Norman England,

[1] i.e. of the same holding, on the death of the father.

[2] '*Relever*' – hence '*relief*' = a taking up.

quickly turned into an obligation – a tax. It was at first fixed by bargaining between the two parties, or simply by the lord, but was more or less speedily standardized by regional customs.

Historians have not paid enough attention to the geography and chronology of the incidence of *relief*, and we still have only a rough knowledge of them, as also of the different rates which were charged.

In Germany the *Lehnware* was uncommon and collected only on fiefs held by vassals of modest means. It is true that the old system of surrendering the horse and all or part of the armour may be regarded as a *relief*, maintained only for the *ministeriales*; but Perrin, following Marc Bloch, thinks that it was a question rather of a kind of payment in kind, 'as one frequently finds in the Middle Ages, payments related to the trade exercised' by the person in question. It would therefore be an entrance fee paid by the new vassal, rather than a succession duty.

In France, south of the Loire, *relief* seems to have been uncommon, except in Poitou. It was in greatest vogue in western France and the country between the Loire and the Rhine. It therefore occurred in general in the lands most favoured by feudalism, and this is very significant. The Anglo-Norman monarchy developed the use of it all over England.

If the vassals as a whole could hardly oppose the principle itself, which allowed the lord to exercise a strict supervision over the devolution of the fiefs under his jurisdiction, they did on the other hand force customary procedure to fix the sum due at a rate which was not prohibitive, so as not to ruin the heir. The task was a difficult one – since the lord could confiscate a fief if the *relief* was not paid – yet it was often successfully achieved. The first two Norman kings and the Anglo-Norman lords raised very heavy dues from their men; in consequence, from the time of Henry I onwards, there was a strong reaction on the part of the vassals. In the course of the twelfth century this succession-due was lowered and rated at a fixed sum, which was very advantageous at a time of economic expansion. English custom (see Glanville) regarded as an almost obligatory maximum a tax of £5 for a knight's fief, which did not exceed a quarter of the annual income (which has been calculated, it is thought, as an average of £20 sterling). But then, in the second half of the twelfth century and at the beginning of the thirteenth, the Plantagenets assumed the right of laying heavy and arbitrary taxes on their barons; and this led the latter to have it stipulated in *Magna Carta* that the *baronies* should be subjected to only a reasonable succession-due (*relief*), which should never exceed £100 sterling.

In France north of the Loire and in the Lotharingian countries of Hainault and Namur, the succession-due remained more favourable to the lord. It did not consist in a fixed sum but followed the fluctuations of the economy, because it was often equal to the then value of a year's income. This fact was to be confirmed in the thirteenth century by the customary law of Paris. In this region the *relief* remained for centuries an important source of revenue for those lords who had numerous vassals. But the French monarchy was waiting until it was strong enough to tax its great vassals; which it then did in a heavy and arbitrary manner. It was Philip Augustus who inaugurated this lucrative system, which was to last for a long period. An example of his procedure dates from 1222, when he imposed a succession-due of £50,000 on Ferrand of Portugal, who had married Jeanne, the heiress to the County of Flanders. The tax was particularly high when the new vassal was not the son of the old. This was the case, of course, with Ferrand, but it nevertheless drove him to rebel.

The contrast between those regions in France where *relief* existed and those from which it was absent offers the same contrast – and the coincidence is not fortuitous – as that which distinguishes countries where the lord's position had remained solidly established from those where it was less secure, both in respect of his real power and of his resources.

E. Systems of Succession to Fiefs

So far only the simplest situation has been considered, that in which the dead vassal left only one son, and that son already a major. But three rather delicate cases might also arise:

i. The vassal leaves several male heirs. Is the fief divisible or not? How far may the lord intervene?

ii. The heir is a minor. How far has the lord the right of *garde féodale,* that is to say, of assuming the 'guardianship' of the minor and of enjoying the revenues of the fief until the heir comes of age?

iii. The vassal leaves only daughters. Does the lord dispose of the *right of marriage*? Can he choose husbands for the heiress, or the man with whom the widow of his vassal will contract a second marriage?

In principle, the 'right of ward', or guardianship, and the right of marriage were the necessary consequence of adapting the heredity of a fief to feudal customs. It remained necessary for the new vassal to be in a position to provide the service due from the fief, which was always to remain *in law* and for a long time *in fact,* military service, provided therefore by a man. However, all customary laws in the West did not recognize the lord as having this double right. Here, as in the matter of *relief,* there were inequalities in the powers retained or created by the lord, and inequalities in the strength of a lord's control over his vassals.

Indivisibility or Divisibility of the Fief. There was opposition of interests between feudal law and the right of family successions. In the matter of freeholds, a sharing out of the property was generally *de rigueur.* But, in the matter of fiefs, such a subdivision might compromise the service due. The division, hence the multiplication of fiefs, would apparently have put more vassals at the disposal of the lord; but in fact each of these fiefs risked being too small to enable its holder completely to furnish the service due from him. Hence, at the beginning, the principle of the indivisibility of the fief. But this principle could rarely be maintained, or re-established after interruptions. Compromises had to be found, varying from one region to another, between seigneurial insistence on the integrity of the fief and customary practices which favoured a sharing between the heirs; since it was recognized that the sense of solidarity between the members of a family was stronger than that which bound vassals to their lord. It was generally feudal law which had to make the most concessions.

At first, and after some rather unsuccessful attempts by the lords who had tried arbitrarily to select one of the heirs (one of the sons, for example), there appears to have been a trend here and there towards primogeniture; especially in England, in parts of France including Normandy, and in Germany. This at least was the position in the German duchies, marches and counties, and even the Italian (cf. the Constitution of Roncaglia, 1158); and the case of the Empire illustrates a concept to which feudal law held strongly, namely that fiefs involving the exercise of 'public functions' should not be divided. This was also admitted in France for most of the principalities, although the notion of a 'public function' was less operative than in Germany.

In regard to ordinary fiefs, it was thought to safeguard their integrity by instituting a sole heir in several French provinces, especially in the north and west, and in England. This marked the appearance of the *droit d'aînesse*, of which the importance and significance have been exaggerated, because it was often only the invention of an heir who was privileged, but was not necessarily the sole heir. Several customary laws even preferred the *droit de juveigneur*, the youngest son receiving a larger share of the inheritance than his brothers. It was only in England that primogeniture became an unqualified right. 'The eldest son succeeds his father for everything', wrote Glanville: thus, to the indivisibility of the fief was added that of the whole feudal inheritance. This strict right of primogeniture had been developed in a few parts of Normandy, and it was from there that it had been exported to England. The dukes of Normandy and the Anglo-Norman kings were the only great lords to propagate this kind of indivisibility of the fiefs, which maintained the old principle.

Elsewhere, in western and northern France and in several parts of Lotharingia, primogeniture did not operate completely, and then only in the direct line of descent. In the absence of an eldest son, who was privileged, the eldest daughter inherited – in those countries where women were permitted by custom to succeed to fiefs – provided that she had sisters only. If she had brothers, the eldest was preferred to her, or else the eldest inherited the most important fief, his younger brothers receiving the others. The eldest might even receive an additional portion, the castle or the family house, and share the other fiefs with his brothers; he, however, kept at least half of them for himself, but not more than four-fifths.

The pressure of family interests and the fact that fiefs were being increasingly turned into patrimonies favoured the tendency to sharing the patrimony, and this made further progress in large parts of France. Methods were worked out with a view to reconciling – temporarily – the lord's interest in making the fief indivisible, and the vassals' aspiration for sharing out. In lands of primogeniture the outcome was the institution of *parage* or *frérage*: this existed in western France and in Lotharingia in the twelfth century. The fief was divided, but the eldest son resumed it by doing homage to the lord and he alone was to perform the service due. But *parage* could take two forms.

i. *'Parage' without homage*: By this system the younger brothers held their portions from the eldest brother, but did not do him homage. This system could only be maintained between the senior branch and the younger branches of a family as far as the seventh degree of canonical relationship. After that, the representatives of the younger branches had to do homage to the representative of the eldest.

The eldest had to make the younger brothers share in the service of the fief, but this *parage* without homage did not work well, the eldest having few means of bringing pressure on his co-heirs. Only in Normandy, thanks to the duke's power, did the system work in the best interests of the lords.

ii. *'Parage' with homage*: This worked better in principle. It was the method followed in the Parisian basin, including the Ile-de-France, but excluding Normandy. Only the eldest brother did homage to the lord, but the younger brothers did homage to their senior and held their portions from him: they were the vassals of the man who was best able to oblige them to share in rendering feudal service. This system, however, was to turn out disadvantageously for the lord. The younger brothers were only his sub-vassals, and so these branches would owe no succession-dues. Hence an ordinance decreed by Philip Augustus in 1209: the younger brothers were in future to hold their portions from the lord, and no longer from their elder. The decree, however, was not applied everywhere.

All this became too complicated in the end; and so, in the course of the thirteenth century, *parage* tended to disappear except in Normandy and French Vexin. The lords used their influence against it no doubt, since pure and simple partitions were more profitable for them on account of the succession-dues. Henceforward, the financial aspect of services and rights was of most importance for them.

There remains the case of Germany in respect of ordinary fiefs, which were the most numerous and were divisible by virtue of the constitution of 1158. In order to protect the lord, German law had had recourse in the eleventh century to collective enfeoffment (*una manu, Belehnung zur gesamten Hand*). Thus in 1076 the Countess of Hainault and her son Baldwin II held conjointly a fief from the church of Liége. In the thirteenth century this system was still in current use. When they swore fealty and did homage, all the heirs together placed their hands between the lord's hands and then, when they were invested, they all together grasped the symbolical object which he held out to them. They designated that one of their number who would be responsible for the dues and services required. This was still the rule in the thirteenth century, but in later years the fiefs could be shared out among the co-heirs. After a certain delay and in various manners, the trend here, as in the whole of the French kingdom, was towards a multiplication of fiefs.

Fiefs falling to the lot of a minor or a woman. These two situations will be studied briefly, for lack of space. They are less important, since it was a question of temporary situations, and they did not lead to disintegration of fiefs, and so of rural lordships.

Right of ward and right of marriage set face to face two different communities of interest, those of the family and those of vassalage. These were not necessarily opposed to each other, far from it, and yet customary law had to devise compromises so as not to give too much offence either to the lord or the family; except in the centre and the south of France where the solidarity of family interests maintained for many years an exclusive right, the lord being obliged to limit himself to demanding feudal service from the guardian or the husband.

In the northern half of France, in England and in Germany, the dilemma was clear when the heir was a minor. Ward, or *bail,* could be exercised by a relative; or by the lord, acting by himself or through a representative. In this situation one spoke of seigneurial ward, if it were the lord who acted as *baillistre,* or royal ward if it were the king. This did not imply real guardianship, because the temporary administrator took for himself the product or profits of the fief, being simply required to provide for the needs of the child 'under age'.

In the other instance[1] one spoke of *garde noble.* In northern and western France, except in Normandy, 'noble ward' was the most widespread, effected under the supervision of the lord. This was an ancient procedure because a trace of it has been detected in a letter of Loup de Ferrières (860). This involved the establishment of a temporary vassal, until the young man should come of age. Majority varied from fifteen to twenty-one years of age, and cases of deception regarding age were not rare, in the absence of any kind of civil registers.

In Normandy and England, on the other hand, custom retained the use of seigneurial ward. But as the lord owed no account of 'guardianship' to the heir when he became major, he could bleed the fief white during the years of ward. Cases of abuse were all the more frequent as the king, who had very many vassals, exercised this right with great rigour, extracting very heavy *aides* and forced 'gifts' from the inhabitants of a fief. Frequent and numerous were to be the protests against this 'royal ward' from the time of William the Conqueror to the time of Magna Carta; but as the lords also profited from a similar right, they generally contented themselves with demanding – in vain – more moderation. It was,

[1] When a relative of the minor exercised ward (Translators).

in truth, a fruitful source of revenue for the Plantagenets, as it had been for their predecessors; and also for the Capetians from the time of Philip Augustus. He was the first, in this matter as in others, to exploit all the possible means of profit afforded by feudal law. However, after 1186 in the county of Brittany, as in 1205 in Flanders, the power of the king of France was to appear more limited, because 'noble ward', most widespread in France, yielded much less profit for the lord or king than seigneurial or royal ward.

In Germany seigneurial ward appeared, as in France, in the tenth century. Thus Otto I demanded the wardenship (*bail*) of the young king of Burgundy, whereas noble ward was exercised over the small fiefs. But the German lord delegated his right to a third party, instead of exercising it himself, as was the principle in Anglo-Norman law. And there were even two *baillistres,* one for the freeholds, the other for the fiefs.

When a woman inherited a fief, the service was compromised; hence in the earliest period women were excluded from feudal succession. But in southern France, before 1000, they were admitted to hold fiefs. This was a favour which had turned into a right, in France by the twelfth century, and subsequently in Lotharingia; whereas in the thirteenth century it was still a favour, although very widespread, in Germany. It was, however, necessary for the military service to be rendered in her name, and so by her husband. Hence it was to the lord's interest to agree to her marriage with a dependable man, and even to impose such a marriage on her.

After about 1050 examples occur of the lord's consent to the remarriage of widows or the marriage of heiresses in northern France and in Lotharingia. Customary law of this vast sector already admitted – what would persist in the following ages – the dual principle of a woman's capacity to succeed to a fief, and of the obligation on her part to obtain the lord's consent to her marriage or remarriage.

This seigneurial right of marriage had, from the outset, been much more compulsive in Normandy and England. From the time of William the Conqueror the king had made it more rigorous for his own vassals, who were very numerous.

Using his authority as arbiter of the rights of the family, he imposed husbands on all the daughters of his vassals, even during the lifetime of their fathers, and he used this right as a source of revenue, making the suitor pay, or even forcing the heiress to pay, by threatening to marry or remarry her against her will. Obviously the barons never ceased from protesting right up to the time of Magna Carta, and later still; but without much success, since this marriage-right gave the king power and resources with which he would not willingly part.

For a long time the king of France's right in this matter remained theoretical, as witness the remarriage of Eleanor of Aquitaine in 1152, against the wish of her suzerain and ex-husband. Here again, it was not until the reign of Philip Augustus that the right was exercised effectively in respect of the great vassals (cf. the marriage of the heiress of Flanders with Ferrand in 1212).

F. The Right of Alienation of the Fief

The 'patrimonial' character of a fief did not merely include rights of inheritance. It also meant that one could give, sell, exchange or pledge the fief, like a freehold. And, except in countries where feudalization came late or remained incomplete, freeholds often became fewer and fewer, their characteristics passing over, in a large measure, to the fiefs.

A vassal might come to the point of demanding the right to alienate his fief, or even take forcible possession of it. The demand for this right, however, did not become pressing as early as the demand for the rights of inheritance. The reason for this is clear enough. During the early Middle Ages the market in land had been depressed, and it grew progressively more active only with the expansion of the economy, and the growing circulation of money, that is from the eleventh century on, and generally after 1050 or 1075.

The right of alienation of the fief, far more than right of inheritance which, of itself, did not remove the fief from the vassal's family, was contrary to the bonds of vassalage. Alienation of the whole fief did not necessarily prejudice the service due. But a partial alienation was more serious. In cases of 'abridgment' (the term belongs to the twelfth century), the service of the fief was threatened by a diminution in the vassal's revenue.

The lord, therefore, had a first reason for intervening: alienation could damage him by compromising the service of the fief. But his intervention was justified for another reason. Since he had retained in principle the *proprietas* of the fief, it was only to him in law that the vassal could cede the fief, as there was no other way of disposing of a piece of land over which he had only the right of usufruct. In the eleventh century and even later (until 1150–1185 in the Ile-de-France), customary law did not therefore admit the right of alienation, except in the case of sale to a relative of the vassal. Family bonds thus effected the first breach in this law. But circumstances soon hastened this development. The expansion of the economy, as much as the natural desire to bring more of the fief into the vassal's patrimony, also favoured the possibility of alienation for fiefs, as they had for rural tenures.

Despite the maintenance of prohibition in principle, fiefs had in fact changed hands well before 1200. As early as 1150 vassals in the Paris region sold fiefs outside the circle of their relatives. The land was first offered to the lord, and if he did not wish to acquire it, permission was requested to sell it to a third party. Under the pressure of financial need, or coerced by lords who were short of money or desirous of making a donation to the Church, the lords were not able for long to oppose alienation of their fiefs, either freely or on terms. It only remained possible for them to exercise some control over the operation, such as requiring the vassal to obtain their permission – usually in return for a fee; or they themselves might redeem the fief in question.

The practice of total and final alienation began before the end of the first 'classical' age of feudalism. On condition of remaining vigilant, in 'detecting changes of the men in possession', the lord had one obvious means of exerting pressure: as, in the case of succession to a fief, there was a change of vassal, the sale dissolved the former bond of vassalage, obliging the purchaser to do homage to the lord before he could obtain investiture.

It was evidently in the territories where feudalization was oldest, most deep-rooted and most complete, that the lord's right to intervene was best asserted and in the most profitable way. In nearly all the regions between the middle waters of the Loire and the Rhine, a ceremony known as *report de fief* (transfer of fief) was devised. Appearing in the lord's court, the seller announced his intention of surrendering possession, of *transferring* or restoring to the lord his fief, which was then reinstated in the lord's patrimony; it being tacitly understood that the seller was by that act freed from his obligations as vassal. Immediately afterwards, the buyer offered to do homage and asked for investiture, which the lord granted as soon as the former promised fealty and did homage. The lord was indeed 'at the centre of the affair' (Perroy) at the time of this procedure of *vest et devest,* which was also called *disseizin and seizin,* and of which there were many examples in the twelfth century. But from this period on, the procedure began to be replaced by the simple consent of the lord. In England *enfeoffment* was also to fall into disuse, but only in the next century.

Although customary law between the Loire and the Rhine had not recognized it, the lord disposed in fact of the possibility of recourse to the *retrait féodal,* or 'feudal withdrawal'. This was a right of preemption. Refusing the restoration of the fief, the lord recovered his land after settling with the buyer and freeing the seller from his feudal obligations. But this right came into conflict with the right of *retrait lignager* ('family withdrawal') which enabled the relatives to prevent the land from escaping from the family's patrimony. In various provinces, and notably in western France, there grew up a hierarchy between these competing rights, to the advantage of the family interest.

It does not seem that *retrait féodal* was often exercised. Like the right of preemption, which the Department of Registration possesses in France, it was rather a means of ensuring an open deal, since, traditionally, the lord always charged a fee for his consent; as in the matter of succession to a fief, the *relief*. In the earliest period, the two parties made their own terms. Later on, custom – oral at first, and then recorded, under the influence of the territorial princes – fixed the rate of this real, if occasional right; which, as Perroy has so well said, contributed to 'make it profitable to have enfeoffed vassals'. But the geographical occurrence of this right did not coincide with that of the rights of *relief* (or succession-dues), of ward and of feudal '*aide*'. In Anglo-Norman lands, where custom favoured the lord's interest, it did not exist, and it was indeed rare to require the homage of the buyer; and this was because, from the end of the eleventh century, the patrimonial or personal nature of fiefs was more firmly established there. It was then, with exceptions, only in the northern part of France that the lord exercised rights over 'conveyancing'. Sometimes the name of these rights recalled the ceremony (*vestitio, investitura*). Sometimes the words used were the same as for changes of peasant tenures (*laudes, lods, venditiones, ventes, lods et ventes*). Or again, the right might be called a *relief*. The fixing of the tax was in proportion to the sum paid by the buyer. In Paris one reads of the *quint* (the fifth), or the *quint-denier*, the tax, which was heavy in the Ile-de-France, being often as high as twenty per cent. And this tax was in general to be levied for a very long time, as in the Parisian region, where, as early as the thirteenth century, customary law had recognized that the whole fief could be alienated, and had in 1239 fixed the rate at the *quint-denier*, the payment of which became the only condition required for the lord's assent to the sale.

There remain two kinds of alienation which were more complicated: donations and 'abridgments' of the fief. Donations were mainly those made in favour of the Church, and these were particularly numerous during the first 'classical' feudal age (1000–1160). They were the result of an intense religious feeling, even among the most warlike and quarrelsome, who were very prompt to believe that a man could easily put himself right with God by an act of great generosity towards the clergy. But such gratuitous alienations seriously endangered the service of the fief, when they did not compromise it entirely. If all the ancient houses of religion had their vassals, if many prelates, often younger sons of noble families, behaved like lay lords and even took part personally in certain military operations (examples of this were not rare, notably in the entourage of the Capetians), the same did not apply to the new abbeys, established after the first period of classical feudalism. These new abbeys wished to hold their lands *en franche aumône* (which after 1100 was synonymous with freehold). Then the ancient foundations, imitating the new ones, and influenced also by Gregorian ideas, were no longer willing to hold the new lands that were given them as fiefs, like the old temporalities, and preferred donations of freeholds. Hence a loss for the lord, both in men and services.

Being naturally unable to flout the religious feelings of the time, the lord had to agree to donations. But in the twelfth century, and still more in the thirteenth, customary law took measures to make the lord's assent explicit. Severe sanctions were promulgated against any eventual contraventions of the procedure of *disseizin-seizin*. And in regions where laws governing changes of property prevailed, that is, particularly in France north of the Loire, the lord, by way of compensation for his future loss of the *quint-denier* or the *lods et ventes*, received the right to impose a tax called *mainmorte* on the religious establishment which had received a donation. This tax proved very profitable, especially for the kings of France who actively extended its application. Another means by which the lord was not frustrated of his rights was to appoint a man described as 'living and dying', so that, when he did die, the religious house in question would have to pay the succession-dues.

In respect of *partial alienations* – whether by sale, gift, legacy of a part of the fief, or temporary loan of the fief – distinctions must be made. Donations to the Church of a portion of the fief were generally permitted at an early date, under the same conditions as donations of the whole fief. But conditions were not the same for the other kinds of 'abridgments'. The custom of Paris was, however, especially favourable to both lords and tenants. Towards 1250 this customary law maintained in principle a lord's arbitrary right to consent to or refuse any move to free his serfs, or to subdivide the fields in the reserve-domain, or to any partial sub-enfeoffment; *a fortiori*, if the fief were pledged or sold in part. As to what happened in practice, there was a difference between the two 'classical' ages of feudalism, and it was only during the second (1160–1240) that the lords tried to control cases of 'abridgment'. During the first 'classical' age (1000–1150) on the other hand, they do not appear to have realized the gravity of the danger, especially if the fief had been 'put in pledge' – we should say mortgaged – which, at least in the eleventh century, represented about the only form of credit. This was because land-values were continually rising, and also because a vassal raised a loan from among his peers, or from the lord himself, or from a wealthy Church. It was only at a later date that loans were raised from the burgesses of the neighbouring town or city, and if the loans were not repaid, these townsmen would find themselves in possession of fiefs.[1]

From the Carolingian age to the end of the thirteenth century, the importance of the fief and its value as real estate were constantly increasing in inverse proportion to the personal bond it represented. But the latter was not always weakened as rapidly and as fundamentally as is supposed. Towards 1300 the 'mystique' of the act of homage was by no means forgotten.

Even so, the lord was gradually losing the right to choose his own vassals, while military service was again, and increasingly, becoming an obligation to the advantage of the State. As under Charlemagne, the lord in many regions was little more than an intermediary between his own vassals and the king, to whose army he had to bring his men. This was the situation in thirteenth-century France, as it had already been at an earlier date in England. Seigneurial power had thus

[1] Hence the problem of the bourgeoisie and the fiefs, a problem which became serious from the thirteenth century onward. The nobles, who were the most subject to financial difficulties, were the most numerous borrowers, and were also those who were least often able to repay. There were also the cases of pure and simple sales to burgesses and also to clerics.

suffered an erosion. On the other hand, the lord had found some profitable compensations in England and in the countries between the Loire and the Rhine: here 'the vassal's obligations were on the way to becoming chiefly fiscal duties' (Perroy): dues which could bring in for the lord a great deal of money. From the thirteenth century there are records of actual figures; and these – although historians of feudalism have not hitherto given much attention to them – will undoubtedly facilitate an estimate of their importance in assessing the sum-total of the lords' resources.

Chapter 5

RURAL LORDSHIP[1]

'In the dark ages of the tenth and early eleventh centuries', writes Duby, 'the system of landholding had been gradually superseded, giving place to lordship, which was itself destined to undergo other transformations'.

There were several kinds of lordship, the term being understood in different ways, since a lordship could assume various aspects. Two examples may be given. Lordship could be a great landed estate, what had been formerly the *villa* in Carolingian, and the *manor* in Anglo-Norman lands, with a territorial basis; still divided into the 'reserve' and the tenures. Or it could mean the power to exercise judicial and economic rights over the region.

But it is difficult to trace the continuity of the changes, because written documents are rare from the tenth century until about 1150. To uncover the successive stages of these changes, very patient investigations are needed, like those which Perrin has conducted for Lorraine. But after 1150 or 1180, the documents becoming more numerous, the position is clearer. One may therefore concentrate on the two principal aspects of lordship, in other words, that of landed lordship and that which involved the right of ban.

[1] R. Boutruche, *La crise d'une société: seigneurs et paysans du Bordelais pendant la guerre de cent ans*, Paris, Belles-Lettres, 1947. – *The Cambridge Economic History of Europe*, Vol. I, 2nd ed., Cambridge Univ. Press, 1966 (also concerns social history). – O. M. Fourquin, *The Oxford History*, op. cit. Chs. III and IV. – C. E. Perrin, *Le servage en France et en Allemagne* (*X. Congr. Intern. di Scienze Storiche*, Florence, Sansoni, 1955, pp. 213–45). – A. Plaisse, *La baronnie du Neubourg; essai d'histoire agraire, économique et sociale*, Paris, Presses Universitaires de France, 1961.

I. THE TWO ASPECTS OF LORDSHIP

A. Landed Lordship

What was the extent of the lordship, viewed in its entirety? What were the extents of the *reserve*[1] and of the *manses*?[2] Had the *manses* of the earliest medieval age survived?

Historians have believed that there was a process of 'dismemberment of the *villa*', ever since the work of J. Flack, who described the history of the temporality of Saint-Vaast of Arras between 866 and the end of the twelfth century. Devastations, usurpations and partial enfeoffments had combined to disorganise many *villae*. In some of them the monks had preserved only a few pieces of land or a few rights. In others there had been a division and sharing, now of the lands, now of the rights, between the abbey and the feudal lords. In short, a former *villa* could have given rise to several distinct lordships. Hence the word *villa* was replaced by the word *curtis* (*cour*, then translated back as *curia*) to describe the domain; and it was finally limited in use to designate the *village*.

The example of Saint-Vaast was not unique; many other temporalities suffered the same kinds of transformation. But towards the twelfth century an opposite movement began, a movement of at least partial reconstitution of the former domain. Suger, the Abbot of Saint-Denis, who died in 1151, redeemed or obtained the restoration of the rights and lands of the old reserve in such a way as to re-establish lordships of a very fair size. The Gregorian Reform unquestionably played a great part in this trend to reconstitute ecclesiastical estates, the only ones of which we have a fairly good knowledge.

A well-founded contrast has been drawn between 'the vast lands tilled by the slaves of the great Carolingian abbeys', and 'the reserve of limited size, situated near the lord's dwelling, a reserve from which he drew the provisions for his

[1] The *reserve* was the portion of the estate reserved for the personal use of the lord, as distinct from the tenures of vassals and the tenures of peasants (Translators).

[2] *Manse* (from vulgar Latin mansus) appears to have been a small estate, a small 'manor', probably a sub-division of the ancient *villa* (Translators).

table' (Duby). There were therefore, in Germany as in France and England, many indications either of a dissolution of the reserve or, more often, of its being sub-divided. But the changes were slow. From time to time a small lot was detached and given to a peasant for life or in perpetuity. It had been taken from the lands furthest away from the centre, or from lands recently acquired; or because it was necessary, owing to a shortage of labour, to reduce the area directly exploited by the lord. Moreover, in respect of lay lordships, not only were fiefs established for vassals (a practice in which the Church, too, was involved), but also and especially there was a sharing of land among the heirs. Hence, properties were further sub-divided. One can see that this was due to necessity on the part of the family, and not to any deliberate desire to reduce the reserve, or personal domain. 'One must therefore, in general, regard the sub-divisions of the *indominicatum* as an accidental phenomenon, often due to the simple increase in size of the patrimony' (Duby), at least in the case of clerics. One should add that the agricultural yield of land had improved and that the provision of food and other domestic needs of the lord and his household was now to require areas under cultivation less extensive than formerly.

One should not, however, regard this reduction of the reserves as a general phenomenon. Certain lords wished to increase their reserves in order 'further to improve the profit immediately derived from them'. The monastic orders which wished to maintain something of the ideal of a hermit's existence, Cîteaux in the first instance, cultivated their fields and vineyards themselves, at least until about 1150. In their early days the Cistercians had divided their estates into reserves, known as *granges,* each one being entrusted to domestic workers directed by the monks. Other monks, like those of Cluny or Saint-Denis in the twelfth century, increased their reserves. To some extent, laymen acted in the same way. The clearing of forest-land, which they controlled or directed, gave rise to further reserves and peasant tenures, as is shown by the foundation of '*villeneuves*' and contracts of *pariage*.[1]

[1] Or 'paréage'. The sharing by two lords of the one property and its rights of justice (Translators).

Thus in the eleventh and twelfth centuries there were, with a few exceptions, no lordships without a reserve, the extent of this being many times greater than that of a tenure. As in former days, it comprised fields for crops, meadows, vineyards on occasion, as well as woods and waste land. There was no lack, either in England or on the Continent, of reserves of several hundred *hectares*,[1] equal to the total area of the *manses*. One must remember also that, as formerly, the cultivable part of the reserve could be in one portion or else composed of many separate fields scattered over the estate. But many estates had been cleared of forest-land; hence, in those which were old, 'the relative area of the reserve and its economic importance' had been reduced in face of the increase in the number of peasant-tenures (Perrin).

What now remained of the former economic links between the reserve and the tenures? These links had been very close under the Carolingians in the regions between the Loire and the Rhine. To answer this question one must consider the eleventh and twelfth centuries, but only in respect of ancient estates which were not yet benefiting from 'extensive exemptions'.

There remained for the master three of the former possible ways of exploiting (or, as we should say, farming) the reserve: recourse to the *familia*, recourse to the tenants, recourse to paid labour, or the use of all three methods. Were the relations between these methods the same in each district, as under the Carolingians?

The most direct means of exploiting the reserve involved cases where the lord lodged his own *familia*, that is, his 'domestic servitors'. The part played by the *familia* had often remained of first importance, the slaves having been replaced by serfs. The significance of all this is seen in the fact that the labourers or 'prebendaries' were regarded as forming, together with the agricultural implements and the draught-animals, the basic equipment of the *courts*,[2] in the Ile-de-France, in Burgundy and Italy. Other servitors, more

[1] As an *hectare* = 2·47 acres, this means that some estates comprised apart from the peasant-tenures, over 1,000 acres of land (Translator).

[2] i e. estates or domains, originally *villae* (Translator).

numerous than under the Carolingians, came every day to work on the reserve, while possessing a house and a small tenure of their own: these were the *servi quotidiani* who received distributions of food to supplement their meagre income. Finally, for work of a superior kind there were the *ministeriaux,* men provided with a 'fief', which was small but exempt from dues. To them also the steward distributed food and other produce.

Recourse to paid workers, engaged on a temporary basis at harvest times, seems to have become more frequent and more extensive. The Cistercians themselves had to obtain assistance for their lay brothers from paid labour. The English tenants who had the poorest holdings, *bordiers*[1] and cotters, hired themselves out to the lords or the well-to-do peasants.

How far did the forced work of the tenants – the third alternative – still play an important part? This was obviously dependent on the size of the reserve. As there no longer existed any vast reserves, forced labour was generally reduced, even in provinces which had made the greatest use of it. In attempting to outline the geographical distribution of these services, Duby contrasts the northern half of the West with the southern.

In the northern regions requirements of forced labour remained fairly heavy, although far less exacting than formerly. They had not varied in kind. They consisted in cultivating two pieces of land (in countries where a triennial rotation of crops was the rule) in seasonal services and work in the woods, etc., But these exactions were declining. The abbey of Marmoutier in Alsace even replaced them by a due in money, on the ground of 'negligence, uselessness and indolence of those who were serving' (Perrin). One should perhaps ascribe the trouble to a certain ill-will, a more or less concerted movement among all the tenants of the lord in question. There were other causes, such as the splitting up of lordships and reserves, the expansion of trading, and the increase in the need for coinage on the part of those lords who preferred to replace labour by a tax in money. This

[1] A small farmer owing part of his products to the lord (Translators).

could be paid by peasants who disposed of cash, thanks to the sale of crops more abundant than of old; agricultural techniques having so far improved as to require fewer workers. As for manufactured products, these were becoming less necessary, owing to the increasing number of rural artisans. England, however, occupies a place apart in this matter, because there, in the twelfth century, the organic connection between the reserve and the tenures had been better preserved. Two kinds of tenants were living on the manorial estates: certain tenants were required to perform specified services, as in northern France and in Germany; others, the *villeins*, were, on the contrary, subject to real forced labour. The *weekwork* imposed on them three days of service apart from seasonal work.

South of the Loire, and also in the West, in the Midi and in Italy, the situation was quite different. Most of the tenures were either exempt, or required to render very light services when work was urgent as at times of ploughing and harvest. In these regions demands for obligatory work had always been less exacting than elsewhere.

What had become of the *manse* in the course of ages? Subdivisions had already begun to appear in the early Carolingian era and had become general. The evolution can be followed most clearly in Lorraine (Perrin). Half-manses and quarter-manses were still rare in the ninth century; but in the twelfth 'the quarter had become the standard unit of a tenure' and formed the new basis for the assessment of dues. One wonders how a family could live on it, since its area was usually only from three to four hectares,[1] and the increased yield of the land could hardly enable a family to find compensation for this reduced holding. Except for a time-lag, the situation was identical in the region of Namur (L. Genicot), where after about 1200 there is no mention of manses, but only of quarters (of about four to eleven and a half hectares). In England, the *hide* as a land-unit remained in use for many years, being replaced only in the thirteenth century by the *vergée* (a quarter of a *hide* or one and a quarter roods) and the *bovée* (an eighth of a hide). This

[1] About nine acres (Translators).

delay was due to the fact that the royal tax, which was imposed earlier here, was based on the tenure as a unit. In Germany, which was less behind the times, the *Hufe* was fairly soon subdivided into *Halbehufe* and *Viertelhufe*. The time-lags are definite; Lorraine and the region of Namur are average examples, while as early as the tenth century in Normandy, the manse was replaced by the *charruée*, whereas the English *hide* was discontinued only in the thirteenth century.

Once the manse had disappeared, and next its subdivisions, which rarely lasted very long, there remained no territorial unit for the assessment of dues or taxes. These had now to be calculated individually, each piece of land, whether built on or not, being subject to dues. But this logical outcome of the situation did not apply everywhere. In north-west Germany and in Bavaria, a sharing out of tenures was forbidden and the rule of primogeniture was imposed on the peasants, which safeguarded the unity of the tenure. In the region of Namur the lords prevented any change, in the thirteenth century, by imposing the quit-rent on the quarter manse, even when it had been again subdivided. On the other hand, the evolution reached its final stage in Suabia, in Alsace, in Flanders and in the Paris region as early as the twelfth century. But the lords were obliged to have very detailed *censiers* drawn up in order to establish periodical lists of all the pieces of land, with the names of the holders and an indication for each tenure of what was due from it. This work was indispensable, and the records have provided historians with an almost inexhaustible mine of information for drawing a picture of rural life.

B. Bannal Lordship

The peasants not only owed dues to the lord, or the landed proprietor, but, when occasion arose, services also. There existed a whole hierarchy of 'lordships', sometimes concentrated in the hands of the same lord. The tenant, as responsible to the landed proprietor, was subject to the judicial lordship exercised by the person who had the right of adjudicating, at least for those cases which came before an inferior court; and often also for cases pleaded in a middle court and what might be called a high court of justice. Landed lordship and judicial lordship were very often combined in the hands of the same man, and a lord, by virtue of being a landowner, had the right of 'landed justice'. This right was of very ancient origin, because the Roman aristocrats had already possessed powers of coercion over the inhabitants of the *fundus*; and this 'landed justice' differed very little from justice administered in the lower courts. Above it in authority came *bannal lordship*,[1] so called by Georges Duby because its possessor disposed of the right of *ban*, wholly or in part. The *bannal* lord imposed his authority over the whole of the territory he controlled: he could therefore impose supplementary obligations on the peasants dependent on the 'landed' and 'judicial' lords. Finally, and still higher, the holder of *castellan* lordship exercised power over a wider territory. The castellan could exact from all the inhabitants of the '*sauvement*' dues or services for the maintenance of the castle, of the garrison and horses; and also taxes for the passage of men and merchandise through the territory. If at the beginning bannal lordship had coincided with castellan lordship, the former had become more and more widespread after 1000.[2] In the twelfth century many nobles who were not castellans had arrogated to themselves or seized the right of ban. The bannal lords were often 'high justicers' like the castellan lords, only a few prerogatives remaining the apanage of the castellans.

The effects of this development had weighed heavily on the peasants. The obligations due to the 'landed' lord – the immediate landowner – had been lightened since the Carolingian era, but this improvement in the peasants' condition had been more than offset by the new obligations resulting from the ban; the lords using their powers to exercise authority in the judicial field as well as in the economic.

The Carolingian *dominus* had not in principle extended

1 More or less corresponding to immunity (Translators).

2 Perhaps more quickly and less completely at first than Duby has supposed, when we have regard to the great number of *mottes* (mounds surmounted by the manor of an inferior lord) which archaeologists are now discovering (see above p. 91).

his powers of constraint over the free men of his domain, at least when he did enjoy immunity. But subsequently the *potentes,* beginning with the castellans, had manoeuvred for themselves lordships which were often both judicial and bannal; so that the exercise of private justice was often confused with the right of ban. At the same time the tenants and small freeholders had been obliged to ask for, or to submit to, the domination of the lord, thus falling into a state of dependence more rigorous than that of the former free peasants of the *villa.* They were now the *homines de potestate,* subjects of a *potestas* (from *pôté,* as the land administered by the bannal lord was called in Burgundy). And the judicial employment of the ban weighed heavily on the weak for many years.

Its effect was, however, probably less severe than the economic application of the ban. Whereas the old dues rendered in services were diminishing through disuse or from being bought out, the lords now assumed other and greater powers. They could, for example, revive former services, like that of *cartage,*[1] and, furthermore, they could impose new obligations on all the peasants within their jurisdiction. 'Regulating the economic life of the lordship', the lord could fix the order of rotation of crops, assign dates for major work on the farms, ploughing and the various harvests, and regulate the peasants' use of the forests and waste-lands. He constrained his men to use only his oven and mill and wine-press, and pay for it. The right of ban was a source of direct profit – in the form of 'banalités', some of which were to survive until 1789 – and also of indirect profit, by reason of the fines imposed through 'any disobedience to the ban' (Perrin).

The exercise of the ban reinforced a very ancient right, that of the 'general protection' which the master had exercised over his dependants for centuries. Just as the vassal owed pecuniary *aide* to the feudal lord, so the dependants of the rural lord had to aid him by every means in their power, including money. This was a kind of poll-tax (*petitio,*

[1] The obligation to furnish regular returns or lists of produce, etc. (Translators).

precaria; in German, *Bede*), payable on the 'prayer' of the master, who fixed the sum arbitrarily, as he did for the rights connected with the ban.

The 'burden on the peasant economy of this system of requisitioning' is not easy to estimate. One thing is certain: rights of ban and justice, with taxes, constituted a burden 'incomparably heavier' than the dues strictly based on the land. Judiciary fees, above all, weighed heavily: hence the harsh manner in which both lay and clerical lords clung to their right of administering justice; hence also their attempts to extend this right. One of the first 'franchises' demanded by the peasants was for the competence of seigneurial judges to be limited and the rate of fines fixed at definite figures.

England, however, presented a different picture. Here the Crown had managed strictly to limit the lords' powers of exaction, and the taxes they levied and the justice they administered brought them lower profits than elsewhere. As the dues and services were so much smaller, the English lords, especially from the end of the twelfth century, worked persistently to increase the agricultural production of their reserves (Perroy). On the Continent, however, it was the administration of justice which brought in the big profits. But to fulfil his functions as justicer, and also to collect the taxes and obtain the services due to the ban, the bannal lord was obliged to depend on numerous '*ministériaux*' (estate officials), who were generally recruited from among the members of the *familia*, where this still subsisted. These men – the miller, the baker, the master of the wine-press, the judge, the provost and the bailiff – had the means of enriching themselves. Being provided with a 'fief', a piece of land conceded without charge or rent, and receiving a percentage of the taxes and fines, they ended by forming 'a little rural aristocracy' (Duby). In the Mâconnais in the thirteenth century, the fifty odd families of senior *ministériaux* and the hundred and fifty families of small nobles 'both seem to have been living on virtually the same economic level'. Some of the *ministériaux* even ended by becoming the effective masters of the lordships, at least when the titular lord was negligent or often absent.

II. THE SITUATION OF THE PEASANTRY UNDER THE SEIGNEURIAL SYSTEM FROM THE ELEVENTH TO THE THIRTEENTH CENTURY

The economic condition of the peasantry was not the only factor that determined its real situation. The decisive factor was 'the combination of their juridical status with their social condition (human relations between dependants and lords). . . .' (Genicot). If 'the status of the peasants has not bemused research scholars', it is none the less very important, because it could aggravate or ameliorate the lot of the rural masses.

In the earliest period the new powers of the feudal lords proved onerous for the peasants; but in the next period, owing to the great clearing of the forests, a definite improvement was generally felt, as much in the juridical domain as in matters economic and social. In the last two fields this improvement did not last beyond the end of the thirteenth century, because in very many regions the population had increased beyond the level compatible with its well-being.

A. The New Juridical and Social Stratification Associated with the New Powers of the Lords. The Example of France

After the year 1000 a great change took place in the status of the peasant population. Its condition became more uniform, as is shown by the terms generally used to describe the peasants: *manentes* (inhabitants in general), *villani* (villeins, dwellers in a village), *rusticani* (country folk) – all words which were sooner or later to acquire a pejorative sense in a society which always regarded the peasants as at the bottom of the social scale. This is also proved by the inexact use of ancient words like *servus* and its feminine *ancilla*, which ought to have been used only of serfs, but which were sometimes misapplied. Towards 1060 the abbey of Cluny obtained from a lay lord a domain with 'the *serfs* and the *serves*, whether free or unfree'. This was because, if some were born free, but not all, they were still regarded as 'serfs' (=unfree), because dependent on a lord. General opinion was in fact inclined to regard dependants as deprived of freedom when under the control of a lay lord, and therefore subject to heavier burdens that the dependants of churches, who, for their part, were regarded as free. Eventually, towards 1100, the old words of *servi, ancillae* and *liberi* disappeared from the charters of many regions.

The old distinctions had therefore been effaced. This movement, which had begun at the end of the first medieval age, was completed owing to the decay of public institutions. This change was to make it impossible to establish in law a status of either freedom or of servitude, of slavery in the first instance and then of serfdom. But within this peasant class which had become more uniform, shades of difference could not fail to persist or to appear. If the distinction between freedom and servitude was no longer a clear one, if one could speak of men who were half-free, there were several kinds of peasants who were, in differing degrees, subject to their lord. All the new exigencies, derived from the higher ban or the lower, weighed proportionately on the rural population. They were not a proof of servitude, but they were a proof of dependence, more or less strict according to the weight of these exactions. Thus there were still degrees of liberty.

There existed, however, within this general condition of dependence, as twelfth century texts bear witness, a group of men with no freedom at all. They were more numerous than the Carolingian slaves, and fairly well defined in northern and eastern France, where they were known as *hommes de corps* or *hommes propres* – *men* who were once again described by the word *servi*, which became 'serfs' in French.

Historians have differed as to the criteria that define serfdom, and the matter is important, since any calculation of the numbers of serfs depends on it. In Marc Bloch's view the majority of French peasants were serfs in the twelfth century and the first half of the thirteenth, because, according to him there existed three burdens or dues characteristic of serfdom: *chevage*,[1] *mainmorte* and *formariage*, of which the

[1] *Capitagium*. A kind of poll-tax levied on the unfree rustics; more especially if they sought to leave the lordship.

two last at any rate were certainly paid by the greater number of peasants. Other historians have thought of the poll-tax as a criterion. Later still, the views of L. Verriest have been partly accepted by most students of the age. For Verriest, all the seigneurial exactions weighed on the serfs in the twelfth century; but other men in a state of dependence, and yet free, were also unfavourably situated. There remained therefore one characteristic feature: the serf belonged wholly to his master, his condition was hereditary, and, like the slave of ancient times, he could be bought or sold. But if Verriest regards these serfs as descendants of the Carolingian slaves, Duby argues with more likelihood that the last slaves had disappeared and that it was a question now of groups of 'protected' men who had 'commended' themselves to a powerful lord and who, unlike those of higher rank who had commended themselves, had lost their former freedom by taking an oath of fealty. The best proof of this lies in the fact that the hereditary transmission of serfdom did not operate in the same way as the transmission of slavery. The bond between man and man, to the exclusive advantage of the master, implied that the serf could not leave the lord's domain without permission; failing this, the lord had the right of pursuit and could bring back the fugitive by force. This right of pursuit was evidently only effective within a limited area. In an age when population had become much more mobile, consequent on the clearing of forest-lands and the expansion of city life, many serfs contrived to free themselves from the mark of servitude by seeking refuge at a distance; and, as early as the twelfth century, the groups subject to serfdom showed signs of diminishing in numbers, despite the general increase in population.

There resulted an approximation of status between serfs and 'villeins', recalling the earlier one between slaves and *colons*. This was due to several factors, such as the frequency of mixed marriages, the subjection of all the dependants in a lordship to the lord's tribunal, a similar way of life, and so on; so true it is that material conditions tended increasingly to make for uniformity. This approximation had 'consequences of considerable import for the future lot' of the serfs (Perrin). It led to two contradictory results in the thirteenth century, sometimes as early as the twelfth.

In several provinces, burdens which without being obvious symbols of serfdom were increasingly incompatible with freedom, were suppressed or lightened; either by payment in instalments or by pure and simple redemption. The poll-tax was an example. From the lightening of this levy the serfs profited like the free men; at the same time the movement for emancipation was acquiring wider proportions. In western and north-western France serfdom disappeared at an early date; even in Normandy there were no serfs after about 1120. In the Ile-de-France the two movements occurred simultaneously, but only towards the mid-thirteenth century. The serfs were able to buy out their personal liberty, while general exactions like the poll-tax, which were associated with serfdom, were limited instead of being, as formerly, at the lord's discretion. In other regions serfdom as a status was affected by villeinage, in Burgundy for example. In 1105 the term *servus* was applied for the last time in the Mâconnais, in a written document, to describe a status both social and juridical. The lords now recognized only one group, treating all their peasants on the same footing. At the end of the twelfth century the term 'serf' had gone out of use except as an insult. This does not mean that from the early twelfth century all the peasants of the Mâconnais were wholly free. Twelfth-century freedom, then known as *franchise* – not peculiar to the Mâconnais – simply meant that exploitation by the lord had been mitigated. '*Liberty* is no longer a title; like the former *nobility*, it is a quality varying in degree' (Duby), according to the degree of alleviation obtained. Between 1160 and 1240, not much earlier than in the Ile-de-France, most of the 'churls' in the Mâconnais had managed to win full freedom by limiting the burden of exactions and, in general, the arbitrary power of the lords, with or without obtaining charters of *franchise*. In certain provinces '*affranchissement*' in the sense of emancipation might be no more than a concession of the *franchise*, not liberation from a servile status properly so-called. The very early date of the fusion of serfdom and villeinage in the Mâconnais, and the disappearance of the first kind of serfdom, without the grant of charters of *franchise* as required in western France, confers an exceptional interest on the history of the Mâconnais. The charters did not appear until 1160, whereas the serfs had disappeared for more than half a century – without mention, one might say.

One outcome of the fusion between the free and the unfree had been the disappearance of the first form of serfdom. But there was a reverse movement. By affecting villeinage, serfdom increased and became more constraining. This is what happened to the north and east of the Parisian region, in Vermandois, Champagne, Franche-Comté and central France.

Formariage, a levy on the serf who marries a woman from outside the lordship; *mainmorte*, or succession-due; the poll-tax and forced labour; and also *chevage* – all these exactions were in appearance those of the serf. To those subject to them there were applied the judicial and canonical limitations reserved in principle for serfs: in short, as nearly all the peasants were sometimes subject to them, serfdom looked like becoming the common lot of all the country folk. The date when, in certain regions, the peasants came to be treated almost as serfs certainly varied; but it has been generally placed in the second half of the thirteenth century. It was a question here of the second serfdom, which was to last longer than the first. Its features were very different. Its basis tended to become more a question of material conditions rather than of personal status, the serfs being often bound to the soil – '*attachés à la glèbe*', according to a stereotyped formula – an expression which would have been inappropriate to describe the first kind of servitude. This state of attachment to the *glèbe* existed even in the Mâconnais where, however, it was less common; its members there forming an economic and not actually a juridical group. But they were subject to taxation and arbitrary forced labour, and were required to '*tenir feu et lieu*', that is, to live on their tenure day and night. This new kind of serfdom was not unknown again in the south-west. In the country round Bordeaux the unfree man, known as a *questal* (from *queste* = poll tax), was subject to obligations similar to those of his brothers in the Mâconnais, and he also belonged to a small group. But there was a vast difference here in the fact that serfdom in the south-west was hereditary, like the first kind of servitude, unlike that of the Mâconnais, which was fundamentally a much less thorough-going version of the system.

Lack of space prevents the author from making a detailed examination of serfdom in other western countries. A few brief observations, however, and points of comparison may be made.

Perrin has undertaken a comparative study of serfdom in France and Germany.[1] He regards the serfs in both countries as connected with the Carolingian *servi*. But whereas in France the serfs were presumably descended from the *servi casati* of Carolingian times and never formed other than small groups before their condition was to have this effect on the villeins, in the thirteenth century, serfdom in Germany was much more widespread. It took two different forms. 'The tenants who tilled or worked on the lands of rural lordships had been grouped at an early date into a single class of *hörig*, a class formed largely of *servi casati*. As to the 'hommes de corps', or *leibeigen*, they were in part, descendants of the *mancipia* of the reserve-domain, it being understood that they had passed through an intermediate stage, corresponding to the class of the *censuales*.' After the thirteenth century, the changes and reductions in the burdens of serfdom were not to be granted by the lord but were to originate in customary law, and be related to the practice of the Weistümer. On the other hand, serfdom was unknown in the lands colonized in eastern Germany, except sometimes at the end of the Middle Ages.

There remain the questions of Italy, northern Spain and England. One should note, also, that slavery of the ancient kind persisted in Mediterranean countries, although the slaves had generally become few in number.

Certain regions experienced great progress, at least in an early period: Spain, for example, where the grant of *fueros*

[1] *Le servage en France et en Allemagne* (at the 10th International Congress of the Historical Sciences. Florence, 1955).

was needed to support the colonizing and peopling of zones liberated from the Moors; Lombardy and Tuscany, too, where the 'great cities led the movement'. 'Taking over from the nobles in the countryside in order to bring pressure to bear on those who refused to submit to them, to win partisans for the popular faction, and to increase the number of taxpayers: and also, no doubt, in response to moral and religious considerations' (Genicot), many cities abolished every form of personal, and subsequently of material subjection, thereby removing the obstacles to freedom and suppressing or reducing the exactions of the lords. But such changes were neither general nor always very lasting. The Italian princes did not follow the example of the great cities; and the latter were too often more oppressive than the lords, using every means to lower the peasants' standard of living, at the same time granting them juridical freedom.

In certain countries, as in England, the number of serfs was to remain high. The *villeins* (English serfs) at the end of the thirteenth century still composed a quarter, a half or even three-quarters of the rural population, and could not in theory leave their tenures or dispose of them without permission of the lord, who could still tax them and impose forced labour at discretion. Even 'free tenants' had to defend themselves against attempts to impose on them obligations to which only serfs were legally subject; unless they were forced to accept the status of *villeins* in order to obtain a tenure. In the thirteenth century the 'land famine', consequent on over-population of the countryside, caused a deterioration in economic conditions, and also affected the juridical status of certain peasants, not only in England. Serfdom reappeared in Germany and northern Spain, and in certain French provinces, connected no doubt with the shortage of available land.

B. The 'Franchises' and the Consequences of Land-clearing

In face of the lord's exactions, the peasantry did not always remain inactive; they were at times able to present a united front, which the master had to reckon with. Serfdom was in fact only one aspect of peasant history; the other side of the picture, a very different one, was connected with the great movement of forest-felling and marsh-draining.

This land-clearing could be, for the peasants, an excellent opportunity for immediately improving their lot and an efficient means of exerting pressure. 'It is undeniable', writes Perrin, 'that colonization contributed to improve the condition (of the country folk). This followed the lords' need to attract men to clear the forest-lands, and for this purpose they were obliged to grant them favourable conditions, especially as concerned the exercise of the right of ban. It often happened that a charter for land-clearing had the same value in law as a charter of franchise. But land-clearing was also of indirect advantage to those peasants who had remained on their own tenures, and taken no part in the work. . . . Under threat of seeing the dwellers in their own lordships joining the flood of emigrants to the newly available lands, very many lords had to grant them *franchises*'.

This was very apparent in Germany, where records make it possible to follow the movement of colonization eastward. Being threatened, in the twelfth century, with depopulation of their lordships by the departure of many colonists, the lords of western Germany succeeded in obtaining important advantages from their own masters. In twelfth-century France, charters of franchise in favour of the older villages became numerous at about the same time as charters for the foundation of new towns (*villeneuves*). Thus the movement towards a diminution in the number of serfs is to be connected with the clearing of forest and other lands, which made it easier and more profitable for many of the serfs to escape from their former dwellings.

France and Germany may be taken as examples. They were, however, somewhat different, because in France the peasant reaction dates from the second quarter of the twelfth century, and in Germany from the end of that century, while the methods used to limit the arbitrary conduct of the lord were not identical.

The relatively effective emancipation of the peasants in matters economic and social was accomplished in France by charters of franchise. The most famous, also one of the oldest, was that of Lorris-en-Gâtinais (1108–37). The number of these charters then increased. Granted by the lord (by the king in the case of Lorris) to the inhabitants of one or several of his lordships, they were not usually the outcome of a trial of strength, but of a bargain. The capital needed to obtain the charter was often advanced by the burgesses of the neighbouring towns, who in this way managed to obtain a footing in the open country. The forms and clauses of these charters varied a good deal, because they depended on local and even regional conditions, and on the degree of goodwill shown by those who granted them. Many franchises, however, were the same in dozens or even hundreds of old domains adjoining the lands covered by the charters of the 'new towns'. Some of them covered a wide area: that of Beaumont-en-Argonne, for example, covered a much greater area than the charter of Lorris.

Since the charters to establish new towns guaranteed freedom to the 'guests' who came to share in the clearing of the land, and an assurance that they would be exempted from arbitrary taxation; and since it was necessary to prevent the inhabitants of old villages from seeking better living conditions in the newly populated regions, charters of franchise had been drawn up to accord with charters of the new towns. If, on certain points, it was thought enough to codify local custom in order to prevent the lord and his *ministériaux* from abusing their interpretation of it, on other points the king's or prince's jurists went further by specifying 'the conditions and limits within which in future the lord could exact dues and services' (Perrin). Dues required by the ban, tolls, *tonlieux*, poll-taxes and fines were fixed at standard rates (generally lower), while services were reduced. But as the object of these charters was only to put an end to arbitrary abuse of the ban, they contained nothing in principle affecting landed lordship. The burden of taxes connected with this was, however, to be modified, following the example of the charters of colonization.[1] Sometimes charters of fran-

[1] i.e. for occupying the lands recently cleared or drained (Translators).

chise, like that of Beaumont-en-Argonne (1182), which affected all the regions from Champagne to Lorraine and Luxembourg, even recognized the right of the rural communities to elect representatives who would take part in administering the lordships and raise taxes to benefit the communities.

Charters of franchise were granted in the Rhineland under the name of *Handfeste*, while charters for founding new towns began to appear in the lands that were being colonized beyond the Elbe. However, in Germany and Lotharingia the enactments mainly responsible for fixing customary law and improving the condition of the peasants, from the end of the twelfth century, were of a different nature. They were called *rapports de droits* in Lorraine (Perrin), *records de coutume* in the region of Namur (Génicot), and *Weistümer* in Germany. They derived from the vigorous growth of the institution of advocacy within the Empire.

The *Weistum* was a solemn declaration made by the peasants of the domain at the lord's request, at one of the three courts which assembled annually. Its object was to specify the master's rights in accordance with the custom of the particular place. Although the lord took the initiative in the *Weistum* the court did not usually favour him, but rather the subjects making a declaration of their rights. The lord could demand a statement of all customs and precedents to his advantage, and the peasants could not protest about any 'unfair' practice; but, on the other hand, they could insist on some innovation that was favourable to them. 'It is remarkable', writes Perrin, '. . . that in Lorraine, where charters of franchise co-exist with records of rights, the latter were often actually of benefit to the subjects of those lordships who had not yet been freed, and they thus profited from the privileges acquired by neighbouring lordships, already provided with a charter of *franchise*'.

The social consequences of these charters were not, however, the same as those of the *Weistümer*. In France, the men who were protected by a charter of *franchise* from the arbitrary exactions of the lord, were reputed free; whereas in Germany the consequences were far more limited. It was only the economic results of the charters that were common to the two countries.

III. ECONOMIC ASPECTS OF LORDSHIP IN THE THIRTEENTH CENTURY

For most of the country districts of the West, the thirteenth century represented the heyday of prosperity. Lords and peasants had never, in principle, experienced such favourable conditions for the sale of country produce, although here one must discriminate. The peasants, who had increased in numbers, held tenures more and more limited in size, while the changes in their juridical status was not always, or for long, accompanied by an equal economic improvement. As for the lords, possession of the right of ban and even landed lordship often brought in less than before. To make up for this, they strove, whenever possible, to increase the yield from the reserves. From these came the better part of their resources, about which, from now on, much more is known, owing to the very many accounts of income and expenditure that have been preserved.

A. Estates Cultivated by the Nobles

As reserve and tenure became more loosely attached, the economic history of the former can be traced much more easily than in the earlier centuries.

1. *The seigneurial reserves.* The history of what were called *granges* in the Ile-de-France is bound up, for the most part, with the question of personal fortunes. What had become of the wealthy and moderately comfortable landowners?

The temporalities of the Church generally continued to increase as a result of gifts, legacies and purchases, the funds for which came from charities or investments from yearly income. This was the situation at Saint-Denis, among many establishments of the kind. But the temporalities of poorer religious houses seem to have remained static. The personal fortunes of laymen suffered from subdivision or from lordly extravagances. Crusades and military expeditions had become very costly. Some historians have alleged that the nobility were poor administrators, without however advancing indisputable proof of this theory. Hence the idea – which can also be disputed – that the fortunes of the nobility were suffering a general decline to the advantage of the burgesses who were well provided with capital and were good administrators.

What is certain is that in provinces where the right of primogeniture was not established and where fiefs could be divided *ad infinitum*, as in the Ile-de-France, many heirs ended in possession of no more than a 'rump lordship' and such men swelled the ranks of the 'plebeian nobility'. A small noble of the Paris region could well finish up, towards 1300, with having no more than a reserve containing a house and two or three hectares of land (five or seven acres) – as little in fact as many peasants – and a '*copyhold*' tenure which brought in only a few pounds a year. The thirteenth century did not, however, witness a general collapse of the material fortunes of the nobility. Both on the Continent and in England there remained many lordships of considerable extent in the hands of the knights. When one of these estates changed hands, it was often a noble and not a burgess who acquired it. There was no general 'invasion' of the countryside by the bourgeoisie except in parts of Italy. Moreover, the knights were no longer solely dependent on their lands for a livelihood. The rise in the power of the Crown and of the great princes, as well as the increasing centralization of the Church, enabled older as well as younger sons to obtain official positions or receive fruitful benefices.

In Marc Bloch's view, the lords of the thirteenth century were now only '*rentiers*', one might also say 'annuitants of the soil', victims of great economic changes. As a consequence of the clearing of forests and the reduction of bannal exactions, a lord's income might be reduced to various sums of money, fixed in perpetuity, while the cost of commodities was going up. It will be replied that a lord's resources included also the income derived from the reserve, and that these nobles had become simple husbandmen rather than rural lords.

Save on the lands newly colonized, as in eastern Germany, there were no longer any immense lordships or huge reserves in western Europe. But there remained many reserves of a good size despite some parcelling out, resulting from the pressure of population and the need to concede more tenures to the peasants. The vast estates, like those of the Carolingians, had been divided into groups of domains. Thus in the Ile-de-France, the Bishop of Paris, the Abbot of Saint-Denis and the Montmorency family shared out their estates in castellany-provostries,[1] of which the local capitals were both centres of rural administration and feudal centres for the fiefs dependent on the lordship.

Reserves of about one hundred hectares (two hundred and fifty acres), or larger still, were not uncommon. But in the thirteenth century, especially in the northern parts of the Continent, a direct exploitation of the reserve was often replaced by farming it out (a habit not absent from the Midi, although there *métayage*[2] was the system mainly in use). This was from motives of efficiency and not because the lords were moving away from their estates. In England, on the other hand, the practice of farming out the reserve, which had been in use earlier, was replaced in the great ecclesiastical lordships by direct management, hence the new and more active use of the *weekwork* which was owed by the tenants. But if indeed direct management was once again the rule in England, it was still only the most extensive reserves of the Church which returned to forced labour on a large scale.

2. *The Seigneurial Accounts.* After the early 1200s many registers of accountancy, still not well known but certainly quite considerable, have been preserved. In country districts there already existed professional accountants, which explains the remarkable competence of many of these accounts. From the receipts they record one may learn the sources of income of the great lords; but a study of them is only beginning in France, whereas it is much more advanced in England.

Here, income from the reserve does not seem in the thirteenth century to have represented a really preponderant

[1] '*Châtellenies-prévôtés*'.

[2] The proprietor provided the seed and animals, and the *métayer* paid him in kind (Translators).

portion of the receipts; and this portion was tending to diminish, no doubt because here, more than elsewhere, pieces of land had been parcelled out to the advantage of the peasants. Thus the reserves which provided the Cathedral Church of Ely with fifty per cent of its resources in 1255 were furnishing no more than forty per cent in 1298.

On the Continent, however, if one considers the seigneurial receipts as a whole, the income from the reserves shows a clear preponderance. In the temporality of the abbey of Saint-Denis about eighty per cent of the total receipts came from the *granges* (and, it is true, from the seigneurial dues farmed out with them); yet it was still a question only of income in money, to which must be added the value of produce used or consumed, and not sold. The remaining part of the receipts was derived from the woods, tolls and *tonlieux* more than from the 'copyholds'.[1] But the rights of ban, of justice and of the levy of succession dues brought in relatively greater sums than the rents from the copyholders.

This situation was to last after the thirteenth century. In 1332 Philippe VI of Valois was drawing more money simply from his rights of ban than from the copyholds on his domain between the middle waters of the Seine and the Loire at Orleans. The conclusion is evident: in spite of the limitations which bannal lordship had been obliged to accept, it still remained more profitable than landed lordship.

B. The Cultivation of Peasant Tenures

The *manse* and its subdivisions having disappeared, they were replaced by other forms of tenure. The origin of these new types is little known, because it goes back to an age with few written records; but it is at least certain that the new tenures were widely granted in connection with the great clearing of the forests and the charters for founding new towns and with the charters of *franchise*. They were finally to be encountered in all regions. In many French provinces the *hostise*, a tenure granted to a newcomer, who in the regions cleared of forest was always a free man, and the

[1] For this translation as an equivalent of '*censive*' see Translators' Note.

censive or copyhold, a new tenure on the old cultivated lands, were practically equivalent terms.

Two major types of holding can be distinguished: the *censives*, which were subject to fixed dues in money, in kind, or in both; and the lands subject to *champart*, a charge proportioned, at a fixed rate, to the harvest. It will be observed that the *agrarium* or *champart*, a system practised under the Romans and Merovingians but not much in Carolingian times, came once again into use after the eleventh century. It seems, however, to have been less favoured than the *censive*.

1. *Rent Tenure*. This is the term used today, but the Middle Ages spoke of *censive, hostise* or *tenure en vilainage* (although in England this last expression was reserved for the holdings of serfs). This was the most typical kind of tenure. While the institution of the *manse* was based on oral tradition, the *censive* originated first as a collective contract, and subsequently as an individual *written* contract, of which tens of thousands of copies survive in the archives, especially after the years 1200–50.

Since the *censive* was a tenure, it was not property in the Roman sense, and until the French Revolution two forms of complementary rights coexisted in connection with it, exactly as with the fiefs: the right of the *domaine éminent* (in Guyenne, the right of *Senhoria*), which was to the advantage of the rural lord; and the right of the *domaine utile*, which was to the advantage of the tenant. After the eleventh and twelfth centuries the *domaine utile* generally became the more common, as in the case of fiefs.

The *eminent* rights, which represented fairly heavy charges, usually belonged both to landed lordship and bannal lordship. Some of them were specified in the *bail à cens*, the first in importance being the rent. The others, which were not stipulated, were based on prevailing local custom. They were all charges or impositions of an economic kind (dues and, in some instances, certain obligations of service still in existence), while to these were added judicial obligations, since the lord had at the very least all legal rights both in the property- and lower-courts.

Certain variations may be noted. Here are two examples, one taken from a province in the *pays d'Oil* (the Ile-de-France), and one from the *pays d'Oc* (the region of Bordeaux). The comparison illustrates a significant difference in terminology. In Guyenne, as very often in the Midi, the vocabulary of rural lordship resembled that of the fief. *Bail à fief* is used to describe the grant of a peasant tenure. In the Ile-de-France, on the contrary, and in many northern regions, there was a clear distinction: the expression *bail à cens* and others similar, were current.

The growing changes in the status of this 'copyhold' tenure, apart from chronological irregularities here and there, ran parallel to those occurring in the fief. There was mainly involved, after the eleventh century, a movement in the direction of perpetuity, right of inheritance, and liberty to alienate the tenure: these tendencies were to reach fulfilment at dates more or less variable.

In the eleventh century grants were still only made for life or for a short period, generally speaking. This is what was done, for example, by the abbey of Saint-Denis or by the chapter of Notre-Dame de Paris, when they had to let lands on condition of clearing them of timber. But the interests of both parties, and not simply of one, as in feudal conditions, were soon to induce these lords to make grants in perpetuity. How were they to attract pioneers, how keep them on the spot and induce them to build themselves houses if, on the death of the father, the new holding did not pass to his children? This was understood by many lords and recognized in many charters. Even more than in the case of fiefs, bargains between the lord and the heirs led to recognition of an hereditary right, which, as one might expect, was followed by recognition of heredity in law. The heirs, direct and later even indirect, requested a renewal of the grant, and this was generally accorded. As early as the first half of the twelfth century the decisive step was taken in the Ile-de-France with the appearance of grants of copyhold 'for ever'. In the next century, grants in perpetuity were to become the rule and those conceded for a limited time, which would be called leases today, were the exception. With some delay, by comparison with the Paris region – where such changes took place more quickly than elsewhere – the same process has been observed in most regions. Right of inheritance and perpetuity of copyhold tenures accorded much better with the logic of things than when the same issues were involved in feudal conditions, where the *intuitus personae* was the important consideration.

The lord found it all the more to his interest to agree to a new grant, first for life and later on a permanent basis, since the heirs would offer him payment for it. Custom transformed this payment into a succession-tax, similar to the *relief* paid by the heirs of a vassal. Such payments, indeed, were often called *reliefs* (*relevationes*, and also described as *relevamentum*). After the end of the twelfth century, it became the custom of Paris to cease to make this due a necessary condition for perpetuity of tenure. The grant in itself had become hereditary; or else the *relief* became voluntary, as in the region of Namur; or it was replaced by a simple tax in recognition of the holding of the tenure. The *seizin* in the Paris region amounted only to twelve deniers. It had become no more than a means of making the heirs recognize the lord's eminent right over the land.

As in the matter of fiefs, the right to alienate a copyhold was won belatedly. Even in such regions as the Ile-de-France, where custom particularly favoured the tenant, the holders of many such tenures in the years following 1150 were still forbidden to dispose of their land, either freely or in return for payment, although this prohibition was sometimes modified in the event of a sale or a gift to someone from outside the lordship. But such restrictions could not survive very long in an age when men and goods had become very mobile. As this feature of life was particularly marked in the Ile-de-France, freedom to dispose of the holding was to become complete before 1250. There had evidently been an intermediate stage, when there had been bargaining and the lord had received some payment by way of compensation.

What allowed the tenure to become fully transferable was the right, universally recognized as belonging to the lord, to raise a tax whenever the tenure changed hands, freely or in return for payment. But in the case of a free transfer, the new holder had to pay only the succession-due, or the *seizin*, which amounted to very little or even nothing. If the tenure was sold, one had to pay, apart from this symbolic due, a fairly heavy tax assessed in proportion to the value of the land: 8·33 per cent in the Ile-de-France, 12·50 per cent in the Bordeaux region. Such taxes were called *lods et ventes* in the region of Paris, and often *ventes* and *services* elsewhere.

Medieval law never regarded the right to inherit, or even the completion of a written contract, as sufficient for the new tenant in legal possession. A ceremony was needed – very simple in point of fact, and reminding one of investiture in a fief, though without the solemnity of that occasion. It was the Paris *ensaisinement*, the Gascon *investiture*, the *dévêture-vêture* around Namur, and so on; consisting in an oral declaration by the lord or his representative and the handing over of a symbolical object, usually a piece of straw. It was sometimes a mere formality, as in the Paris region, where the right of the lord to recover the tenure was not recognized. In the region of Bordeaux, however, he enjoyed the right of *retrait censuel*, which meant that, if asked to grant *investiture*, he could in reply mark disapproval of a transfer by increasing a fine, and himself resume possession of the tenure by reimbursing the purchaser. The principal object here, as in the matter of fiefs, was to prevent any concealment of the real price. On the other hand, since the right of *retrait lignager* was in force almost everywhere, the peasant could also prevent a piece of land from being sold to a stranger outside the family.

The grant of a tenure for rent had been concluded, in the early period, before the court of the local lord, but more and more often, as the jurisdiction of the prince or the king was enlarged, before a judge representing the count, the duke or the king, as the case might be. Rented tenure was distinguished by one feature: the owner would owe an annual fee in the form of a small sum of money (generally a few *deniers*, sometimes only a few *sous*) or a due in kind, also assessed at a permanent figure, or a little of both. This sum (paid in rent or kind) represented a due recognized as a perquisite of lordship. In the Ile-de-France, where the vocabulary of seigneurial courts was more strictly judicial, one reads of *chef cens*, of *fonds de terre* or of *menu cens*. The vocabulary was less adequate in the Midi where, moreover, the quit-rent was sometimes omitted. Where it was due, as in the Bordeaux country, *esporle* (from two to twelve deniers) was the term used. *Esporler* a person was to recognize that you were his tenant.

It is doubtful whether the rent was anything like the same figure as that of the rental value of the land when the grant had first been made. In the thirteenth century the rent fixed was always very much lower than the rental value, as Genicot's calculations in respect of the Namur region have shown. But the lord mainly counted on filling his purse from other sources, such as those derived from the right of ban, or from the money due when properties changed hands. Was there any connection at all between the amount of the rent and the value of the property? In a single region the irregularity of the rate among various houses, lands, meadows, vineyards, and so on, appears disconcerting. This may be explained by the fact that the houses and lands had not been assessed at the same time, and that the rate must have varied from one period to another, even for properties of quite comparable value. One notices, however, that the rent for a house, a garden, a meadow or a vineyard, was frequently higher than that for a simple land allotment.

Except when a large area had been cleared for cultivation, or was parcelled out in lots, or escheated (in default of heirs), a grant in 'copyhold' rarely gave the peasant a completely rounded holding, but only one of its component parts, for example a house, a kitchen-garden, a piece of land or of vineyard, because the juridical unity of the tenure had disappeared at the same time as the *manse* and its subdivisions. Except in a few districts, like the region of Namur, where the rent continued in the thirteenth century to be levied on the whole of a 'quarter' (shared, it is true, between various owners but destined to remain the 'standard for dues' until the end of the Middle Ages) – except in such districts the due for each holding was assessed individually.

The contract stipulated that the *cens*, that is the rent, carried 'lods et ventes, saisine et *amende*'. This was because the rent gave the lord who conceded the tenure certain rights in law over the land. This formula recalls the two great prerogatives of the lord, the right of seizin and of sale, in case of changes of ownership, and also the right of levying a fine in case of non-payment of rent.

In the Ile-de-France the fine for such default, in the thirteenth century, was usually five Paris *sous*, a rate which was not modified subsequently. It was therefore a question of only a small sum, representing a quite mild means of coercion. But if the tenant was obdurate, the owner who had granted the holding could 'put his hand' on it by practising *saisie censuelle*. If it was a house, he would have the seals affixed, or the doors and windows removed. If it was a property not built on, he would proceed to the *brandonnement*, that is seizure of the crops whether cut or still standing. There was nothing specifically Parisian in all this; the practice existed in many regions. Often, too, custom permitted the seizure of furniture or some such moveables, though not in the Ile-de-France. But as the lord could not actually appropriate, for example, the harvest, *saisie censuelle* was not always effective. Hence custom admitted that this method of threatening seizure should be changed into *saisie définitive*. It was then called *commise* and was authorized after years of non-payment of rent.[1] In the thirteenth century it was still usually automatic, but was not always to remain so, as from the fourteenth century onward. In the Paris region, after the early 1300s, the landed lord was no longer able to effect the *commise, jure domini*. He would have to appeal to the high justicer to get him to 'decree' it. Then, if a tenant appeared in court to oppose the appeal, the *censive* would be assigned to him at the *chef-cens*, that is the highest rate of rental; or, it would be adjudged to the lord who was prosecuting him. Even if the latter were himself a high justicer, he would still have to proceed by way of a 'decree', but in

[1] It is interesting to compare these means of coercion with the means of which the feudal lord disposed, in dealing with unsatisfactory vassals.

his own court, so as to enable the opposing parties to make themselves known. The procedure had two objects: to protect the tenure as a patrimony of the family – for this was the point reached in 1300 and even earlier – and to defend the interests of the rent-payers[1] in regard to the lord because, by this time, as will be seen, payments of *rents* was seriously beginning to encumber the holdings.

Until the beginning of the fourteenth century the above procedure was rarely put into practice. If delays in payment were frequent, refusals were exceptional, since the rent was so small. On the other hand, when France was devastated by the Hundred Years' War, prosecutions for non-payment became more common. This applied also to 'decamping'. At a fairly early date tenants had asserted their right to abandon their heritage if they so wished, and the lord had agreed on condition that the peasant paid off any arrears and left the property in good condition and the fields under cultivation. A further condition required the lord to be warned in advance. Such 'abandonments' of holdings were naturally exceptional prior to the mid-fourteenth century, because available land was scarce. They became numerous during the Hundred Years' War. Tenants then 'decamped' without more ado, leaving the lord to face a *fait accompli*.

The other important prerogatives of lordship were *seizin* and, on occasion, control of sales. In the Ile-de-France, for example, within the week stipulated for a contract to 'sell', the contracting parties had to appear before the seigneurial court. The vendor declared to the provost, mayor or bailiff, as the case might be, that he was *disseizing* himself of the property to the benefit of the lord; he then asked the lord to give the buyer *seizin* of it, offering to remit to him the letters, or contract, of sale, as evidence of the price paid. After payment of the *seizin* fee and, in this case, the *lods et ventes*, the lord's officer gave the buyer *seizin* of the tenure

[1] *Rentiers*. This word normally means an annuitant, in receipt of an annual income. The context shows that the author is referring to the *censitaires* who paid rent. *Rentes* = rent, and is therefore synony mous with the *cens* (Translators). But it is also used to mean an annuity.

by handing him a straw and also the 'letters of seizin', setting out his tax liabilities.

2. *Tenure à Champart.* This kind of holding was less widespread and more short-lived. It varied a great deal from one region to another, certain districts, which contained many such tenures, maintaining them over a long period; in others there were fewer and they were more ephemeral. The term *campi pars,* meaning a share of the harvest, denoted that this tenure was encumbered by a due, proportionate to the size of the harvest. As the *champart* concerned cultivated land, synonyms like *terrage* were used in the greater part of northern France, and *agrière* (from the Latin, *ager*) in southern France. For vineyards, which were less frequently *tenures à champart,* the word *pressurage* was current in the Ile-de-France.

It was a purely rural tenure – whereas copyholds existed in towns as well as in the country – and its importance, even more than the copyhold, lay in connection with the clearing of forests. But there are fewer records in writing of this kind of tenure, because contracts of *champart* remained oral over a long period. It was, moreover, less current in ecclesiastical lordships than in lay ones, because there the tithes supplied the clergy with most of the agricultural produce which they needed. *Champart,* however, was practised in areas where the forests had been cleared, equally with other regions.

As a due proportioned to the size of the harvest, the *champart* on agricultural land was payable only every two years in districts where the rotation of crops was biennial, and every three years where it was triennial. It was collected every year on the meadow-lands, as along the Garonne, and in the vineyards around Bordeaux and in the Ile-de-France. It was not a matter of perpetual *métayage,* since the lord did not contribute to the cost of working or tillage. His agents, the *champarteurs,* limited themselves to collecting, on the spot, before any of the harvest was removed, a percentage of the hay, some sheaves after the wheat-harvest, and some barrels after the end of the grape-pressing.

The lord's quota varied a good deal from one region to another, hence the *champart* could be more or less onerous for the tenant. Usage in the Ile-de-France was again the most favourable for him. The lord's share varied from one sheaf out of nine to one out of fourteen, but usually one out of eleven or ten, like the tithe, the rate of which was always the same as that of the *champart*. The percentage for vineyards was sometimes much higher – one pot of wine out of three or four – but more often one out of nine or ten. But in the south-west, in this matter, as in many others, the tenant's lot was harder, since he usually owed one sheaf of wheat out of five, from twenty per cent to thirty-three per cent of the wine, from twenty-five per cent to thirty-three per cent of the hay, of the osier or the *aubarèdes* (willow-plantations). On the other hand, in Lotharingia, a peasant who was subject to *champart*, which rarely happened, owed still less than his contemporary of the Ile-de-France – only one sheaf out of twelve or fifteen.

As regards the peasants' rights over his tenure, and the lord's rights, lands in *champart* were subject to the same rule as those for rental tenure.

3. *The Other Kinds of Tenure*. In addition to the two kinds which have been described, others appeared or continued to obtain. Some of them were not held in perpetuity and were even contracts for hiring out. The *libellus*[1] of the early Middle Ages remained in current use, while the *emphyteusis* of Roman law was widespread in Mediterranean lands, especially in Italy. Another kind of temporary tenancy was the *ferme muable* in the Norman district of Neubourg.

A curious form of tenure to be considered apart was the *bail à complant*. Appearing in France from as early as Carolingian times and surviving even today in a few districts, it became current from the ninth century in wine-growing regions. During the first five years the tenant performed all the operations of culture, from the breaking up of the ground to the planting of the vine-stocks and their cultivation. After this period the vineyard was divided into two equal parts, one half being retained by the vine-grower as a tenure for life, or in full ownership, on condition of yielding as a due

[1] A charter or deed (Translators).

a quota of every harvest. But after the late twelfth century the portion retained by the tenant became increasingly larger than half the vineyard and was changed into a permanent tenure. This evolution of the holding shows how far the right of inheritance and the power to transfer a tenure were a natural growth.

4. *Dues other than those of the Domain.* Whatever the kind of tenure, there were always other dues: first and foremost the tithe, which the Church was almost the only institution to levy, since it had recovered a large part of the enfeoffed tithes; next, the taxes due for redemption from serfdom in certain cases, and all those connected with the power of ban which, though it had diminished, survived none the less into the thirteenth century.

The old arbitrary rights had not disappeared everywhere; some persisted in the region of Bordeaux. But they were very often fixed, 'subscribed'.[1] Instead of forced labour, poll-tax, and arbitrary dues under the ban, the tenant paid a permanently fixed sum. Other customary dues remained commonly in force, like the fixed dues called *droitures, coutumes, tauxements* and so on, which were levied either in money or in kind (bread, capons, eggs, etc.) or both in kind and money. The poll-tax was also '*abonné*', particularly in northern regions. In the Ile-de-France, following concerted movements by the peasantry, which the Crown sometimes backed up, the poll-tax was 'subscribed' (that is, fixed) after the period 1250–70. Instead of being, as formerly, irregular in amount and in the dates when it was levied, it was henceforth payable annually. Hence the peasant could foresee what his expenses would be in the coming year. As a basis for this '*abonnement*'[2] and in certain cases for other taxes, two methods were in use, both current round Paris. Either the sum due for every dwelling, field or vineyard was fixed once for all and recorded in the contract; or the total due by those peasants who were interested parties had to be

[1] *abonné*.

[2] =The fixing of a limit to the dues owing to a lord. From *borne*= a limit.

shared out annually among all the tenants. It then varied for each one since, when the total due for which the village had been assessed was fixed, its sharing out also varied according as the population of the lordship increased or decreased. In both instances it was nearly always the delegates of the rural community who proceeded in the matter, by collecting the fixed sums in the first case, and, in the second, by assessing the individual sums due and then collecting them. This usage raises the question of how far the peasant communities carried weight in their dealings with the lords. Little is known of this, from lack of records, but the peasants must have played an important part, at least where they were living in large villages.

If one asks what other charges encumbered the peasant's tenures in the thirteenth century in addition to those which he owed as a subject of the king or the prince, it will be shown that the only form of agricultural credit then current actually had the effect of increasing his liabilities. Tenures were dwindling in size in the thirteenth century, and the clearing of forest-land was coming to a halt, while the population was on the increase. Thus, even before the fourteenth century, there was a problem of survival for the rural masses. It became more acute as tenures were often subject to new charges. The price of land, every foot of which was fiercely disputed, was continually rising (as witness the higher profits drawn by the lord from the dues on transfer of property). In face of this rise in the price of land, peasants in straitened circumstances were tempted, even before 1200, to incur further debts; with the result that towards 1300 most of their tenures were subject not only to the rent and customary dues, but were also 'mortgaged' in return for an 'annuity'; that is, the peasants added to their liabilities, the giving up of their tenures as security for a *rente perpétuelle* – a kind of annuity.

The clergy and the burgesses, rather than professional money-lenders, acted as agents for this kind of credit. The practice of 'annuities', which had appeared in France towards the end of the twelfth century, came into universal use in the West after about 1250, for the tenure recognized as capable of being transferred, an indispensable condition for the concession of an 'annuity'.

This practice, which gave some relief to the tenant, could take two forms:

a. Annuities granted in perpetuity.[1] By this arrangement the tenant, who made the offer, handed over to the other party the usufruct of his holding. The latter then entered into possession of the land against payment to the former tenant of an annuity on the land, and he also had the obligation of paying the lord's dues. By this means peasants could round off their holdings, while the well-to-do, the clerics, burgesses and even nobles, who might acquire the tenures by inheritance, or more often by purchase, found this a good kind of investment. But it was not strictly a credit because the tenant had to give up his holding.

b. Annuities granted with usufruct.[2] In this arrangement, apart from its being a means of investment for holders of capital, there was a real kind of agricultural credit; it was the one in most frequent use. By this means the new owner, who had to pay the annuity, did not take over the produce of the holding, whilst he still allowed his creditor the right of collecting, 'in perpetuity', an annual amount ('*rente*') for the holding. This annual payment, as it might be called, was generally fixed at some figure between 5 per cent and 8·33 per cent of the property value.

The two kinds of contract had certain features in common: the annuity in both was permanent and represented an immediate credit. Customary law decided that this fixed payment, either in money or in kind, did not prejudice the lord's position. It was, in fact, necessary to reassure the lord, who at the outset had regarded this re-handling of the tenure with no friendly eye. For the second type of annuity, that is, where the peasant retained the usufruct, the law early recognized the lord's right to levy *lods et ventes*, since there was involved a partial alienation of the land, and it thus had a lower saleable value. For the first kind of contract, in which the peasant abandoned the usufruct, the lord long retained

[1] *bail à rente perpétuelle.*

[2] *constitution de rente.*

the right of authorizing or refusing the conclusion of such an agreement, though this was partly due to the language in use, for example in the Ile-de-France, where *rente* (annuity) was sometimes described as *cens* (rent). The lords, however, ceased to oppose these agreements in the Paris region well before 1300; they were recognized as enjoying the right not only of collecting the dues payable on the transfer of a holding, but of making use of the adage: '*cens sur cens ne vaut*'; so that an erstwhile tenant could never acquire *seigneurial* rights over a holding, that is reverse the feudal relationship.

It was in fact very often a lord, and not a burgess, who benefited from these annual payments. One significant example may be cited. Towards 1300 nearly all the tenures in the Ile-de-France were encumbered in this way, and usually to the advantage of the lord; because, at the time when the franchises were granted and the total payments agreed to, it had been the lord who advanced the funds to his own tenants. Only those peasant families in a comfortable position could have neglected this offer. In other words, the lord had taken back with one hand what he had just given with the other, and his grants for copyholds brought him in nearly as much as he had received before the concession of franchises.

The tenure of average size, small as it was and subject to renewed taxation, could not of itself support a peasant family; the latter had some cattle or swine to send to pasture in the lord's forest or on the fallows. The rustics were obliged to obtain additional resources by hiring themselves out at harvest-times on the *granges*, or by working as artisans or craftsmen. If the juridical status of the majority had improved, their economic situation, despite the prosperity of the age, was once again deteriorating.

PART FOUR

DIVERGENCIES BETWEEN THE EVOLUTION OF LORDSHIP AND THE EVOLUTION OF FEUDALISM

Fourteenth and Fifteenth Centuries

Chapter 6

DECLINE AND RECOVERY OF RURAL LORDSHIP[1]

I. DECLINE OF LORDSHIP AND LIMITS OF THE DECLINE (FROM ABOUT 1300 TO ABOUT 1450)

The extent of the difficulties experienced throughout the fourteenth century is well known. There were economic troubles, aggravated in the countryside by the distortion of prices in general and the collapse of prices for cereals, while other costs continued to rise. There were demographic difficulties, because not only was the countryside now underpopulated, but labour was in short supply and farm wages had gone up. There were also political and military troubles, especially in France, owing to devastation and anarchy. All this could not but result in dire repercussions on the seigneurial system.

The extent and significance of these repercussions have, however, been subject to debate. In the view of Marxist historians like E. Kosminsky, the growing difficulties of the lord cannot be explained simply by reverses in the economic situation. (This had begun in the fourteenth century, when a period of expansion had been succeeded by more than a century of depression). Nor, in their opinion, was the trouble due to the decrease in population, or to wars and disturbances.

[1] In addition to the works already cited, see J. M. W. Bean, *The Estates of the Percy Family, 1416–1537*, Oxford Univ. Press, 1958. G. A. Holmes, *The Estates of the Higher Nobility in XIVth Century England*, Cambridge Univ. Press, 1957. *The Oxford History of England*, Vol. V (The XIVth Century, 1307–1399, by M. McKisack 1959), and Vol. VI (The XVth Century, 1399–1485, by E. F. Jacob, 1961).

For the Marxists there was no general decline in the rural economy, as most historians believe; but there was a collapse of the prosperity of the lordships which the Marxists incorrectly identify with feudalism. Movements of the labour-force took place, according to the Marxists, to the detriment of the lords but to the advantage of the peasants, and this in turn brought about renewed prosperity in the countryside in the second half of the fifteenth century.

It is very difficult to follow this interpretation of history. The 'decline'[1] (the word is Duby's) in the fortunes of the lords did not extend to the whole of western Europe. Even in those regions where it was most marked, the lords nearly always came into their own in the course of the fifteenth century.

A. *Difficulties Experienced by the Lordships: The Example of France*

The provinces where lordships appeared to suffer the sharpest decline were naturally those regions in which the effect of the war was added to the economic, demographic and social troubles. It was therefore in the first place a question of those parts of France which were the worst hit by the Hundred Years' War. Outside France, the regions which suffered from wars and disturbances were few in number; and in any case none of them underwent damage comparable with what was experienced in France.

The extent of the decline can be gauged from the fall in the yield from the *granges* (or *reserves,* as the personal domains were usually called), and from the rents. The former were of most concern to the lord's standard of living, the latter to the peasant's. But this decline was not continuous before the mid-fifteenth century, because periods of devastation alternated with periods of short-term reconstruction. The chronology of these periods, in the regions of Bordeaux and Toulouse, and in the Ile-de-France, is now known in detail.

As soon as a respite was in prospect, sometimes when danger was still threatening, lords and tenants tried to bring the land back into cultivation and to rebuild what had just been

[1] *Défaillance.*

sacked and ruined. Their courage is one of the outstanding features of the moral outlook of the end of the Middle Ages. The oral and documentary evidence on record confirms the extent of the ravages, the most serious of which were suffered by the lords' granges. These were often isolated and less easy to defend than the villages. The measure of their devastation can be found in the seigneurial accounts. Take, for example, the situation of the monastery of Saint-Denis, near Paris and in the heart of a devastated province. Between 1342 and 1343 and again between 1374 and 1375 (war having been interrupted for ten years), the receipts fell by fifty or sixty per cent, as much in money as in kind. All receipts, from whatever source, were equally reduced. This meant that the *granges* produced only a half or a third of the farm produce in the decade 1340–50, and that a third or a half of the tenures were abandoned or were occupied by peasants who were not solvent; a situation confirmed by the grants of land to new tenants – when any could be found! – grants which described the state of the holding for the purpose of rent assessment.

The lord had always possessed the right to recover a tenure which had been abandoned, if there were no heir to claim it, while the tenant had always disposed of the right of 'decamping', in which event the lord could re-assess the rent of a property which was without a legal tenant. But custom had sanctioned and formulated the procedure in force, in the event of seizure of a tenure subject to rent. The property had to be 'decreed' by whatever lord was high justicer in the region, in 'default of duties not performed and rents not paid'. After this, the lord had to wait for a certain time before declaring the property '*en criées*' – the expression used to mean 'before announcing it was to be put up for auction'; and it was obviously the highest bidder, the one who offered to pay the heaviest dues, who secured the holding. But what would happen if, one day, the tenant, who had been driven away by war, returned, or the heirs of that tenant? His 'decamping' had in general been a simple departure in fact, and not a deliberate and juridical abandonment. Strong pressure was exercised by the peasants who had remained on their holdings for the '*criées*' to be delayed for longer periods. Their former neighbours, or the heirs, might one day return, and they should then be able to recover their properties. The result was that in order to '*subhaster*'[1] properties which were vacant or ruined, the lords were encouraged to appeal to the power of the prince or the king; but this was not usual before the year 1450.

The work of bringing the land back into cultivation and of partially restoring the buildings, was greatly hindered by the difficulty of finding labourers willing to apply, at a time when the population had greatly decreased. There were occasional immigrants, particularly in the Bordeaux region; but it was usually the neighbours who took over the abandoned vineyards and paid the rent. In those provinces which had vineyards, like the Ile-de-France and Guyenne, the peasants did not much concern themselves with the abandoned huts and lands.

These attempts at restoration, during lulls in the warfare, were very backward-looking, since the lords were anxious to draw from the tenures which had been re-assessed and which represented only a part of the vacant properties, the same returns, in value and in composition, as before the war. They do not seem to have thought of unifying in one tenure the charges and dues on the cottages with those on the land or with those on the vineyards. They clung no doubt to the hope of finding purchasers for everything that had been abandoned; perhaps also they hoped to recover, in the way of receipts, the same amounts as before 1430. Although supply was much greater than demand, new purchasers rarely found the charges or other dues any lighter than formerly. The old charges no doubt still remained lower than the rented values, but these had gone down, following the decline in the property's market value. Moreover, it happened more often that the tenants were irregular in their payment of rents and other dues; all this added to the financial difficulties of the lord, who could rarely threaten defaulters with fines or seizure of their holdings.

[1] Sell legally, as by authority of a court, e.g. the lord's tribunal (Translators).

The greater part of a lord's resources continued to come from the *granges.* In regions where farming of the *grange* had been well established after about 1250, it remained as widespread as then, the lord still preserving the right to resume direct cultivation of his domain in the event of the farmer's defaulting or abandoning his task, while awaiting a new tenant. The sums received for farming, which are recorded in the accounts, tended to recover when there were attempts at partial reconstruction; but without ever reaching their pre-war levels. The *grange* of Saint-Denis at Tremblay affords an example. Before the war it had been farmed out for five hundred Paris pounds and eighty barrels of grain, half wheat and half oats. In 1368–69, at the beginning of the lull, two hundred and five pounds and thirty-nine barrels were charged. Towards 1400, after thirty years of relative calm, the figures rose to two hundred and seventy pounds and fifty barrels. Thus it is known that in 1404, about a few years before the resumption of disorder and warfare, the total receipts of the monastery of Saint-Denis still amounted to only half the level of 1340, or even less, when one recalls the monetary inflation which had taken place in the interval.

The resulting improvements from this temporary recovery were everywhere on a small scale. Yet there was no resignation to failure on the part of lords or peasants, although royal or princely taxation had drained country districts of capital of which they were sorely in need. Further, the results of all their efforts were to be annihilated during the last and most terrible phase of the Hundred Years' War, which began soon after 1410 and ended only in the period 1450–53.

This first half of the fifteenth century witnessed a real impoverishment of the seigneurs, matched by a further impoverishment of the peasants, already stricken. In order to maintain or restore their husbandry, lords and peasants had to face greater hardships than before. In the case of *granges* which had been farmed out, the forced abandonment by the farmers compelled the proprietors to resume, almost overnight, the direct exploitation of the land, while awaiting new tenant-farmers. Each time the land was raided and pillaged, the livestock had to be renewed and the farm-implements replenished; and the workers had to rebuild, as far as possible, what the soldiery or 'free companions' had demolished, both in the *granges* and in the peasant tenures. Though the reserves were rarely abandoned, very many tenures became 'vacant and ruined'.

A few examples may be given. In the Norman district of Neubourg the herds of swine belonging to the peasants, herds which fed in the forest of Neubourg, decreased by seventy-five per cent between 1397–8 and 1444–5. In the same half-century the remission of dues payable by tenants still in occupation but too poor to pay, and the 'unproductive' tenures, that is dues payable from abandoned holdings, went from three per cent to sixty-six per cent of the total of the seigneurial dues. In the Ile-de-France the same slump in receipts from the tenures resulted from the 'decampings', the general lack of resources or the ill-will of the tenants still in occupation. The lords had to 'moderate' the charges on the tenures still occupied, such decreases in rent and dues being agreed to 'for a time' or 'for always'. The new assessments, which were frequently conceded in spite of the difficult times, were evidently concluded on terms more favourable to the tenants: the rents and dues in money were reduced, while the poll-tax and the dues in kind were often not chargeable at all. In certain respects the Bordeaux country presents an exceptional case. The lords in that region also had to cut their losses, but they went further than many of their contemporaries in the 'defence of their traditional rights', and they were on the whole harsher in their dealings. Not only did the serfdom that survived continue to develop in the 'real' rather than the personal sense, but an attempt was made to tie the free tenants to the soil. Reductions in the dues were less ample and less numerous than in the north. It is true that farming out the land was coming into wide use in Guyenne, which had hitherto seen very little of it; hence the great lords' acceptance of redemption of dues by work on the reserves.

The 'exhaustion of the seigneurial resources [in France] was therefore', writes Duby, 'in great part the result of the war'. But not exclusively so. If, in respect of France, one stresses the consequences of the war and the collapse of revenues, it must be pointed out that in many regions outside France which had been spared the devastation of civil or foreign war the scope and fortunes of lordship also suffered a decline. The inference is, that the collapse in revenues is rather to be imputed to the economic difficulties of the age and the decrease in population. Thus in England the manorial revenues frequently dwindled by more than a third between 1345 or 1370 and about 1450. The same thing happened in Germany, where the collapse sometimes amounted to a loss of two-thirds of the former level, on the reserves as well as on the tenures.

A fundamental problem for the historian is to discover what happened to the seigneurial fortunes, to the patrimonies as a whole. Did the decrease in their income lead the lords to cut into, or even liquidate, their capital in land, which was now bringing in so little and causing so much trouble?

The fate of the seigneurial estates depended in the first place on the master's personality, on his qualities or his weakness. If such and such a lord, lay or clerical, were a very powerful man in the State or the Church, if he were a good administrator, his estate or that of his community would resist the depression. One must distinguish, moveover, between fortunes of a moderate kind and the very great estates. Most historians think that the ecclesiastical lordships and those belonging to the great families were most successful in meeting the shock. This was unquestionably the case for the most important temporalities. No powerful monastery or cathedral chapter was led seriously to reduce its landed properties. Many historians now agree that the principal lay estates also held their ground, contrary to M. Postan's view. Certainly, in England the great families decreased in number, but they concentrated their properties and sometimes succeeded in further increasing their wealth because they acquired great sums of money from their personal association with the kings, and from positions of power in the State. It has long been believed that the situation was quite different in France, because historians have been too much obsessed by the Hundred Years' War and its possible effects; they have spoken to excess of a 'decline of the nobility' and a 'rise of the bourgeoisie'. But the authors of a few careful regional studies have attempted to prove that this is incorrect. In the Ile-de-France the great lay estates were largely successful in resisting the effects of the war and the economic difficulties, the more so as the lords who owned them were living mainly on the emoluments they received as great functionaries, civil or otherwise, of the Crown. They did not have to depend for a living on the receipts from their estates. Why then should they find it necessary to liquidate their fortunes? The matter is important, because the power of the king – or of the princes – by increasing the corps of their 'officers', that is, their functionaries, rescued a number of lordships from decline or disaster. Here was a curious reversal of the situation: the lordships had formerly confirmed their powers at the expense of the Crown, and now it was the Crown which came to their aid!

It was rather 'the middle range of incomes which showed the clearest signs of straitened circumstances'. (Duby, Genicot). Without going so far as to deny this, as Postan does, one should at least draw certain distinctions. The capacity of estates of average importance to maintain themselves varied from one region to another, and it was strongest in those provinces where a centre of royal or princely power could offer public office to a fairly large number of nobles. Here again, the income of some of the lordships, for example, those held by knights, served no more than to make up the balance. To sum up: except in Italy, where the cities dominated their *contadi,* there was strictly speaking no significant bourgeois invasion of landed ownership.

As for the poorest of the nobles, 'the most closely involved in the peasants' way of life', they could get a precarious living whilst serving in the army in time of war. For the rest, they were obliged to manage more carefully their meagre lands, which they could not have sacrificed without losing all their income.

Historians have readily stressed the rapidity of the change in the nobles' attitude to life, a change which they point out as taking place from the thirteenth century onward. The lords were not, as seen above, drawing all their resources from their lands. It is true that 'a great number of the nobles, of the regular clergy and of Church dignitaries were living less frequently at this time in their country homes' (Duby). The offices which many of them held necessitated prolonged absences. They had to live in the cities for a great part of the time, and this appeared less unpleasant to the northern nobles than formerly. The clergy, too, owing to the increased centralization of the Church, devoted less time to their domains. But did this entail a transformation in the mental outlook of lay and clerical lords, a change of attitude which is described as 'profoundly modifying the methods of management or exploitation'? This does not seem to have been the case, or at least only to a small extent. The lords may well have felt, however mistakenly, that the various difficulties which they were experiencing were transitory. The tradition had always been that 'the landed proprietor . . . should watch his harvests ripen, his flocks grow in number, and should drink the wine of his vineyard' (Duby). Psychological resistance was 'a powerful factor for stability'. Thus the seigneurial reserves very often held their own under the storm. There was at times a reduction in the area of land cultivated, in England before 1340, in France from about 1350 to 1450; this also applied to the vineyards. This slight reduction in the size of the *granges* – part of a 'movement of very long duration' – can be explained by economic conditions in England, the sharp decline in the price of cereals and other commodities, and a rise in wage-rates owing to the diminished numbers of agricultural workers. In France it was mainly due to the wars. Since this reduction was only slight, the West was not lacking, towards 1450, as earlier towards 1300, in reserves of considerable dimensions. In England, in France and elsewhere, *granges* of about 100 hectares (250 acres) and more were not uncommon. It was the exception to have estates entirely parcelled out; though these existed in a few regions, as Brandenburg, in the period 1350–90.

The actual development of the reserves was not thrown into any great confusion. It was simply that the management of these estates became less efficient in various countries, especially after 1380, to the advantage of 'farming out' in northern districts and of *métayage*[1] in the south. England witnessed a renewal of farming after the mid-fourteenth century. Almost everywhere the lords farmed out their great reserves, either to a single tenant or to several. Thus between 1390 and 1420 the Archbishop of Canterbury let out for rent forty manors, including their meadows, mills, marshes and 'parks'.

The reasons put forward to explain this first rise of the practice of 'farming-out' on the Continent in the thirteenth century remain valid. It is therefore a mistake to regard the farming out of estates as a desperate solution adopted by lords who – if this were true – would then have abandoned the management of their lands and given up much of their control. On the contrary, every allocation of lands was the outcome of lengthy bargaining; for example, by Canterbury Cathedral. But two additional causes probably contributed to this second expansion of the farming system. Owing to the depopulation of the countryside, those tenants who were already fairly well-to-do were able to take out leases of the deserted lands, make a good profit, and so find it possible to assume the lordship of a large estate. On the other hand, the general decrease in the population naturally reduced the labour-force and automatically pushed up wages. It has been observed that the only parts of Europe where direct management of the domain remained very active – in eastern and south-western Germany and northern Italy – were those where the authorities, of the prince or the city, had taken 'measures sufficiently energetic to maintain conditions of employment favourable to the masters' (Duby).

One must conclude that the new extension of the farming and *métayage* systems, in short, the changes in methods of managing the reserves, were neither cause nor consequence of a weakening of lordship. This weakening was almost everywhere temporary; apart from this, any decline was not at all the rule.

B. Strength of the Lordships in the South and East

In the south of Europe lordship remained generally flourish-

[1] 'Share-cropping' is the modern American term (Translators).

ing and even made further progress. In northern Italy and in Tuscany the mountain lordships retained their somewhat outmoded characteristics. The system of cultivating the reserves by means of forced labour was often maintained without any major change. On the hill-slopes and on the plains agriculture progressed, the wealth of the cities encouraging some expansion in the management of estates. The bonds between town and country, already closer than in other thirteenth-century lands, were still further strengthened after 1300 or 1350. The Tuscan lords were often townsmen, either nobles who had come at some time in the past to live in the city, or burgesses who had bought estates, and they proceeded to 'urbanize the country districts' of the *contado*, procuring capital for their development, outlets for market-produce, and offering the peasants easier kinds of contract. But it is not clear if these townsmen applied to the management of their lands the spirit of initiative which they displayed in their commercial dealings; in other words, if they fostered agriculture while maintaining the outlook of townsmen, or if they acquired or preserved the modes of thought and action of the old landed nobility. What is certain is that the reserves brought in, as did the rents and dues, as much as or more than, in former times. And everywhere *mezzadria* (= *métayage*) came into further use in and after the fourteenth century.

In southern Italy and in the greater part of the Iberian peninsula the great lordships were even more flourishing. At an increasing pace, after the end of the thirteenth century, vast *latifundi* – estates huge by comparison with the great lordships in France – were created and extended. This phenomenon can be explained very largely by political factors. In Sicily and southern Italy the struggle between the Angevins and the Aragonese resulted in the disappearance of the smaller vassals and the concentration of lordships in fewer hands. The new 'barons' proved hard masters, closing their forests to access by the peasants and imposing on the latter exactions connected with the ban. All this was to provoke, even before 1450, an exodus from the countryside and peasant revolts, further provoked by the heavy burden of royal taxation. This process, by which the lordships, and also the reserves, increased in size, had begun very early and was connected with the eleventh-century reconquest of lands from the Mohammedans. In Spain and Portugal the political situation produced similar results. Internal wars and dynastic quarrels forced the kings to surround themselves with a party devoted to their cause, and whose services had to be handsomely rewarded. During the second half of the fourteenth century, this state of affairs permitted the formation and continual strengthening of territorial oligarchies, composed of the men who were soon to be called the Grandees of Castille (*Los Grandes de Castilla*). Once calm was restored, these immense estates, which were already closely concentrated, were further enlarged. The kings could not, in default of any counter-support, resist the pressure of the grandees, the bourgeoisie being still without power and not sufficiently numerous. One must hasten to add that the reasons for these changes were not exclusively political. The rise in power of the Iberian lords was due also to changes in the rural economy. The estate-managers abandoned some of the cultivated fields and devoted themselves to the rearing of stock, which were driven in summer to the mountain pastures.[1]

There remains the case of eastern Germany, which was still being colonized. As there was in that part of the country a very marked decrease in population, the lords were able to carve out for themselves vast domains from the lands deserted by the peasants. One of the best known examples is connected with Brandenburg. Towards 1375 the reserves owned by the country squires were still far less extensive than the land held by the peasants. The latter were not subject to forced labour, since the reserves were tilled by free agricultural workers. But during the last quarter of the fourteenth century, the population continued to decrease, while more land was deserted, which made it possible for the lords to add this land to their reserves. But how could they develop these larger reserves at a time when paid labour was becoming scarcer? The Brandenburg squires had one means of action at their disposal. The central government had lost all effective

[1] The system of *transhumance* still commonly practised in the Alps (Translators).

power and from this fact the aristocrats could draw advantages similar to those which their predecessors had won during the decay of Carolingian power. The prince allowed the nobles to take possession of 'royal' rights and recognized the lords, lay and spiritual, as having a kind of new right of ban. Hence the appearance of new exactions and of the 'second' serfdom. The peasantry of eastern Germany, who had formerly been the most free in the whole of the West, now found themselves tied to the soil and forced to render heavy services in labour on the reserves, which were being extended. Like the *latifundi* of southern Europe, the 'vast agricultural enterprises' established in eastern Germany were to prosper for centuries. But they needed a larger labour-force because they were not devoted, as in Spain, to the rearing of cattle or sheep, which involved changing their pasture grounds every summer. Labour was, however, provided by fresh waves of colonists from the west.

In order better to understand the meaning of the consolidation, and even of the progress, of rural lordships in the various countries that have been reviewed, one must revert to their causes. They were in part due, according to the regions affected, to the lack of a dominant central authority and to disturbances of various kinds. But if one asks whether the prosperity of these lordships in the east and in southern Europe was simply the outcome of a more backward development than elsewhere, and whether it was destined, for that reason, not to last for long, the answer is that the real causes were economic. It was the increase in the rearing of livestock which was to assure a long life for the vast lordships in these countries.

II. THE RESURGENCE, AND NEW DEVELOPMENTS IN THE POWERS OF THE SEIGNEURS IN THE SECOND HALF OF THE FIFTEENTH CENTURY

The decline of these powers, where it had taken place, had not been definitive. In France it had been partly caused by the war. But the major cause, everywhere except in France, was the great economic depression. However, at varying dates, generally about the middle of the fifteenth century, the depression was to end, thus enabling the lords to make a new start. All traces of past difficulties did not wholly disappear. In England, for example, the lot of the peasants was still difficult; although there is as yet no agreement among historians as to whether certain *cottagers* were promoted to the higher rank of householder, virgater, small landholder, or semi-virgater[1]; or whether the rural community was divided by the simultaneous growth at the two extremes of the social spectrum, of a group of '*koulaks*'[2] at one end and an overgrown proletariat at the other. The poor peasants would have become poorer, but the prosperous peasants would have been able to take possession of any available lands, if such a split in the peasant ranks had in fact taken place. One thing alone seems certain in England and elsewhere: the village 'cocks of the roost' carried more weight and were to acquire still more in the second half of the fifteenth century, except in southern Europe and eastern Germany, as shown above.

A. Agricultural Recovery in France

Though rural life had never been interrupted, even when most disturbed, several provinces had been very badly devastated, and the task of all and sundry, whether lords or peasants, proved extremely heavy.

Were the lords still members of the old nobility, or had they often been supplanted by the burgesses? Two preliminary observations must be made. For has it been definitely shown that the nobles were poor administrators? And was the gap between nobles and burgesses as wide as has been alleged? It is impossible to dogmatize and return an affirmative answer to the first question, which has not been well studied, or to the second. Within the great royal or princely administrations, the 'officers', as is known, were recruited both from among the nobles and from the upper bourgeoisie. The same system often prevailed on the regional level. Now

[1] A *'virgate'* was normally about thirty acres, the fourth part of a hide; but it could vary between ten and eighty acres (Translators).

[2] Rich Russian peasants (Translators).

it was this new group of men, called the *notables,* who owned the finest rural lordships. Experienced in business and lacking neither in capital nor in useful connections, they were able to proceed fairly rapidly, in favoured regions, with the work of bringing the land back into cultivation and restoring the prosperity of the lordships.

But the *notables* were not the only members of the old nobility. The latter also included the clergy and the minor nobility. As regards the clergy, it has long been supposed that the poor recruitment of the religious houses from the time of Charles VII, and still more under Louis XI, had had a disastrous effect on the temporalities. This should not be exaggerated, as the history of the Ile-de-France bears witness. It was rare that prelates so mismanaged their affairs as to put at risk the mainstay of their wealth. Moreover, the real administrators of these estates were not the abbots and bishops, but jurists, known as '*pensionnaires*', that is, salaried officers. These men, like many of the prelates, came from families of notables. Finally, in the case of the minor nobility, who held no permanent public office, it will be agreed that they had fewer adequate means of successfully restoring their lordships and recovering their rights over the peasants. But it does not appear that there was any far-reaching upheaval. Those fortunes which did suffer decayed only slowly, and the great notables or, more frequently, since it was a question of fairly unimportant lordships, the 'gentlemen of the robe' in the secondary jurisdictions, were only beginning to buy their lands from impecunious knights. Hence there was no bourgeois invasion at the expense of old noble families which can be described as widespread.

Since the ranks of the nobility received no great renewal from below, it is not a matter for surprise that the lords' behaviour was markedly conservative. The lords – even those who were laymen – were not always short of adequate capital; far from it. They not only invested in their reserves, they even advanced money to their old tenants and to the newcomers, for in certain devastated regions immigration assumed great proportions. Such loans enabled the peasants to bring their tenures back into cultivation. This new resurgence of lordship found the conditions most favourable to its purpose only rather late, in the second half of the fifteenth century, from the time when a further rise in the population was so to increase the demand for land as to render the offer more and more advantageous to the lord who made it.

It is not necessary here to go into details about the new wave of forest-clearing in the provinces most affected by wars. It must only be recalled that the start and completion of this new work of land-clearing varied from one region to another, and, inside the same region, from district to district. In a general way, the renewal of agricultural activity took place, as was natural, earlier and more quickly in the regions most favoured by nature, and where the power and wealth of the lords and a growing population facilitated the task.

As for the tenures, they continued to share only to a small extent in the seigneurial prosperity. But from the social point of view they were very important because they provided sustenance and a living for the majority of those Frenchmen who remained peasants. In this connection two problems are outstanding. How were the lords able to re-let property which had apparently been abandoned by their former tenants? What had become of the dues, in money or kind, formerly levied on the tenures, whether or not these dues were still owing from the former tenants?

After the restoration to order, legal obstacles arose in the case of a lord wishing to grant to a peasant a tenure which had been deserted, for very few former tenants had 'decamped' according to the legal forms. It was not known how many of the unoccupied tenures in 'copyhold' had been definitely abandoned, and whether they were indeed vacant and without occupiers. While some of the peasants were dead, others, or their heirs, might one day return. Could the holdings which were in fact vacant be once again conceded by the lord to new tenants? Or, on the contrary, if such tenures had been granted in perpetuity, did that fact exclude their being restored and recultivated? Since the fourteenth century at least, in the Ile-de-France, a lord could no longer recover possession of a deserted tenure *jure dominii*, but was obliged to follow the procedure of obtaining a 'decree', involving the '*criées*', that is an announcement of vacancy. This had already been the custom at the time of partial restoration of tenures during the wars. But after the period 1445–50 the problem became of much greater concern. Faced with the vast number of properties to be announced as vacant, the lords in general thought it best to seek the help of the Crown. This was a new development because, save in the matter of private lawcourts whose functions were being steadily encroached on by the monarch, kings had never, since the Carolingians, been involved in problems of lordship except as they concerned the status of the peasants. Charles VII now took action, but only slowly, since many of his special enactments date only from 1447; thus his declaration authorising the high justicers of the kingdom to put deserted properties on the open market. In the Ile-de-France, at least, after six years during which agriculture had been slowly recovering, the lords found themselves confronted by discontented rural communities who were hostile to the system of 'decree' and 'subhastation'.[1] Hence Charles VII and Louis XI were obliged to issue new orders, general and particular, at more frequent intervals, over a period of some thirty years. One should add that the power of the lords began to be threatened not only by the continuing ill-will of the village communities, but also by the monarchy, eager to increase its own power. By virtue of the old adage, 'no land without a lord' current in northern France, the king could arrogate to himself the 'eminent' lordship of lands to which no lord had stated a claim. Thus Charles VII and Louis XI caused enquiries to be made in all quarters affecting the rights which the lords alleged that they possessed in respect of vacant properties; and the king then proceeded to 'announce' publicly, to his own advantage, those properties which were 'uninhabited or vacant'. In other words, the rural lords were caught between two fires, the discontent of peasants who had remained on their tenures, and the encroachments of the Valois dynasty. It was urgent to have the unoccupied lands 'decreed' as such by the high justicers.

The conditions fixed by the kings for the *mises aux criées*, that is the public announcement of vacant tenures, varied in time and place. Generally speaking, they were as follows: in conformity with customary law, as it prevailed in the area in question, the lord might proceed to four *criées*, one every fortnight. There was no question as yet of putting up the land for auction, but simply of announcing the vacancy four times. In the year following the last of the *criées*, the person concerned could declare the rights which he claimed over one or other of the properties announced, on condition of paying the dues, if successful; in default of this, under pain of foreclosure. After this delay, and if no one had appeared to prove any counter-claim, the lord could grant the unclaimed tenures in perpetuity. But although, in certain instances, the new purchaser was secure against any further claimant, in others, the king laid down, for example in a decree in favour of the chapter of Notre-Dame de Paris, that the former tenants should still have two years in which to claim possession on condition of paying all the arrears and of reimbursing the evicted purchaser for the expenses which he had incurred. But this last condition was early omitted, since it was too discouraging to eventual purchasers.

What was the fate, after the mid-fourteenth century, of the various dues chargeable on the tenures? As the number of 'huts', fields and vineyards which were offered were, at the outset, much greater than the demand, there was frequently a marked fall in the dues assessed in relation to the pre-war level or to the first years of the century, while the dues in kind were more and more replaced by fixed taxes in money. 'Copyhold' tenure became more widespread, and *champart* tended to fall into disuse – no doubt because the latter did not encourage the holder to clear the land, whereas a tax in money could be exacted even if the tenure remained neglected. Lastly, the amount of the dues chargeable was fixed at the lowest level in each region, the original tenants now paying only as much as the newcomers. It was only towards 1500 that the charges on the tenures again began to rise, obviously because offers of land were fewer, while demand was increasing in consequence of the increasing population of nearly all parts of the country.

The great impetus of agricultural recovery obviously gave a new lease of life to the rural lordships. But it also favoured a better standard of living for the peasantry. The decrease in rent was not the only concession which the lord had had to make. He also accepted, at a moderate price, the annulment of many of the dues which had not so far been *abonnés,* for example, those still chargeable under the ban. And where in former times the peasants had not received long-term grants of tenure, these were now lengthened. Contracts became either perpetual or for the term of two or three lifetimes – as witness the colloquies of Quercy and the *baillées à trois têtes* (grants for three lifetimes) of Maine. The Roman *emphyteosis,*[1] which had formerly been valid for a short period – from nine to twenty-seven years – became a perpetual lease, and now came into wide use in Languedoc and Provence. Did not all this mean that in fact the return to a healthy agricultural policy accompanied a further decimation of seigneurial power rather than any increase of it? The answer is in the negative. The lord's profits were of necessity reduced, but the seigneurial dues were now collected more strictly and defaulters were prosecuted. There remained, moreover, numerous rights which had fallen into oblivion owing to the wars, the poll-tax for example, and these dues the lords contrived once again to levy. The administration of the lordships seems to have improved; it became more efficient and more probing. Some reassertion of lordly privilege did indeed take place and kept back the improvement in agriculture; while available tenures became gradually more rare, and therefore more expensive, for peasants desiring land. Again, the size of rural holdings was progressively reduced, mainly in prosperous regions; and the beginning of the sixteenth century heralded a new age of impoverishment in several provinces, like the Ile-de-France, so that once again the lord was able to impose harder conditions for the lands which he rented out, and subsequently royal or princely taxation was regularly added to the burden of seigneurial dues and became progressively heavier in most parts of the West. The peasant was forced to lay aside twice the earlier amount of money or produce, for the king as well as for the lord, and

[1] A tenure in which the tenant enjoyed the usufruct (in classical Latin spelt 'emphyteusis') (Translators).

not simply for the advantage of the latter, as had so long been the case.

The *granges*, which the lords had endeavoured to maintain in production, continued to provide their principal resources. But the yield had fallen very low during the first half of the fifteenth century. The freebooters had made a point of pillaging them and they had suffered more damage than the peasant tenures. In order to find small nobles who would administer their lands, merchants to handle the produce and, above all, labourers to work for them, the lords who had previously farmed out their estates, including the reserves, *en bloc*, and, with some exceptions, handed over their seigneurial rights, now divided their estates among their tenants, either on a part-time basis or in perpetuity. This did not entail any lack of control in general management, because the lord now exercised stricter supervision, and methods of accountancy were improving.

The practice of farming out estates had become the rule rather than the exception, for example in upper Normandy and even in some of the southern regions, like the Bordeaux country. It is noteworthy that the contracts for tenures now included larger consignments of grain, indicating that the lord had by no means lost interest in his lands, and that, as in the past, he meant to live on his own produce and sell the surplus. 'Annuitants' were not more numerous than they had been in the thirteenth century.

The picture one has of the countryside in 1500 reflects the final stages of a return to prosperity, particularly on the part of the lords. Compared with the standards obtaining in 1430, 1440 and 1450, their position had improved considerably. Even so, it remained, towards 1500, very much below the peak years between 1300 and 1340. The rents and other dues brought in much less, as did most of the seigneurial rights. The reserves furnished less food and money. In 1519–20 the monetary receipts of the abbey of Saint-Denis barely reached the figure of 20,000 Paris pounds, as compared with under 15,000 towards the year 1400, but with 30,000 pounds before the wars. In addition, there had been inflation in the interval and money had now indubitably lost about half of its purchasing power. For receipts in kind a similar devaluation was apparent.

Notwithstanding these circumstances, at the beginning of the sixteenth century land had once again become a good investment in France. In general, the importance of this fact has not been sufficiently taken into account, but it affords an explanation of the following facts: viz. if the commercial bourgeoisie tended to invest little of their capital in land, this was because land for them yielded little return. On the other hand, if the nobles did not sell as much landed property, as alleged, to city business men, it was because the latter made no pressing requests for it. It is thus quite possibly for these reasons, negative as they appear, that most of the small estates, and those of average size, held their own. In fact the so-called 'seigneurial reaction' was perhaps only a phenomenon affecting the great patrimonies.

B. Changes in the Rural Economy, and the New and Important Role of the Lord

In certain regions of the West, sometimes even in France, the changing status of lordship, with other circumstances, led to changes of the economy. The lords and also the peasants had grasped the fact that other kinds of produce could be more profitable than grain. Hence the great landowners often reduced the area for corn-growing and so brought about a depopulation of the villages. This movement took place most markedly in England and in the Mediterranean countries (though not in northern and central Italy), where the great increase in stock-rearing affected the extent and the management of the property owned by the lord. In England it was from the fourteenth to the nineteenth century that the 'open field' system gave way to that of enclosed fields, and this change began to take effect very rapidly in the fifteenth century. The system entailed enclosing the whole area in a single block, leading the peasants to abandon the villages, since the land was being converted into pasturage. English historians like W. H. Beresford and R. H. Hilton explain this success of the lords by the declining lack of community-feeling on the part of the villagers. The lord of the manor was able to 'liquidate' the peasants by appropriating their common lands, and also farming out to some wool-merchant or butcher his reserve-domain, which had been excessively enlarged and completely turned over into pasturage. By degrees the tenants, thus deprived of the right of pasture on the commons, had to leave their holdings, and the small enclosures between the strips tilled by the tenants were replaced by a single enclosure comprising the whole of the manor. It was mainly in the north-east of the kingdom that this process reached its most advanced phase, and this before the end of the fifteenth century.[1]

The English enclosures prove that the reserves, instead of gradually decreasing in size as they had done for centuries past, could once again increase. As a great area for cultivation, the reserve was not doomed to disappear by the natural evolution of things. The area of the lordship and the area of the reserve might even coincide, for the first time since the origin of the lordship.

In Mediterranean countries it was also stock-breeding – although here it was a matter of flocks being moved from pasture to pasture[2] that helped to maintain the estates. From olden times there had been a constantly recurring conflict between settled husbandmen and shepherds of moving flocks. And the former had given way whenever the villages had been too poor to band together; the fields were then despoiled by the herds or flocks which drove out the tillers of the soil. This is what happened at the end of the Middle Ages in Provence and in the Pyrenees, and even more so in Spain and in the 'Mezzogiorno', that is the south of Italy. The incursions of sheep and cattle constantly on the move reinforced the hold of the great lords in these two countries, after 1450 even more than before. The Spanish grandees formed powerful associations like the *Mesta* or the *Veintana*, which allowed in the poorer folk but gave policy direction to those at the top. The bands of shepherds who led the great flocks belonging to these associations deprived the husbandmen both

[1] But it was not completed in England until the eighteenth century (Translators).

[2] '*Élevage transhumant*'.

of pasturage and the land they crossed. Great numbers of villages were depopulated before being transformed into *cortijos,* vast domains for rural development. Tenants were forbidden to protect their cultivated fields, villages were demolished. All this was done with the approval of kings and popes who saw a personal advantage in it. The same kind of thing took place in the 'Mezzogiorno' where, however, there existed no associations of stock-breeders as powerful as in Spain. The *latifundi* increased, the rural communities disintegrated, tenures disappeared and the countryside was depopulated, as was for example the Roman Campagna. These changes were to continue until modern times. The centuries-old conflict, or competition, between the great domain and the village seemed to be ending badly for the village in Mediterranean countries.

The characteristics of northern and of central Italy were quite different. Here the power of the city business man became increasingly felt. One aspect of this phenomenon was to be found in all Mediterranean countries, namely the hold of the burgesses over the rural economy through their control of markets and exchange rates. The power of the cities over their *contadi* gave them more definite control in northern and central Italy. The second aspect of bourgeois power was, however, peculiar to these parts of the peninsula. In order better to assure the supply of provisions for his family and his city, the Italian business man sought out every possible means of acquiring land. This was all the more desirable since, contrary to the situation in France, land in fifteenth-century Italy was one of the best investments. It yielded an average of from four to six per cent per annum, a rate equal to the usual interest on money, in Genoa for example, while certain profits on land might rise to twenty-five per cent and more, which very few financial and mercantile operations were then bringing in. The burgesses, therefore, who had been acquiring land since the thirteenth century at least, now exercised strong pressure on the impecunious nobles, and many fine domains passed into bourgeois hands, attracting not only the powerful business man but also the modest burgess. It is clear that the changing conditions of lordship in these regions were mainly engineered by the burgesses, and less so by the nobles, as in most parts of the West. That these powerful townsmen promoted the cultivation of a greater variety of crops, and even changed the appearance of the countryside, would have little significance here, if it had not affected the modes of property-holding and of cultivating the land. The areas under cultivation increased in size and brought in more. Fine villas (in the modern meaning of the word) were built on these estates. The system of *métayage* was now preferred mainly for small holdings. The *libellus*, however, came into wider use and lasted for longer periods: the *libellarii*[1] no longer held land for twenty-nine years but for life, and later on an hereditary basis.

To sum up: the 'bourgeois invasion' of the countryside, to the prejudice of the landed nobility, took place only in a part of Italy. Elsewhere the nobles and the clergy remained landowners. In general, the effects of these changes in lordship were the same everywhere, but the agents of change were burgesses as well as lords. The changes did not proceed at the same pace everywhere, and they may have been counterbalanced, as in France, by the decline in the number of private tribunals and so of the profits which they had brought in for the lords, the royal or princely lawcourts reaping the benefits of this change.

[1] Registered tenants.

Chapter 7

DEATH OR SURVIVAL OF FEUDALISM?[1]

I. FEUDALISM AT THE END OF THE MIDDLE AGES: APPEARANCE AND REALITY

A. Appearance

It has been justly observed that up to the end of the Old Regime the oath of fealty and act of homage had to be repeated yearly, hundreds or even thousands of times.

The ceremonial, in principle, was perpetuated. Here is the custom of Paris, drawn up in 1510 and amended in 1580 in view of the changes which had taken place at the end of the Middle Ages. It still imposed on the vassal 'mouth and hands' (that is 'homage') with the oath of fealty. However, the great jurist Dumoulin criticized this ancient ceremonial. One should only kneel before the king; to kiss him was

[1] In addition to the works cited in earlier chapters, see R. Boutruche, *Rapport sur la seigneurie et la féodalité en Occident* (IVe Congrès intern. des Sc. Histor, t. I, Rapports), Paris A. Colin, 1950, p. 455 sq. – R. Cazelles, *La société politique et la crise de la royauté sous Philippe VI de Valois,* Paris, d'Argences, 1958. – R. Fedou, *Les hommes de loi lyonnais à la fin du Moyen Age; étude sur les origines de la classe de robe,* Paris, Belles-Lettres, 1964; *Le terrier de Jean Jossard,* Paris, Bibl. Nat., 1966. – B. Guenée, *Tribunaux et gens de justice dans le bailliage de Senlis à la fin du Moyen Age,* Paris, Belles-Lettres, 1963. – S. Painter, *Studies in the History of the English Feudal Barony,* Baltimore, 1943. – E. Perroy, *La guerre de cent ans,* Paris, Gallimard, 1945. Eng. trs. *The Hundred Years' War,* London, Eyre & Spottiswoode, 1951. – M. Rey, *Le domaine du roi et les finances extraordinaires sous Charles VI (1388–1413),* Paris, A. Colin, 1965; *Les finances royales sous Charles VI; les causes du déficit (1388–1413),* ibid. Cf. pp. 15 et 16 pour les travaux de R. Mousnier.

indecent. But it was only in 1580 that amended custom took account of these objections. One has indeed also to recognize that the bond between man and man was steadily growing weaker. Homage had always to be paid at the principal manor, or at the place of which the fief was a dependency. The lord had to be present, or to send someone empowered to represent him. If no one were present, the vassal could, after calling on his lord three times in a loud voice, make the declaration of fealty and homage at the door of the principal manor. If there were no manor the offers were to be notified to the nearest neighbour, and this act would be equivalent to the actual oath of fealty and act of homage. In the fifteenth century a vassal who had not been able to find his lord or the latter's representative at the centre of the principal fief, had made a show of paying homage: he knelt, bare-headed, and kissed the bar of the lord's tribunal in the presence of a notary who recorded the ceremonial. The great majority of homages were, however, paid personally to the lord or his representative. The bond between man and man was therefore more than a memory.

But as in the period preceding the fourteenth century, a vassal usually paid homage in order to take possession of his fief, or to be maintained in *seizin* of it. It is unnecessary to remind the reader that the fiefs continued to exist until 1789. The mode of investiture persisted, too, while written records became more numerous. Acts of recognition between vassal and lord, lists drawn up, and inscriptions in 'books of fiefs' or 'books of feudatories' proliferated. As Ganshof remarks, the formalities involved when a holding was transferred, and the lawsuits occasioned by conflicts about the rights to be exercised over the fief, gave a constantly increasing importance to the tribunals competent in these matters and to the feudal courts officered by men of the fief.

It certainly cannot be maintained that homage and fealty had become mere formalities. One has only to take, for example, one of the vassal's duties, that of giving counsel. This not only gave birth to the Parlement de Paris and, subsequently, to the provincial Parlements and the Council of Flanders. It played an essential part in creating the institutions representing the 'orders' of the kingdom, both the Estates in France and the Parliament in London. In these developments one must concede that the nobility does not seem to have lost any of its influence.

There remained the great fiefs in France (the apanages of the Crown above all) and in Germany: their princes always had to do homage to the king. Moreover, within the Empire the institutions of feudal-vassalage continued to play a notable part, amongst other spheres, in public law. The small princes, the knights of the Empire, defended themselves against the threat of absorption by the more powerful princes by asserting their status as dependants of the Emperor (*Reichsummittelbarkeit*). But the rôle of the German states is less relevant here, since historians are agreed in recognizing that feudalism persisted longer in that country.

To return to the history of France: in their efforts to keep the Burgundian-Flemish state within the kingdom, the kings of France tried as much and as long as they could to have their right of suzerainty recognized by the Valois of the junior branch, who held Flanders and Artois. There is the case, for example, of the arguments respecting the homage to be done, or not to be done, by Philip the Good, both before and after the Treaty of Arras in 1435. Here it is true that it was specifically a question of public law, and not a simple question of the private code reserved for the bond between vassal and lord.

B. The Real Situation

To appreciate the last phase of feudalism at the end of the Middle Ages it is preferable to stress its two main features, viz. the question of the personal bond and the impact of its observance on the State.

On the first point Boutruche has rightly protested against those 'historians who regard the personal bond, after the thirteenth century, as only an empty ceremonial, a simple formality'. The bonds of vassalage certainly retained some significance at the end of the Middle Ages. If Philip the Good refused to do homage to Charles VII, it seems that it was not only for reasons of high politics, but also because he regarded the 'King of Bourges' as having instigated the murder of his father, John the Fearless. If the bond of vassalage was broken by the felony of the lord, one could not, *a fortiori,* become vassal of a felon. Other very significant examples are not lacking. There were 'the wrangling which preceded Edward III's consent to do liege homage; the excursions of the Black Prince across the principality of Aquitaine to receive in person, in 1363 and 1364, the oaths of fealty of more than twelve hundred vassals'. In this last instance it was not simply a question of public law (that of applying the provisions of the Treaty of Brétigny – Calais) but also of establishing bonds between lord and vassal, all the more necessary since, as will be seen, their repudiation by the French was to create an impossible situation for the English. One can go further. Is it certain that a band of 'free companions' during the Hundred Years' War was attached to its captain only by greed of gain and pillage, and that personal bonds of vassalage did not unite them, at least in certain cases? Again, if so many castellans resisted the Valois or the English kings, it was no doubt partly because they had the support of their vassals, vowed to their service. It cannot be doubted that the significance of the bonds uniting man to man survived in part until modern times. Ernest Lavisse has noted their significance in the seventeenth century.

But in so far as feudalism was a menace to the interests of the State, it inevitably declined as the State grew stronger. This decline certainly proceeded more rapidly at the end of the Middle Ages, except in Germany, although one can 'detect transitional stages between the system of 'classical feudalism' and the new aspect assumed by States and society as modern times drew nearer'. There may, on occasion, have been a real break, and not a transition.

It seems certain that in France, as in England, it was not in order to return to feudal conditions that the upper aristocracy fought against monarchical power, but to control it, to take a hand in government, and to advance its own influence and wealth. This has been said of the English baronies, although these, as we know, were not exactly 'great fiefs'. It has been more correctly asserted of the great apanages of France. In the fourteenth century the great French fiefs had experienced 'an evolution parallel to that of the monarchy'. Organized as veritable States, they possessed all the administrative machinery and all the great corps of officers who, in the nature of things, vied with those of the Crown. 'In order to describe the heads of these great apanages', writes Perroy, 'the history books continue, to save themselves trouble, to use the word *feudalism*. They still speak of the "feudal rebellions" of which Charles VII and Louis XI had to face the successive assaults. Nothing conveys a more false idea of the situation in the French kingdom in the fifteenth century'. The princes concerned were obviously vassals of the Crown. 'But the feudal bond was no more than an empty word; it no longer represented the real structure of society and the real nature of politics. The struggle was not, as it had been in the twelfth and thirteenth centuries, between a feudalism jealous of its autonomy and a monarchy whose encroachments it endured with impatience, whose officials it hated and whose sovereign power it denied'. The fact is that these territorial princes did not actually want to destroy the edifice of a monarchy which had triumphed over the ancient feudalism. They were themselves 'monarchs – or very nearly so – in their own domains', and they wished to dominate and control the State and the royal administration, in order to enrich themselves and share the spoils of the country. Loyalty to the monarch, however, was growing in strength as against 'feudal' loyalty to the princes, and was to prove a weapon for the king; not always effective because of the existence of the rival loyalty in the apanages.

After the first defeats in the Hundred Years' War, those suffered by Philip VI and John the Good, whose armies have been described as 'feudal mobs', the nobility lost a good deal of its prestige in public opinion. Warriors *par excellence*, the nobles had not been able to stop the invasion or prevent the king from being taken prisoner. Their prestige, however, was subsequently restored, though only in part. For the nobles were not the only fighting-men, and the military service due from the vassals was no longer sufficient to fill the ranks of the army. *Soldiers*, in other words professional fighting-men who received wages, had appeared in the fourteenth century, but the *companies* thus established gave little satisfaction to Charles V. It is to Charles VII that belongs the honour of having created an army that was to be permanent and 'paid'. On 26 May 1445 he issued the order which is regarded as constituting the new standing army. Nevertheless, the formation of fifteen companies, called companies of 'the decree', did not mean, for the king and his counsellors, that a permanent force had been established. The king, writes R. Fawtier, 'did not so much create a permanent army as an army which became permanent' by the force of circumstances. At all events, it involved the corresponding establishment of permanent taxation.

Even so, if the nobles – the *bellatores* of old – no longer enjoyed a monopoly of the profession of arms, this was still, and for centuries to come, their favourite profession. And certain of the nobles gradually regained a part of the prestige which they had lost, by becoming officials of the king in increasing numbers and occupying the governmental organizations in which new official posts were proliferating; while at the same time they retained the titles and other honours that belonged to all rural noblemen. Moreover, respect and consideration would always be attributed to the nobleman of many vassals, even if he drew no lucrative dues from them. But many lords, as well as the king, continued to do so in regions between the middle waters of the Loire and the Rhine, until the end of the Middle Ages as in earlier times.

II. THE ORGANIZATION OF SOCIETY IN 'ORDERS' IN FRANCE

The division of society into three orders is admittedly of old standing. It was both a Christian concept and a *de facto* form of classification. But, even before the end of the Middle Ages, the divisions went deeper. The orders, which had hitherto existed only in fact, began to change into juridical orders recognized and utilized by the monarchy. This classification of the system is prefigured in a declaration of Philippe de Vitry, secretary of Philip VI of Valois: 'The people', he said, 'in order to try and avert the evils which it foresees, formed itself into three parts. One was to pray to God; the second part was to trade and labour; and after these, knights came into the world to guard the other two parts from injury and crime'.

How far was the 'trinitarian society' stratified at the end of the Middle Ages? The first Estates, whether or not they were Estates General, go back only to the middle of the fourteenth century. Did the three orders then become part of public law or did they still have only a *de facto* existence (of which the Crown was beginning to make use)? It must be said at once that there had been no real Estates at an earlier date. Thus the Assembly of the Louvre convoked by Philip the Good on 12 March 1303, at the height of the struggle against Boniface VIII, was still only a consultation of public opinion (and one of the first). However, in addition to the prelates and barons, it may have already included some delegates of the cities. In the decades that followed one still could not describe as Estates General the various assemblies that were convoked, because their recruitment was too limited in both the social and geographical senses. It seems none the less true that, prior to the first Estates General, those of 1355 to 1358 – when what was later to be called the Third Estate (that is, delegates of the cities and minor officials) made the law, while the nobles and clergy remained silent – there were assemblies which certainly included representatives of the three orders and which were therefore beginning to recognize that they had a legal existence. In 1347, for example, Estates had been convoked, *bailliage* by *bailliage*. In the provostry and viscounty of Paris (that is, the *bailliage* of Paris) churchmen, nobles and non-nobles had taken their seats.

Thus, as early as the first half of the fourteenth century and even before the first Estates General, a stratification of the orders had in some sense become a reality; certainly *de facto* and perhaps also *de jure*. At the same time there appeared a new and conspicuous social group, made up of the king's officers, 'gentlemen of the robe' in particular, which increased rapidly as the royal administration and justice grew in scope concomitantly with the growing power of the sovereign. It would be worth while to discover the relations, for example, of cause and effect, which probably existed between the stratification in orders and the expansion of this social group.

Had the royal officials in general, and the lawyers in particular, a feeling that they formed a social *class*? To ask this is practically to ask whether a society of orders can also be regarded as a society of classes. R. Mousnier thinks that in many respects the two are fundamentally different. Since then, J. Ibarrola has brought up the question anew, by advancing again Marc Bloch's argument. In Ibarrola's view, 'the seeming contradiction of equating social classes with juridical classes is only for the purpose of analysis'. Classification by orders is valid 'only as it is in line with the law', and that is the supreme criterion in considering the structure of the social edifice.

The social structure is a cross-section of classes. Thus the nobility, in the view of J. Ibarrola, was first a social class before becoming a juridical class, the change occurring when it wished to close its ranks and become a clearly defined order. But this 'nobility in law' continued, it is argued, to be at the same time a social class. Its way of life, which consisted of spending the 'surplus accumulated by the peasants', was the source of its unity, since all the nobles were allegedly 'annuitants of the soil', 'courtiers' or 'king's officers'. But the expression 'annuitants of the soil' is not acceptable or correct. One cannot follow J. Ibarrola when he speaks in this way of 'courtiers'. These were not yet the days of Louis XIV and the word had scarcely any meaning in the Middle Ages, despite the intermittent occurrence of the term 'court', in the modern sense of the word. Ibarrola's reasoning is not very convincing, because a whole world separated the wealthy nobles with their great domains from those nobles who for long past and for one reason or another had been impoverished. There was, in reality, no one way of noble living but several, and so it is very difficult to speak of the nobility as a single social class. The word 'class' takes no account of the real situation, as does the word 'order'.

In the same way, the bourgeoisie did not form a single group. Mousnier has recently recalled what is often overlooked, namely that there existed at least two types of 'bourgeoisie': one represented by a man of law who improved his social standing by the adoption of law as a profession, organized social relations on a legal basis, and thereby contributed an added firmness to the social structure; the other represented by the 'merchant who was responsible for the supply of food and precious metals'. Intellectual occupations being most highly considered, the man of law was placed higher in the social hierarchy than the business man. Similarly, among the many nobles who were officers, that is officials of the king, there were now jurists. This means that the bourgeoisie occupying official posts, and the nobility also enjoying such occupations, were often nearer to each other than the former were to the merchants, and the latter to the nobles who were not legal and administrative officials.

If there was no noble 'class' and no bourgeois 'class', there unquestionably existed at the end of the Middle Ages a group of men who lived by their official positions in the royal service, for example in the administration of justice, and so on. The question arises whether this group had the consciousness of forming, not a class (because all class divisions are 'related to one's position in the economic system', and the king's officers, whether or not they were jurists, did not, properly speaking, perform an economic function) but a social group which had a certain tendency to close its ranks; its position in the hierarchy of *degrees*, which composed the *orders*, being not yet clearly defined, as it was still in process of formation. To describe this group, one may provisionally use the term 'notables', until medieval and modern historians have agreed on the choice of a term more appropriate and of wider geographical application.

If it is asked whether the bourgeois notables and the notables of noble descent were really united among themselves, whether they felt that they formed together one and the same group, the answer is very definitely in the affirmative. This may appear surprising if one recalls that at the time when Henri Pirenne, Marc Bloch or François Olivier-Martin were writing, historians were anxious to assert that there was a 'water-tight' division between nobility and bourgeoisie, that they were altogether separated, beginning with their different ways of life. But in consequence of recent research, like J. Lestocquoy's on Arras and J. Schneider's on Metz, it is clear that one must greatly modify this traditional notion.[1] In the eleventh and twelfth centuries, when city life was developing in extent and importance, nobles had sometimes been sons of bourgeois and bourgeois had been sons of nobles. Even within the ranks of a bourgeoisie engaged in commerce and craftsmanship one must bow to the facts. The 'patricians' and the common folk were at opposite poles, but the bourgeoisie were of a mixed character from their origins. If this is not recognized, how can one explain the decline of the nobility and the rise of the bourgeoisie, dating from about 1200? This movement, of which 1789 marks the epilogue, must have progressed extremely slowly, since it took more than half a millenium to reach its last stage. There cannot have been a continuous decline of the nobility, for in France and elsewhere the nobility must have received a fresh impulse to survive, however slowly and imperceptibly. In all countries, when one dynasty succeeded another, there was created a new nobility[2] (Genicot). Alliances, moreover, between noble houses and bourgeois families were probably much less rare than is supposed.

In the Ile-de-France, for example, at the end of the Middle Ages, there was infiltration between members of both groups, of the noble families provided with estates, and families of landless commoners, both living on the proceeds of certain royal offices. Even before 1300 the group which controlled the principal machinery of the State (the *Chambre des Comptes* and especially the *Parlement* with its many counsellors, advocates, public prosecutors and so on) and of the Church (the chapter of Notre-Dame, the bishopric of

[1] In fourteenth-century England Chaucer was clearly a 'notable', owing to the various services, material and diplomatic, which he performed for the government (Translators).

[2] In England, under the Tudors for example, the rapid rise to eminence of the Cecil family (Translators).

Paris and the great abbeys of the region) – this large group doubtless contained knights or sons of knights and prominent bourgeois or sons of such; and many of these were, sooner or later, to be ennobled as individuals by royal decision or because the offices they filled were eventually regarded as conferring nobility. The monarchy was not particularly averse from ennobling bourgeois, at least those commoners who held public office, though it was more parsimonious in thus honouring merchants or business-men. Just as the d'Orgemont family were already more than ordinary bourgeois even before being ennobled – as Marc Bloch has shown – so the Braque, the Bureau, the Budé, the Briçonnet and the Jouvenel families, and others were already aristocrats *de facto* before becoming nobles *de jure*. And it was to be the same, though in a lesser degree, with a number of notables 'of the robe', of the second rank, that is the principal lawyers in the secondary courts (in Paris, the Châtelet, seat of the *prévôt-bailli's* jurisdiction), such as the Piédefer family. Whether ennobled or not, they were able to acquire lordships of considerable extent. The notables were as yet far from being a social group closed to newcomers.

In certain parts of France, then, the 'gentlemen of the robe' formed a homogeneous social group; a hybrid group, however, of a status which was debatable, and which *was* debated, in this society's 'orders', where these 'orders' were clearly defined and their constituent *degrees, ranks* or *subaltern orders* had finally crystallized out, that is at the beginning of the modern era. R. Mousnier has cited Furetière's definitions (1690): 'Estate[1] is also used of the different Orders of the kingdom. . . . They are composed of the Church, the Nobility and the Third Estate, or the bourgeois notables'. One can see that for Furetière, in his *Dictionnaire universel*, bourgeois and notables have become synonymous. As early as 1610 Charles Loyseau had shown that each of the three orders was subdivided into 'subaltern orders'. In his opinion the Third Estate comprised, at its head, the officers of justice and of finance (although some were noble by virtue of this office); then doctors, licentiates and bachelors; below them the

[1] *Estat* (*État*) also meant State in our sense of the word (Translators).

advocates; then the practitioners (registrars, notaries, procurators); and, on a still lower level, the merchants. The officers of justice and the advocates, although not nobles, nevertheless have the title of 'noble man'.

It was not till the start of the seventeenth century that those who were gentlemen by birth[1] were to thrust 'the nobles of the robe out of the nobility'. At the Estates General of 1614–15 most of the nobles of the robe were to sit with the Third Estate. According to Mousnier, 'a struggle between the orders thus dominates French society', no doubt because, since the end of the Middle Ages, the number of offices conferring nobility had greatly increased and, concurrently, a *noblesse de robe* had arisen in face of the old nobility. With the help of illustrations taken from a novel of the time, from a letter of Guez de Balzac and from the *Mémoires* of the abbé de Choisy, Mousnier shows that 'for the gentlemen of the sword the men of the robe (*les robins*) were only bourgeois'.

But the men of the robe did not so easily resign their pretensions; as witness Charles Loyseau, whom Mousnier recalls as writing that the worthiest service is not 'the service of arms, but the civil service of the State'. In his view, two formulae are essential: 'The magistrature above everything: the magistrature, the true, the highest nobility'. A virulent attack on the pretensions of the nobles and a lively defence of the pretensions of the men of law are followed, in Loyseau's argument, by the suggestion that 'a quite small change, proceeding upward, might, within the same society divided into orders, with the same forms of nobility, make the magistrate the noble par excellence in place of the warrior' (Mousnier).

Why does one find these conflicting claims so marked in the seventeenth century but not nearly so much in evidence at the end of the Middle Ages? The reason is that in the fourteenth and fifteenth centuries a society composed of 'orders' had not yet crystallized out and been recognized in law. A vague, ill-defined intermediate zone existed between

[1] *Gentilshommes,* i.e. real nobles. The word retains its meaning in modern French. Corresponding terms in English have been distorted (Translators).

the nobility and the third order. This can be understood if one recalls what R. Cazelles observed many years ago, that at the beginning of the fourteenth century the tendency was to efface the distinction between nobles and non-nobles and thereby leave a place for a new aristocracy, that of the king's men. This explanation would seem to show that the counsellors of the last Capetians and the first Valois were not far from thinking like Loyseau, three hundred years before his time. But without any violent reversal, this trend was slowed down, because the question of fiscal exemption for the nobility began to set limits to the movement. In the event of an individual's legal status being disputed, it was the business of the Chambre des Comptes to order an enquiry and so, in Cazelles' opinion, the royal system of taxation was 'responsible for keeping the nobility within bounds and turning it into a closed caste'. This last expression, one may object, is inappropriate and exaggerated. Let it be said, rather, that the system of taxation and the fiscal exemptions emphasized the dividing line between nobles and non-nobles. The part which the fiscal system played in embittering relations between nobles and commoners, between lawyers and non-lawyers, must only have made itself felt gradually and have only become a clear issue at a later date.

In the fourteenth and fifteenth centuries the distinction between gentlemen of the sword and 'gentlemen of the robe', between nobles and commoners, was not yet a *fait accompli*, because the 'notables' of noble origin bridged the gap between the old nobility and those officers serving the Crown and the princes, who were by origin sons of commoners. The conflict between the orders was not a medieval phenomenon because their separation, though firmly established in the domain of fact, had not yet given rise to orders and degrees clearly distinguishable and enshrined in the law of the land.

CONCLUSION

About the early years of the sixteenth century rural lordship was reasserting its powers nearly everywhere, in spite of the decline of their private tribunals and the rise of State law-courts, which continued to increase in numbers and authority. The transition from the Middle Ages to modern times was to take place with no perceptible effect on the history of lordship; its existence was to be prolonged for several centuries.

If, on the other hand, the feudal system seemed to be on the way out, it was not yet dead. The system continued to flourish in Germany and it remained active elsewhere. The concept of the bond between man and man probably did not completely disappear in spite of the increasing powers secured by the State. The system had originated in the last years of the Roman Empire and thus before the first dissolving forces of the State. But it cannot be denied that in the long run the bond lost its significance. Apart from the transmission of feudal obligations – which were to retain their *raison d'être* where the fief survived – the 'feudal' Middle Ages have bequeathed two legacies to the modern world: the nobility, many of whose members were to retain a preference for the career of arms; and the division of society into orders. The beginning of the modern era was to witness the confirmation of this division, or separation, into juridical orders, a process not completed in the Middle Ages. The history of feudalism does not stop with the Middle Ages any more than does the history of lordship.

Further Reading

AULT, W. O., *Private Jurisdiction in England,* New Haven, 1923.

BATH, B. H. S. van, *An Agrarian History of Western Europe, 500–1850,* New York, 1963.

BEAN, J. M. W., *The Decline of English Feudalism, 1215–1540,* Manchester, 1968.

BEECH, G. T., *A Rural Society in Medieval France: The Gâtine of Poitou in the Eleventh and Twelfth Centuries,* Baltimore, 1964.

BENNETT, H. S., *Life on the English Manor,* Cambridge, 1937.

BLOCH, M., *Feudal Society,* 2 vols., Chicago, 1961.

——, *French Rural History,* Berkeley and Los Angeles, 1970.

BROWN, R. A., *Origins of English Feudalism,* London, 1973.

CHEYETTE, F. L. (ed.), *Lordship and Community in Medieval Europe,* New York, 1968.

COULBORN, R. (ed.), *Feudalism in History,* Princeton, 1956.

DAVIS, W. S., *Life on a Medieval Barony,* New York, 1923.

DENHOLM-YOUNG, N., *Seignorial Administration in England,* Oxford, 1937.

——, *The Country Gentry in the Fourteenth Century,* Oxford, 1969.

DUBY, G., *Rural Economy and Country Life in the Medieval West,* Columbia, South Carolina, 1968.

GANSHOF, F. L., *Feudalism,* 3rd ed., New York, 1964.

GIBBS, M., *Feudal Order,* London, 1949.

HASKINS, C. H., *Norman Institutions,* Cambridge, Mass., 1918.

HATCHER, J., *Rural Economy and Society in the Duchy of Cornwall, 1300–1500,* Cambridge, 1970.

HERLIHY, D. (comp.), *The History of Feudalism,* New York, 1970.

HOLLISTER, C. W., *The Military Organization of Norman England,* Oxford, 1965.

HOLMES, G. A., *The Estates of the Higher Nobility in Fourteenth Century England,* Cambridge, 1957.

HOYT, R. S., *Feudal Institutions: Cause or Consequence of Decentralization,* New York, 1961.

—— (ed.), *Life and Thought in the Early Middle Ages,* Minneapolis, 1967.

LA MONTE, J. L., *Feudal Monarchy in the Latin Kingdom of Jerusalem*, Cambridge, Mass., 1932.

LEWIS, A. R., *The Development of Southern French and Catalan Society*, Austin, 1965.

LYON, B., *From Fief to Indenture. The Transition from Feudal to Non-Feudal Contract in Western Europe*, Cambridge, Mass., 1957.

MCFARLANE, K. B., *The Nobility of Later Medieval England*, Oxford, 1973.

ODEGAARD, C. E., *Vassi and Fideles in the Carolingian Empire*, Cambridge, Mass., 1945.

PAINTER, S., *French Chivalry*, Baltimore, 1940.

——, *Studies in the History of the English Feudal Barony*, Baltimore, 1943.

——, *Feudalism and Liberty*, ed. F. A. Cazel Jr., Baltimore, 1961.

PETIT-DUTAILLIS, C., *The Feudal Monarchy in France and England*, London, 1936.

POOLE, A. L., *Obligations of Society in the Twelfth and Thirteenth Centuries*, Oxford, 1946.

POSTAN, M. M. (ed.), *The Cambridge Economic History of Europe*, 3rd ed., Cambridge, 1961.

REYNOLDS, R. L., *Europe Emerges*, Madison, 1961.

SOUTHERN, R. W., *The Making of the Middle Ages*, New Haven, 1953.

STENTON, D. M., *English Society in the Early Middle Ages*, 2nd ed., Harmondsworth, 1952.

STENTON, F. M., *The First Century of English Feudalism, 1066–1166*, 2nd ed., Oxford, 1961.

STEPHENSON, C., *Medieval Feudalism*, Ithaca, 1942.

——, *Medieval Institutions*, Ithaca, 1954

STRAYER, J. R., *The Administration of Normandy Under St. Louis*, Cambridge, Mass., 1932.

——, *Feudalism*, Princeton, 1965.

THOMPSON, J. W., *Feudal Germany*, Chicago, 1928.

THRUPP, S. (ed.), *Early Medieval Society*, New York, 1957.

TOPPING, P., *Feudal Institutions as Revealed in the Assizes of Romania*, Philadelphia, 1949.

ULLMANN, W., *The Individual and Society in the Middle Ages*, London, 1967.

WHITE, L., Jr., *Medieval Technology and Social Change*, Oxford, 1962.

Index